CROCHETED DINOSAURS

CROCHETED DINOSAURS

Vanessa Mooncie

10
42
24
52
64
78
92

CONTENTS

INTRODUCTION

Crocheted Dinosaurs is a collection of ten detailed patterns to make popular dinosaurs and prehistoric reptiles. The projects include the three-horned Triceratops, the winged Pterodactyl and the Tyrannosaurus Rex with open jaws of pointed teeth.

The projects are worked primarily in rounds and rows of double crochet. The designs incorporate a variety of decorative stitches and colour-work that are used to create the texture and pattern of scales, armour plating and feathers. Pipe cleaners and craft wire are an optional addition to reinforce legs and wings. To make the pieces suitable as toys for young children, the wire should be omitted and glass eyes can be replaced with safety eyes or embroidered features.

The written instructions are accompanied by charts to make it easy to follow the patterns.

The projects are most suited to intermediate and advanced crocheters, due to the complexity of the patterns. However, for the adventurous beginner there is a comprehensive section at the back of the book with step-by-step, illustrated guides to the essential crochet stitches and techniques. This includes tips on how to get started, joining in new colours, sewing the dinosaurs together and applying the finishing touches, so you will be equipped with the necessary tools to give each prehistoric creation its own unique character.

This colourful collection of archosaurs is perfect for dinosaur enthusiasts and crochet lovers alike. I hope you enjoy making them.

Vanessa

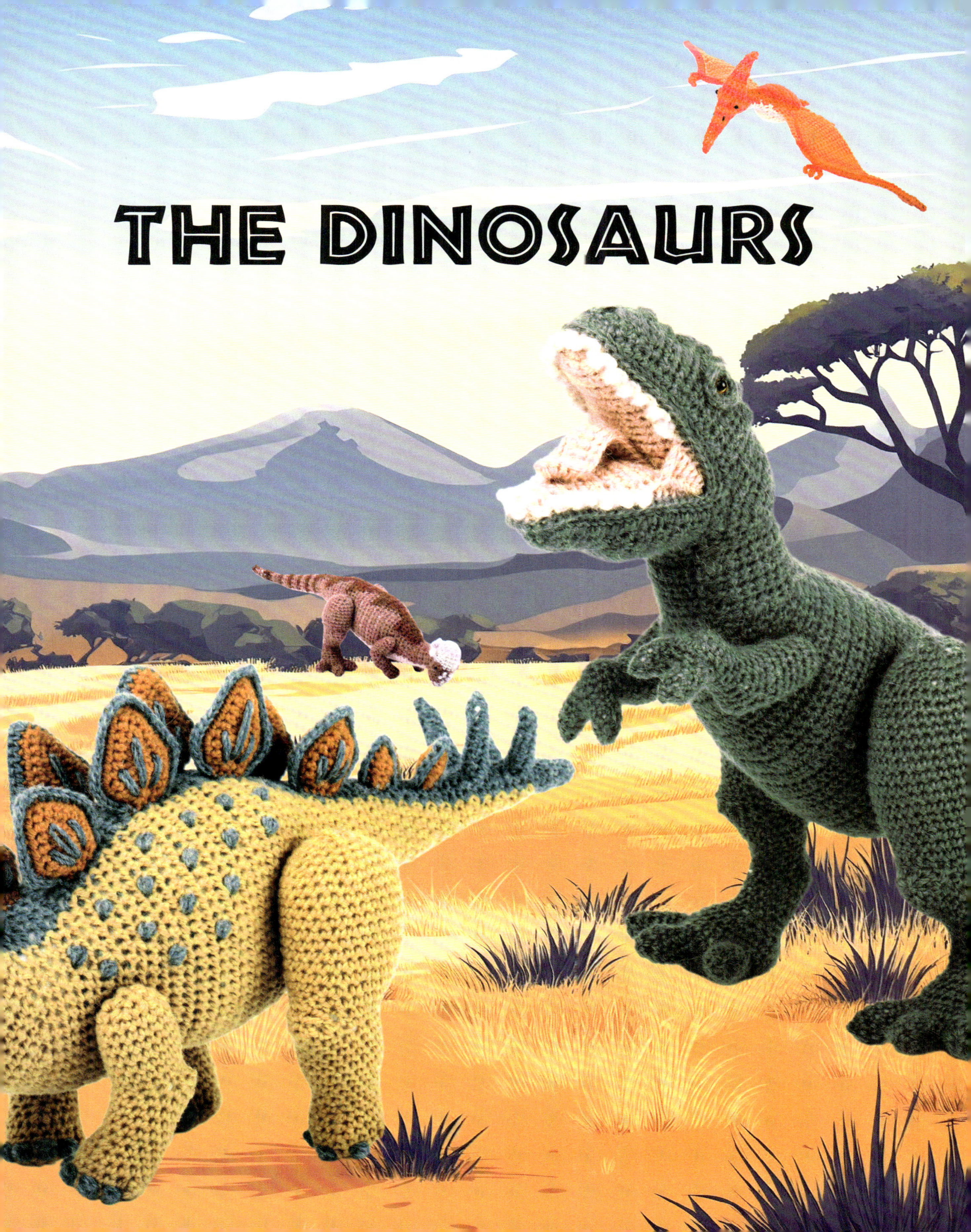
THE DINOSAURS

STEGOSAURUS

THE STEGOSAURUS'S BODY, NECK AND HEAD ARE CROCHETED IN ONE PIECE FROM THE TAIL UP. DECORATIVE DETAILS INCLUDE SIMPLE EMBROIDERY, BOBBLES AND PUFF STITCHES.

MATERIALS

- Scheepjes Metropolis, 75% extra fine merino wool, 25% nylon (219yd/200m per 50g ball):
  1 × 50g ball in 017 Multan (A)
  1 × 50g ball in 035 Seoul (B)
  1 × 50g ball in 065 Liverpool (C)
- 88½in (225cm) length of 4ply yarn in pink, such as Scheepjes Metropolis 052 Bangalore, for the mouth and tongue (D)
- 1 pair of 5/32–3/16in (4–5mm) looped glass teddy bear eyes or safety eyes
- Clear invisible or strong thread to attach the looped glass eyes
- Stranded embroidery thread in black, such as Anchor Stranded Cotton, shade 0403, for the nostrils
- 2.5mm (UK12:US-) crochet hook
- Stitch markers
- Blunt-ended yarn needle
- Toy stuffing

SIZE

Approximately 14½in (37cm) long

TENSION

27 sts and 27 rows to 4in (10cm) over double crochet using 2.5mm hook and yarn A. Use larger or smaller hook if necessary to obtain correct tension.

METHOD

The Stegosaurus's body is crocheted from the tail up and started in continuous rounds. A second colour is joined and continued in rows of double crochet to finish the body, neck and head. Puff stitches create a spotted pattern over the body. The front of the body and the shaping of the beak are formed by crocheting short rows, working into a few stitches of the previous row and then crocheting into an unworked stitch at the end of each subsequent row. The mouth is attached to the beak by working into each stitch of both pieces at the same time to join. The body is stuffed at intervals as it is crocheted and a small gap is left in the head to insert stuffing into the beak before sewing the opening together.

The legs are crocheted in rounds of double crochet. Bobble stitches form the toenails. The bends in the legs are produced by making a length of chain stitches and skipping a number of stitches of the previous row. The stitches of the following row are gathered together to form the joints. The first round of the tops of the legs is crocheted into the skipped stitches and the opposite side of the chain stitches. The legs are attached to the body so that they are movable.

The kite-shaped plates that run along the surface of the dinosaur's back are each made in two pieces that are joined together by crocheting into each stitch of both pieces at the same time. The plates are lightly stuffed and the larger ones are embroidered with lazy daisy stitches.

The Stegosaurus is finished with crocheted spikes sewn to the end of its tail, looped glass or safety eyes attached to a crocheted eye socket, a tiny tongue, and simple embroidery for the nostrils.

1 ch and 2 ch at beg of the row/round do not count as a st throughout.

KEY

- Magic loop
- Chain (ch)
- Slip stitch (sl st)
- Double crochet (dc)
- Dc2inc
- Dc3inc
- Dc2tog
- Half treble (htr)
- Treble (tr)
- 2-htr puff
- Make bobble (mb)

COLOUR

 A

 B

BODY

TAIL

With 2.5mm hook and A, make a magic loop.

Round 1: 1 ch, 6 dc into loop (6 sts).

Round 2: 1 dc in each st.

Pull tightly on the short end of yarn to close the loop.

Rounds 3–4: 1 dc in each st.

Round 5 (inc): (Dc2inc, 1 dc) 3 times (9 sts).

Rounds 6–8: 1 ch, 1 dc in each st.

Join B in last dc.

Carry unused yarn on WS of the work.

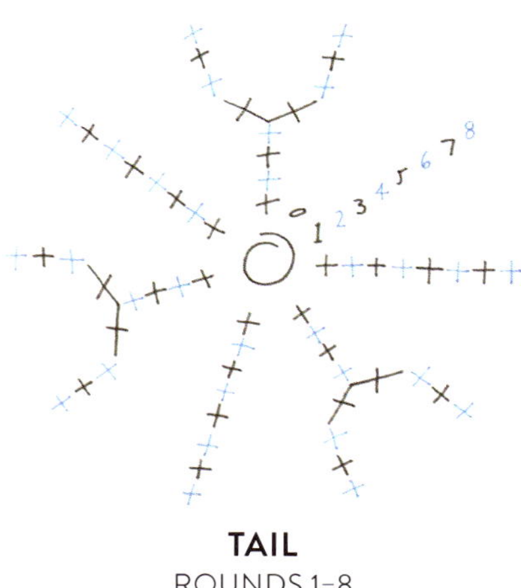

TAIL
ROUNDS 1–8

SHAPE TAIL

The following is worked on rows.

Row 1 (RS) (inc): With B, 1 dc in next dc, dc2inc, 1 dc in next dc; with A, 1 dc in next 6 dc, sl st to first dc, turn (10 sts).

Row 2: 1 dc in next 6 dc with A, 1 dc in next 4 dc with B, turn.

Row 3: 1 ch, 1 dc in next 4 sts with B, 1 dc in next 6 sts with A, sl st to first dc, turn.

Row 4: As row 2.

Row 5 (inc): With B, 1 ch, dc2inc, 1 dc in next 2 dc, dc2inc; with A, 1 dc in next 6 dc, sl st to first dc, turn (12 sts).

Row 6: 1 dc in next 6 dc with A, 1 dc in next 6 dc with B, turn.

Row 7: 1 ch, 1 dc in next 6 sts with B, 1 dc in next 6 sts with A, sl st to first dc, turn.

Row 8: As row 6.

Row 9 (inc): With B, 1 ch, dc2inc, 1 dc in next 4 dc, dc2inc; with A, 1 dc in next 6 dc, sl st to first dc, turn (14 sts).

Row 10: 1 dc in next 6 dc with A, 1 dc in next 8 dc with B, turn.

Row 11: 1 ch, 1 dc in next 8 sts with B, 1 dc in next 6 sts with A, sl st to first dc, turn.

Row 12: As row 10.

Row 13 (inc): With B, 1 ch, dc2inc, 1 dc in next 6 dc, dc2inc; with A, 1 dc in next 6 dc, sl st to first dc, turn (16 sts).

Row 14: 1 dc in next 6 dc with A, 1 dc in next 10 dc with B, turn.

Row 15 (inc): With B, 1 ch, dc2inc, 1 dc in next 8 dc, dc2inc; with A, 1 dc in next 6 dc, sl st to first dc, turn (18 sts).

Row 16: 1 dc in next 6 dc with A, 1 dc in next 12 dc with B, turn.

Row 17 (inc): With B, 1 ch, dc2inc, 1 dc in next 10 dc, dc2inc; with A, 1 dc in next 6 dc, sl st to first dc, turn (20 sts).

Row 18: 1 dc in next 6 dc with A, 1 dc in next 14 dc with B, turn.

Row 19 (inc): With B, 1 ch, dc2inc, 1 dc in next 12 dc, dc2inc; with A, 1 dc in next 6 dc, sl st to first dc, turn (22 sts).

Row 20: 1 dc in next 6 dc with A, 1 dc in next 16 dc with B, turn.

Row 21 (inc): With B, 1 ch, dc2inc, 1 dc in next 14 dc, dc2inc; with A, 1 dc in next 6 dc, sl st to first dc, turn (24 sts).

Row 22: 1 dc in next 6 dc with A, 1 dc in next 18 dc with B, turn.

Stuff the tail to within the last 3 rows before continuing, using the end of the hook to push the stuffing right into the tip.

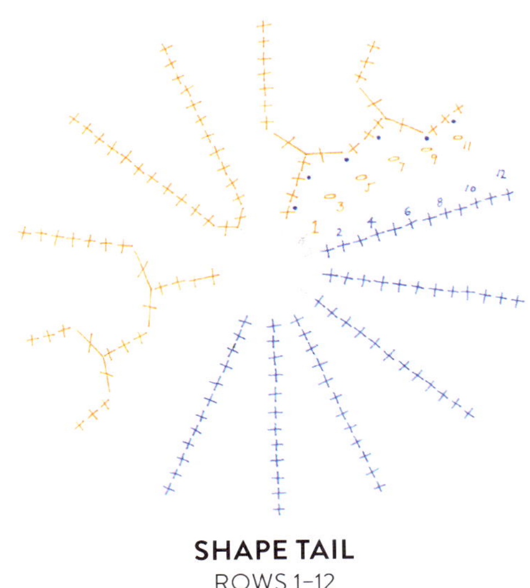

SHAPE TAIL
ROWS 1–12

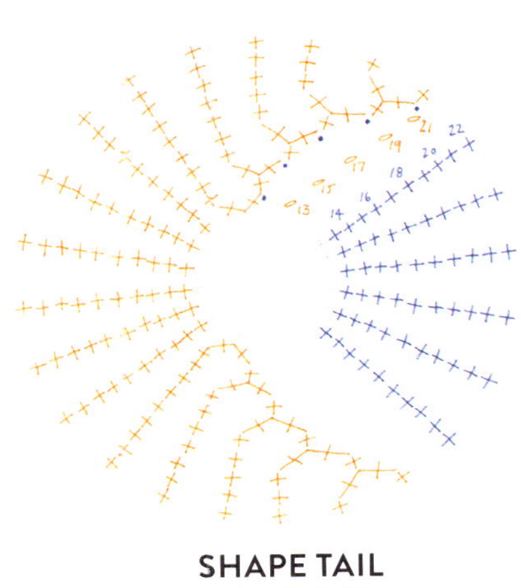

SHAPE TAIL
ROWS 13–22

SHAPE END OF BODY

Row 23 (inc): With B, 1 ch, (dc2inc, 2 dc) 3 times, (2 dc, dc2inc) 3 times; with A, 1 dc in next 6 dc, sl st to first dc, turn (30 sts).

Row 24: 1 dc in next 6 dc with A, 1 dc in next 24 dc with B, turn.

Row 25: 1 ch, 1 dc in next 24 sts with B, 1 dc in next 6 sts with A, sl st to first dc, turn.

Row 26: As row 24.

Row 27 (inc): With B, 1 ch, (dc2inc, 3 dc) 3 times, (3 dc, dc2inc) 3 times; with A, 1 dc in next 6 dc, sl st to first dc, turn (36 sts).

Row 28: 1 dc in next 6 dc with A, 1 dc in next 30 dc with B, turn.

Row 29: 1 ch, 1 dc in next 30 sts with B, 1 dc in next 6 sts with A, sl st to first dc, turn.

Row 30: As row 28.

Row 31 (inc): With B, 1 ch, (dc2inc, 4 dc) 3 times, (4 dc, dc2inc) 3 times; with A, 1 dc in next 6 dc, sl st to first dc, turn (42 sts).

Row 32: 1 dc in next 6 dc with A, 1 dc in next 36 dc with B, turn.

Row 33: 1 ch, 1 dc in next 36 sts with B, 1 dc in next 6 sts with A, sl st to first dc, turn.

Row 34: As row 32.

Row 35 (inc): With B, 1 ch, (dc2inc, 5 dc) 3 times, (5 dc, dc2inc) 3 times; with A, 1 dc in next 6 dc, sl st to first dc, turn (48 sts).

Row 36: 1 dc in next 6 dc with A, 1 dc in next 42 dc with B, turn.

Row 37 (inc): With B, 1 ch, (dc2inc, 6 dc) 3 times, (6 dc, dc2inc) 3 times; with A, 1 dc in next 6 dc, sl st to first dc, turn (54 sts).

Row 38: 1 dc in next 6 dc with A, 1 dc in next 48 dc with B, turn.

SHAPE MIDDLE OF BODY

The puff stitches are crocheted on the wrong side of the work, as they will appear on the reverse side.

See page 159 for instructions to make a 2-htr puff.

Row 39 (inc): With B, 1 ch, (dc2inc, 7 dc) 3 times, (7 dc, dc2inc) 3 times; with A, 1 dc in next 6 dc, sl st to first dc, turn (60 sts).

Row 40: 1 dc in next 6 dc with A, 1 dc in next 2 dc with B, 2-htr puff with A, 1 dc in next 48 dc with B, 2-htr puff with A, 1 dc in next 2 dc with B, turn.

Row 41: 1 ch, 1 dc in next 54 sts with B, 1 dc in next 6 sts with A, sl st to first dc, turn.

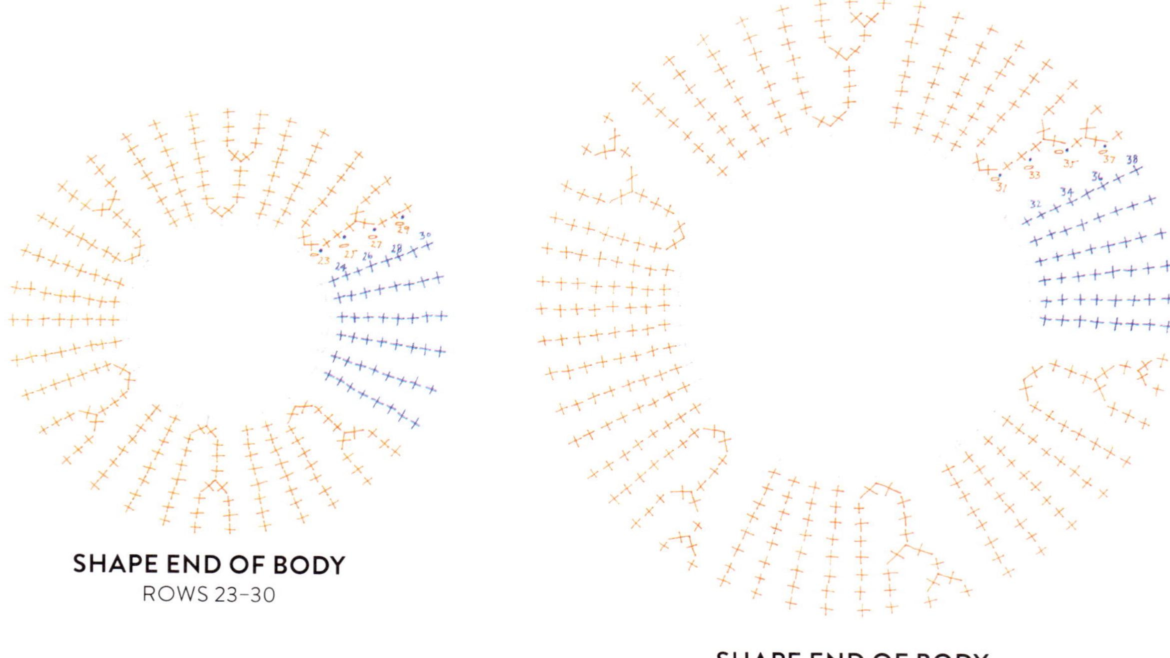

SHAPE END OF BODY
ROWS 23–30

SHAPE END OF BODY
ROWS 31–38

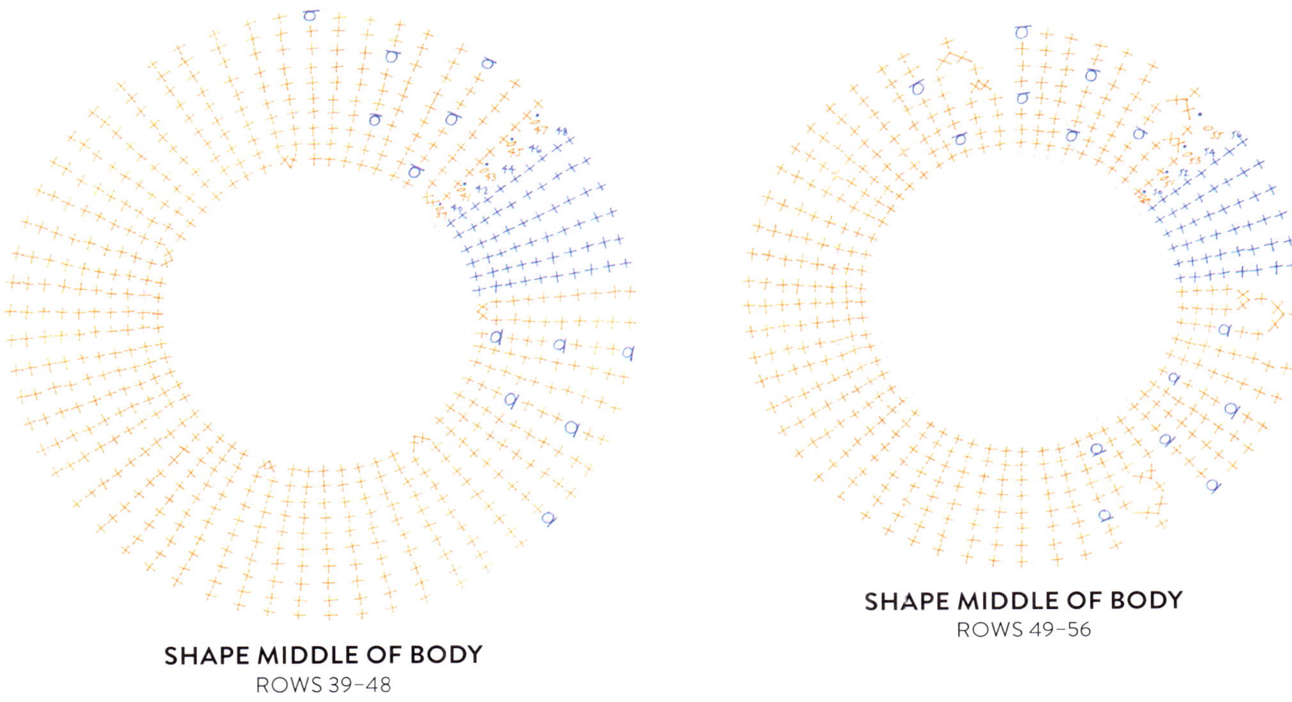

SHAPE MIDDLE OF BODY
ROWS 39–48

SHAPE MIDDLE OF BODY
ROWS 49–56

Row 42: 1 dc in next 6 dc with A, 1 dc in next 5 dc with B, 2-htr puff with A, 1 dc in next 42 dc with B, 2-htr puff with A, 1 dc in next 5 dc with B, turn.
Row 43: As row 41.
Row 44: As row 40.
Rows 45–46: As rows 41–42.
Row 47: As row 41.
Row 48: 1 dc in next 6 dc with A, 1 dc in next 2 dc with B, 2-htr puff with A, 1 dc in next 5 dc with B, 2-htr puff with A, 1 dc in next 36 dc with B, 2-htr puff with A, 1 dc in next 5 dc with B, 2-htr puff with A, 1 dc in next 2 dc with B, turn.
Row 49: As row 41.
Row 50: 1 dc in next 6 dc with A, (5 dc with B, 2-htr puff with A) twice. 1 dc in next 30 dc with B, (2-htr puff with A, 5 dc with B) twice, turn.
Row 51: As row 41.
Row 52: As row 48.
Row 53 (dec): With B, 1 ch, dc2tog, 1 dc in next 7 dc, dc2tog, 1 dc in next 32 dc, dc2tog, 1 dc in next 7 dc, dc2tog; with A, 1 dc in next 6 dc, sl st to first dc, turn (56 sts).
Row 54: 1 dc in next 6 dc with A, 1 dc in next 4 dc with B, 2-htr puff with A, 1 dc in next 5 dc with B, 2-htr puff with A, 1 dc in next 28 dc with B, 2-htr puff with A, 1 dc in next 5 dc with B, 2-htr puff with A, 1 dc in next 4 dc with B, turn.
Row 55 (dec): With B, 1 ch, dc2tog, 1 dc in next 6 dc, dc2tog, 1 dc in next 30 dc, dc2tog, 1 dc in next 6 dc, dc2tog; with A, 1 dc in next 6 dc, sl st to first dc, turn (52 sts).
Row 56: 1 dc in next 6 dc with A, 1 dc in next 6 dc with B, 2-htr puff with A, 1 dc in next 32 dc with B, 2-htr puff with A, 1 dc in next 6 dc with B, turn.

Stuff the body to within the last three rows before continuing.

Row 57 (dec): With B, 1 ch, dc2tog, 1 dc in next 5 dc, dc2tog, 1 dc in next 28 dc, dc2tog, 1 dc in next 5 dc, dc2tog; with A, 1 dc in next 6 dc, sl st to first dc, turn (48 sts).
Row 58: 1 dc in next 6 dc with A, 1 dc in next 2 dc with B, 2-htr puff with A, 1 dc in next 36 dc with B, 2-htr puff with A, 1 dc in next 2 dc with B, turn.
Row 59 (dec): With B, 1 ch, dc2tog, 1 dc in next 4 dc, dc2tog, 1 dc in next 26 dc, dc2tog, 1 dc in next 4 dc, dc2tog; with A, 1 dc in next 6 dc, sl st to first dc, turn (44 sts).
Row 60: 1 dc in next 6 dc with A, 1 dc in next 5 dc with B, 2-htr puff with A, 1 dc in next 26 dc with B, 2-htr puff with A, 1 dc in next 5 dc with B, turn.
Row 61 (dec): With B, 1 ch, dc2tog, 1 dc in next 3 dc, dc2tog, 1 dc in next 24 dc, dc2tog, 1 dc in next 3 dc, dc2tog; with A, 1 dc in next 6 dc, sl st to first dc, turn (40 sts).
Row 62: 1 dc in next 6 dc with A, 1 dc in next 2 dc with B, 2-htr puff with A, 1 dc in next 28 dc with B, 2-htr puff with A, 1 dc in next 2 dc with B, turn.
Row 63 (dec): With B, 1 ch, dc2tog, 1 dc in next 2 dc, dc2tog, 1 dc in next 22 dc, dc2tog, 1 dc in next 2 dc, dc2tog; with A, 1 dc in next 6 dc, sl st to first dc, turn (36 sts).
Row 64: 1 dc in next 6 sts with A, 1 dc in next 30 sts with B, turn.
Row 65: 1 ch, 1 dc in next 30 sts with B, 1 dc in next 6 sts with A, sl st to first dc, turn.
Row 66: As row 64.
Do not fasten off.

SHAPE FRONT OF BODY

The following is worked in short rows.
Row 1 (RS) (dec): With B, 1 ch, 1 dc in next 13 dc, (dc2tog) twice, 1 dc in next 5 dc, sl st in next dc, turn, finishing 13 sts before the end of the row (34 sts).
Row 2 (WS): 1 dc in same dc as sl st, 1 dc in next 13 dc, sl st in next dc, turn.
Row 3: 1 dc in same dc as sl st, 1 dc in next 15 dc, sl st in next dc, turn.
Row 4: 1 dc in same dc as sl st, 1 dc in next 17 dc, sl st in next dc, turn.
Row 5 (dec): 1 dc in same dc as sl st, 1 dc in next 7 dc, (dc2tog) twice, 1 dc in next 8 dc, sl st in next dc, turn (32 sts).

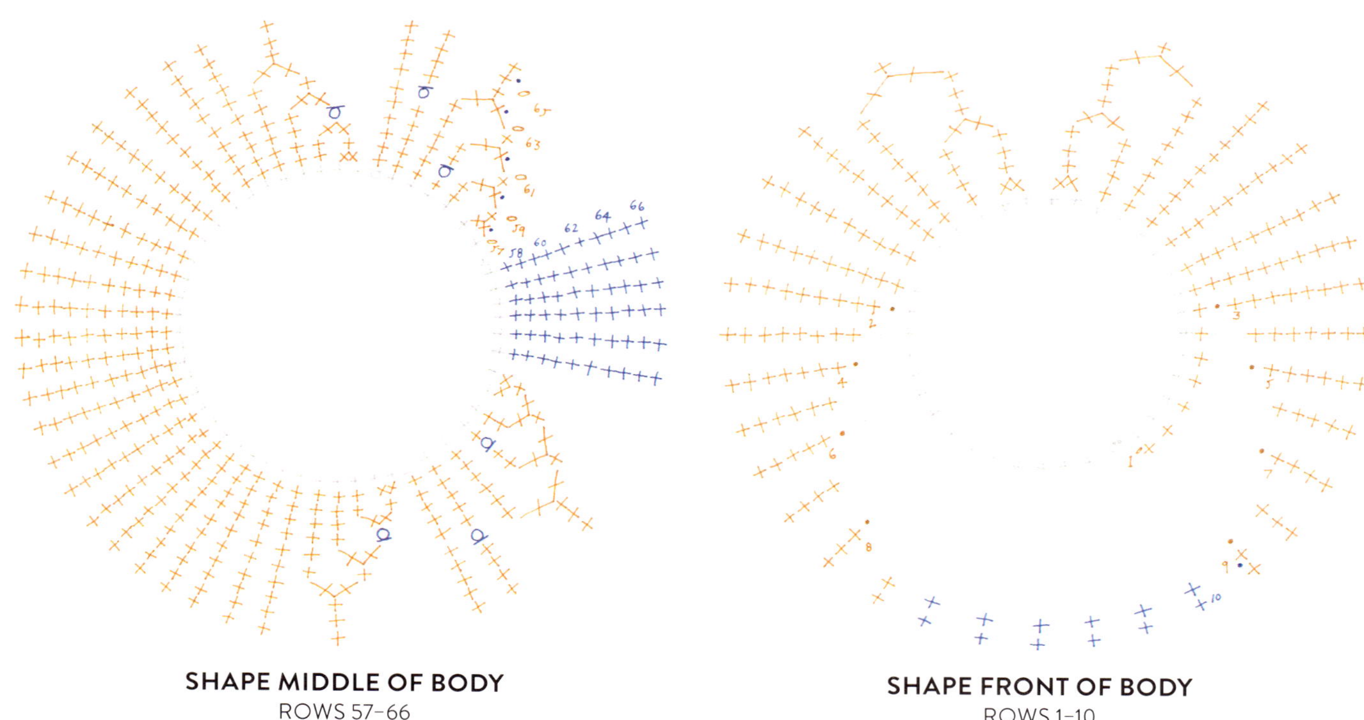

SHAPE MIDDLE OF BODY
ROWS 57–66

SHAPE FRONT OF BODY
ROWS 1–10

Row 6: 1 dc in same dc as sl st, 1 dc in next 19 dc, sl st in next dc, turn.
Row 7: 1 dc in same dc as sl st, 1 dc in next 21 dc, sl st in next dc, turn.
Row 8: 1 dc in same dc as sl st, 1 dc in next 23 dc, sl st in next dc, turn.
Row 9 (dec): With B, 1 dc in same dc as sl st, 1 dc in next 10 dc, (dc2tog) twice, 1 dc in next 11 dc, with A work 1 dc in next 6 dc, sl st to first dc, turn (30 sts).
Row 10: 1 dc in next 6 sts with A, 1 dc in next 24 sts with B, turn.
Insert more stuffing before continuing.

NECK

Row 1 (RS) (dec): With B, 1 ch, dc2tog, 1 dc in next 20 dc, dc2tog; with A, 1 dc in next 6 dc, sl st to first dc, turn (28 sts).
Row 2 (WS): 1 dc in next 6 sts with A, 1 dc in next 22 sts with B, turn.
Row 3 (dec): With B, 1 ch, dc2tog, 1 dc in next 18 dc, dc2tog; with A, 1 dc in next 6 dc, sl st to first dc, turn (26 sts).
Row 4: 1 dc in next 6 sts with A, 1 dc in next 20 sts with B, turn.
Row 5 (dec): With B, 1 ch, dc2tog, 1 dc in next 16 dc, dc2tog; with A, 1 dc in next 6 dc, sl st to first dc, turn (24 sts).
Row 6: 1 dc in next 6 sts with A, 1 dc in next 18 sts with B, turn.
Row 7 (dec): With B, 1 ch, dc2tog, 1 dc in next 14 dc, dc2tog; with A, 1 dc in next 6 dc, sl st to first dc, turn (22 sts).
Row 8: 1 dc in next 6 sts with A, 1 dc in next 16 sts with B, turn.
Row 9 (dec): With B, 1 ch, dc2tog, 1 dc in next 12 dc, dc2tog; with A, 1 dc in next 6 dc, sl st to first dc, turn (20 sts).
Row 10: 1 dc in next 6 sts with A, 1 dc in next 14 sts with B, turn.
Row 11 (dec): With B, 1 ch, dc2tog, 1 dc in next 10 dc, dc2tog; with A, 1 dc in next 6 dc, sl st to first dc, turn (18 sts).
Row 12: 1 dc in next 6 sts with A, 1 dc in next 12 sts with B, turn.
Stuff the neck to within the last three rows before continuing.

The following rows are not joined with a slip stitch at the end to leave an opening for stuffing.
Row 13: 1 ch, 1 dc in next 12 sts with B, 1 dc in next 6 sts with A, turn.
Row 14: 1 ch, 1 dc in next 6 sts with A, 1 dc in next 12 sts with B, turn.
Do not fasten off.

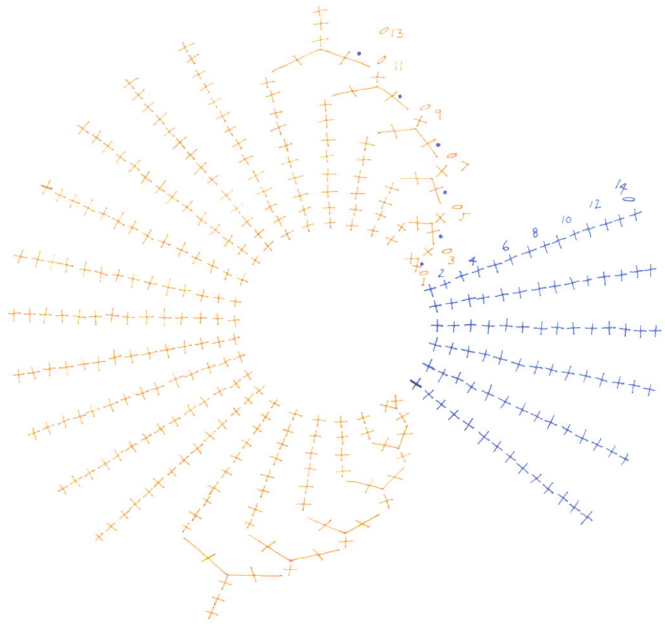

NECK
ROWS 1–14

HEAD

Row 1 (RS) (inc): 1 ch, (dc2inc, 1 dc) 3 times, (1 dc, dc2inc) 3 times with B, 1 dc in next 6 with A, turn (24 sts).
Row 2 (WS): 1 ch, 1 dc in next 6 sts with A, 1 dc in next 18 sts with B, turn.
Row 3 (dec): With B, 1 ch, 1 dc in next 6 dc, dc2tog, 1 dc in next 2 dc, dc2tog, 1 dc in next 6 dc; with A, 1 dc in next 6 dc, turn (22 sts).
Row 4: 1 ch, 1 dc in next 6 sts with A, 1 dc in next 16 sts with B, turn.

The next and following alternate row are joined with a slip stitch at the end.
Row 5 (dec): With B, 1 ch, dc2tog, (5 dc, dc2tog) twice; with A, 1 dc in next 2 dc, dc2tog, 1 dc in next 2 dc, sl st to first dc to join, turn (18 sts).
Row 6: 1 dc in next 5 sts with A, 1 dc in next 13 sts with B, turn.
Row 7 (dec): With B, 1 ch, dc2tog, 1 dc in next 9 dc, dc2tog; with A, 1 dc in next 5 dc, sl st to first dc, turn (16 sts).
Row 8: 1 dc in each st with B.
Fasten off, leaving a long tail of A.

MOUTH

With 2.5mm hook and D, make 10 ch.
Row 1 (RS): 3 dc in second ch from hook, *1 dc in next 2 ch, 1 htr in next 3 ch, place a marker on the second htr st, 1 dc in next 2 ch*, 3 dc in end ch; working in opposite side of each ch; rep from * to * (20 sts).
Fasten off.

TONGUE

With 2.5mm hook and D, make 4 ch.
Row 1 (RS): 1 dc in second ch from hook, 1 dc in next 2 ch, 1 dc in opposite side of each ch (6 sts).
Fasten off, leaving a long tail of yarn.

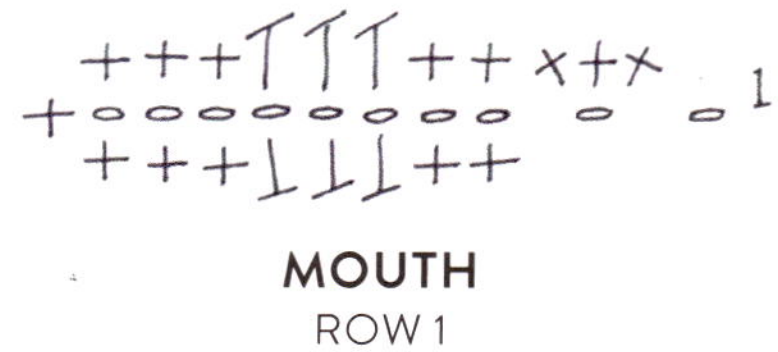

MOUTH
ROW 1

TONGUE
ROW 1

BEAK

LOWER BEAK

With 2.5mm hook and RS of head facing, skip the first 5 of the 16 sts of row 8 of the head and join B with a sl st to the next dc.
The following is worked in short rows.
Row 1 (RS): 1 dc in same dc as sl st, sl st in next dc, turn (1 st).
Row 2 (WS): 1 dc in same dc as sl st, 1 dc in next 2 dc, sl st in next dc, turn (3 sts).
Row 3 (inc): 1 dc in same dc as sl st, 1 dc in next dc, dc3inc, 1 dc in next 2 dc, sl st in next dc, turn (7 sts).
Row 4: 1 dc in same dc as sl st, 1 dc in next 8 dc (9 sts).
Fasten off.

TOP BEAK

With 2.5mm hook and RS of head facing, skip the first 4 of the remaining 9 sts of row 8 of the head and join B with a sl st to the next dc.
Rows 1–3: As rows 1–3 of lower beak.
Row 4: 1 dc in same dc as sl st, 1 dc in next 8 dc, sl st in next dc, turn (9 sts).
Do not fasten off.

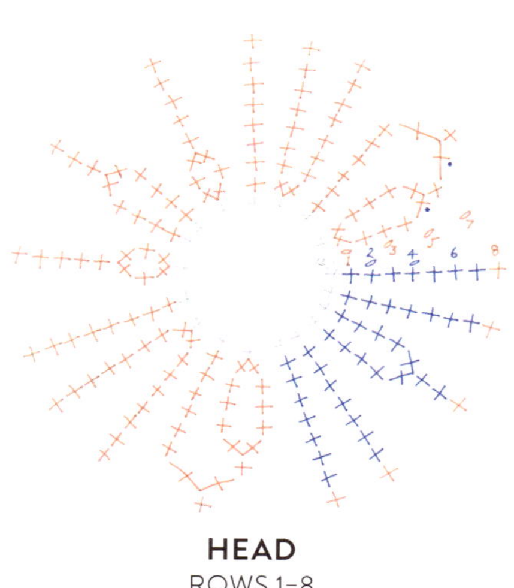

HEAD
ROWS 1–8

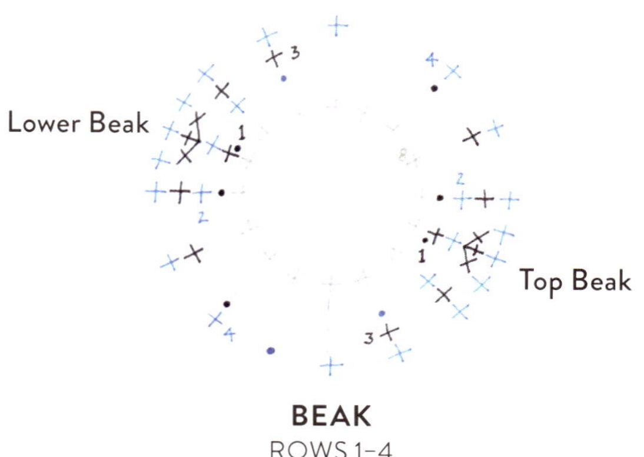

BEAK
ROWS 1–4

Lower Beak

Top Beak

JOIN MOUTH TO BEAK
ROW 1

JOIN MOUTH TO BEAK

Row 1 (RS): Insert the mouth into the head, with WS together, aligning the markers with the unworked stitch on each side of the beak. With yarn B and the top beak facing, 1 dc in the same st as the sl st and the marked htr of the mouth at the same time to join; working into each stitch of the beak and mouth at the same time, 1 dc in the next 4 sts, 1 htr in next st, 1 dc in the next 9 sts, 1 htr in next st at the tip of the lower beak, 1 dc in next 4 sts, sl st to next st and fasten off (20 sts).

EYE SOCKET
(make 2)

With 2.5mm hook and B, make a magic loop.
Round 1 (RS): 1 ch, 6 dc into loop, sl st to first dc.
Fasten off.

EYE SOCKET
ROUND 1

BACK LEGS
(make 2)

FOOT

The bobbles that form the toes appear on the reverse side of the work. This will be the right side. See page 158 for instructions to make bobble (mb).
Starting at the base of the foot, with 2.5mm hook and B, make a magic loop.
Round 1 (WS): 1 ch, 6 dc into loop (6 sts).
Round 2 (inc): (Dc2inc) 6 times (12 sts). Pull tightly on short end of yarn to close loop.
Round 3 (inc): (Dc2inc, 1 dc) 6 times (18 sts).
Round 4: 1 dc in next dc, join A and carry unused yarn on the WS of the work; (mb with A, 1 dc in next 2 dc with B) twice, mb with A, 1 dc in next 10 dc with B, turn to RS.
Continue with B.
Round 5 (RS): 1 ch, 1 dc in each st.
Round 6: 1 dc in each st.
Round 7 (dec): 1 dc in next 11 dc, (dc2tog, 1 dc) twice, 1 dc in next dc (16 sts).
Round 8 (dec): 1 dc in next 10 dc, (dc2tog, 1 dc) twice (14 sts).

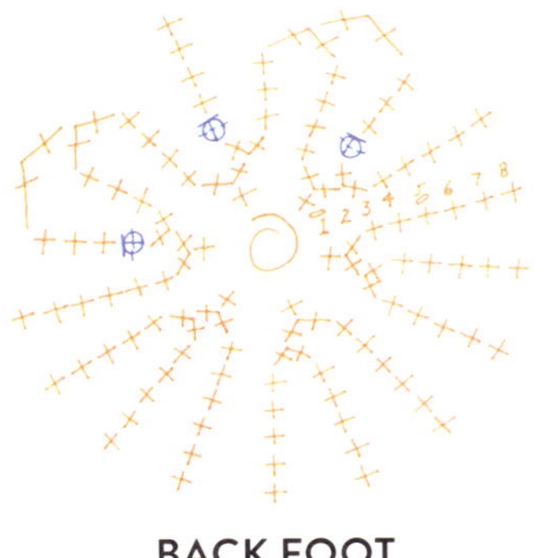

BACK FOOT
ROUNDS 1–8

SHAPE LOWER BACK LEG

Rounds 9–10: 1 dc in each dc.
Round 11 (inc): 1 dc in next 2 dc, (dc2inc, 2 dc) 4 times (18 sts).
Rounds 12–18: 1 dc in each dc.
Round 19: 1 dc in next 4 dc, finishing in line with the first toe, 14 sts before the end of the round.

KNEE JOINT

Round 20: 6 ch, skip next 12 dc, 1 dc in next 6 dc.
Round 21: 1 dc in next 6 ch, 1 dc in next 6 dc (12 sts).
Fasten off and thread tail of yarn through last round of stitches. Pull tightly on end of yarn to close and fasten off.

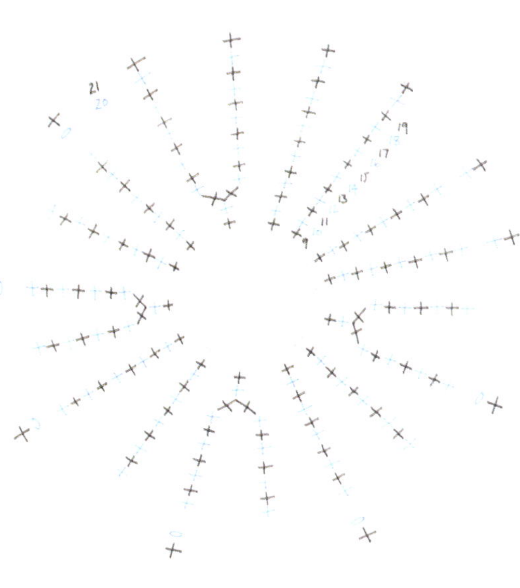

SHAPE LOWER BACK LEG
ROUNDS 9–19

KNEE JOINT
ROUNDS 20–21

SHAPE THIGH

With RS facing, join B with a sl st to the first of the 12 skipped sts of the lower back leg.

Round 1: 1 dc in same dc as sl st, 1 dc in next 11 dc, 1 dc in opposite side of next 6 ch of the knee joint (18 sts).

Round 2 (inc): (1 dc, dc2inc) 3 times, (dc2inc, 1 dc) 3 times, 1 dc in next 6 dc (24 sts).

Rounds 3–4: 1 dc in each dc.

Round 5 (inc): (2 dc, dc2inc) 6 times, 1 dc in next 6 dc (30 sts).

Rounds 6–14: 1 dc in each dc.

Round 15 (dec): (Dc2tog, 3 dc) 6 times (24 sts).

Stuff the leg before continuing.

Round 16 (dec): (Dc2tog, 2 dc) 6 times (18 sts).

Round 17 (dec): (Dc2tog, 1 dc) 6 times (12 sts).

Round 18 (dec): (Dc2tog) 6 times (6 sts).

Fasten off and thread the tail of yarn through the last round of stitches. Pull tightly on the end of yarn to close and fasten off.

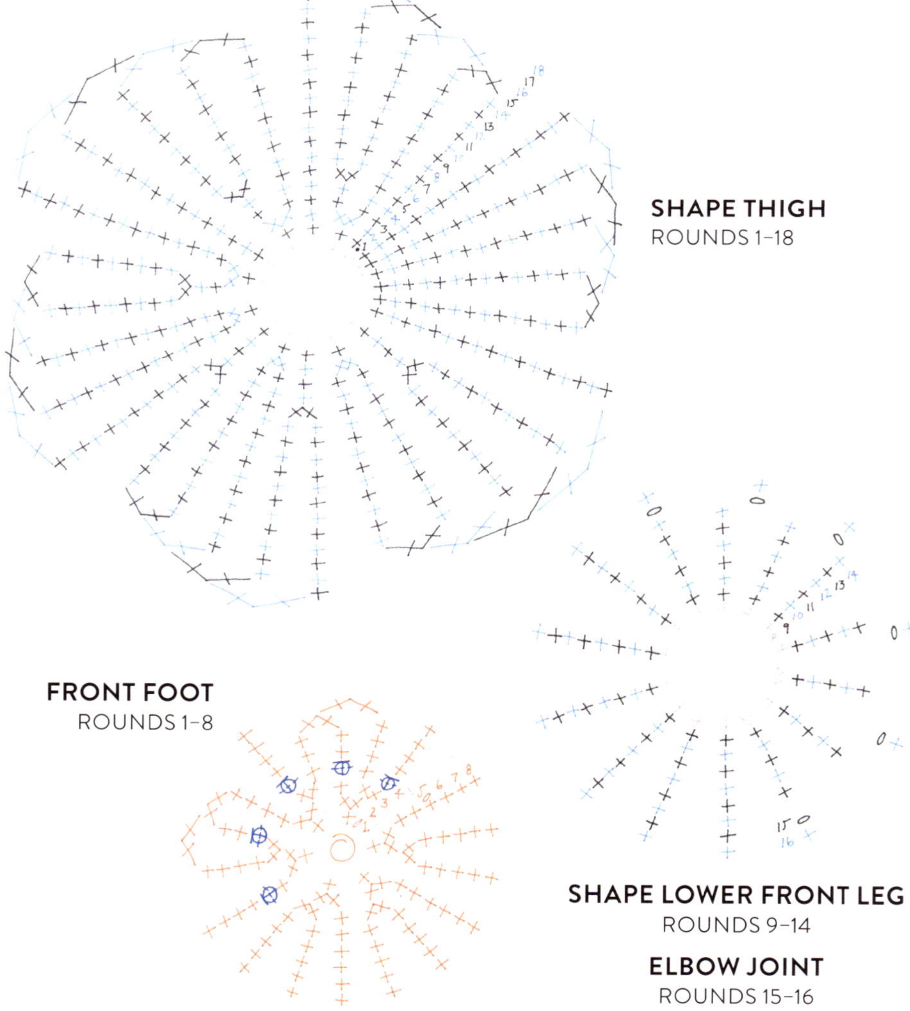

SHAPE THIGH
ROUNDS 1–18

FRONT FOOT
ROUNDS 1–8

SHAPE LOWER FRONT LEG
ROUNDS 9–14

ELBOW JOINT
ROUNDS 15–16

FRONT LEGS
(make 2)

FOOT

Starting at the base of the foot, with 2.5mm hook and B, make a magic loop.

Round 1 (WS): 1 ch, 6 dc into loop (6 sts).

Round 2 (inc): (Dc2inc) 6 times (12 sts). Pull tightly on short end of yarn to close loop.

Round 3 (inc): (Dc2inc, 1 dc) 6 times (18 sts).

Join A and carry unused yarn on the WS of the work.

Round 4: (Mb with A, 1 dc in next dc with B) 4 times, mb with A, 1 dc in next 9 dc with B, turn.

Continue with B.

Round 5 (RS): 1 ch, 1 dc in each st.

Round 6: 1 dc in each st.

Round 7 (dec): 1 dc in next 11 dc, (dc2tog, 1 dc) twice, 1 dc in next dc (16 sts).

Round 8 (dec): 1 dc in next 10 dc, (dc2tog, 1 dc) twice (14 sts).

SHAPE LOWER FRONT LEG

Rounds 9–13: 1 dc in each dc.

Round 14: 1 dc in next 10 dc, finishing at the side of the leg, 4 sts before the end of the round.

ELBOW JOINT

Round 15: 6 ch, skip next 8 dc, 1 dc in next 6 dc.

Round 16: 1 dc in next 6 ch, 1 dc in next 6 dc (12 sts).

Fasten off and thread tail of yarn through last round of stitches. Pull tightly on end of yarn to close and fasten off.

SHAPE SHOULDER

With RS facing, join B with a sl st to the first of the 8 skipped sts of the lower front leg.

Round 1: 1 dc in same dc as sl st, 1 dc in next 7 dc, 1 dc in opposite side of next 6 ch of the elbow joint (14 sts).

Round 2 (inc): 1 dc in next dc, dc2inc, 1 dc in next 4 dc, (dc2inc, 2 dc) twice, dc2inc, 1 dc in next dc (18 sts).

Rounds 3–8: 1 dc in each dc.

Stuff the leg before continuing.

Round 9 (dec): (Dc2tog, 1 dc) 6 times (12 sts).

Round 10 (dec): (Dc2tog) 6 times (6 sts).

Fasten off and thread the tail of yarn through the last round of stitches. Pull tightly on the end of yarn to close and fasten off.

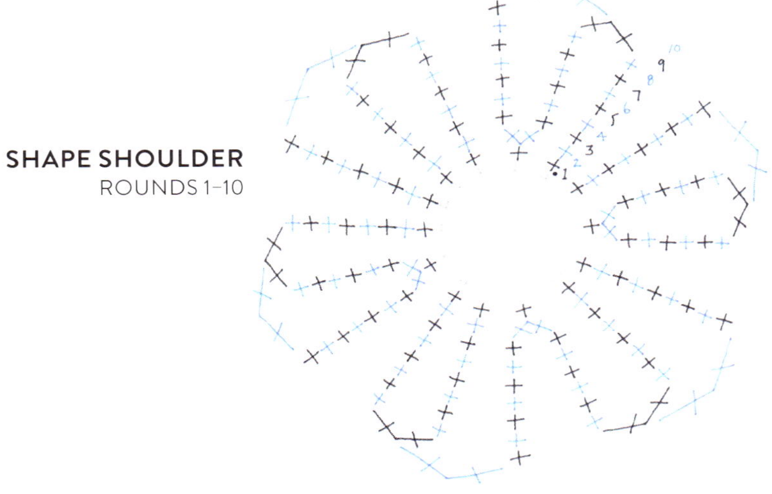

SHAPE SHOULDER
ROUNDS 1–10

BACK PLATES

LARGE PLATES (MAKE 4)

With 2.5mm hook and C, make 10 ch.

Row 1 (RS): 1 dc in second ch from hook, 1 dc in next ch, 1 htr in next ch, 1 tr in next ch, 1 htr in next ch, 1 dc in next 3 ch, 3 dc in end ch; working in the opposite side of each ch, 1 dc in next 3 ch, 1 htr in next ch, 1 tr in next ch, 1 htr in next ch, 1 dc in next 2 ch, turn (19 sts).

Row 2 (WS) (inc): 1 ch, 1 dc in next 9 sts, dc3inc, 1 dc in next 9 sts, turn (21 sts).

Row 3 (inc): 1 ch, 1 dc in next 3 dc, dc3inc, (6 dc, dc3inc) twice, 1 dc in next 3 dc, rotate piece and work 4 dc evenly across the stitches at the edge of the rows (31 sts).

Fasten off.

Make one more piece to match the first and join A in last dc. Do not fasten off.

JOIN PLATES

Place the two pieces with WS together.

Row 4: With A, working into each stitch of both pieces at the same time to join, 1 dc in next 4 dc, dc2inc, 1 dc in next 8 dc, dc3inc, 1 dc in next 8 dc, dc2inc, 1 dc in next 4 dc. Fasten off, leaving a long tail of A and the 4 sts on each side of the open edges unworked (31 sts).

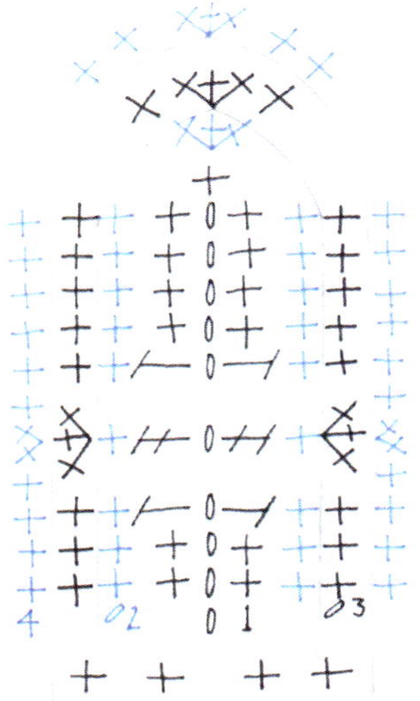

LARGE PLATE
ROWS 1–3

JOIN PLATES
ROW 4
Insert hook into each stitch of both pieces at the same time to join

MEDIUM PLATES (MAKE 4)

With 2.5mm hook and C, make 8 ch.

Row 1 (RS): 1 dc in second ch from hook, 1 dc in next ch, 1 htr in next ch, 1 tr in next ch, 1 htr in next ch, 1 dc in next ch, 3 dc in end ch; working in the opposite side of each ch, 1 dc in next ch, 1 htr in next ch, 1 tr in next ch, 1 htr in next ch, 1 dc in next 2 ch, turn (15 sts).

Row 2 (WS) (inc): 1 ch, 1 dc in next 7 sts, dc3inc, 1 dc in next 7 sts, turn (17 sts).

Row 3 (inc): 1 ch, 1 dc in next 3 dc, dc3inc, (4 dc, dc3inc) twice, 1 dc in next 3 dc, rotate piece and work 4 dc evenly across the stitches at the edge of the rows (27 sts).

Fasten off.

Make one more piece to match the first and join A in last dc. Do not fasten off.

MEDIUM PLATE
ROWS 1–3
JOIN PLATES
ROW 4
Insert hook into each stitch of both pieces at the same time to join

JOIN PLATES

Place the two pieces with WS together.

Row 4: With A, working into each stitch of both pieces at the same time to join, 1 dc in next 4 dc, dc2inc, 1 dc in next 6 dc, dc3inc, 1 dc in next 6 dc, dc2inc, 1 dc in next 4 dc. Fasten off, leaving a long tail of A and the 4 sts on each side of the open edges unworked (27 sts).

SMALL PLATES (MAKE 8)

With 2.5mm hook and C, make 6 ch.

Row 1 (RS): 1 dc in second ch from hook, 1 dc in next ch, 1 htr in next ch, 1 dc in next ch, 3 dc in end ch; working in the opposite side of each ch, 1 dc in next ch, 1 htr in next ch, 1 dc in next 2 ch (11 sts).

Fasten off.

Make one more piece to match the first and join A in last dc. Do not fasten off.

JOIN PLATES

Place the two pieces with WS together and the first piece facing.

Row 2: With A, 1 ch, working into each stitch of both pieces at the same time to join, 1 dc in next 5 dc, dc3inc, 1 dc in next 5 dc (13 sts).

Fasten off, leaving a long tail of A and the 3 sts on each side of the open edges unworked.

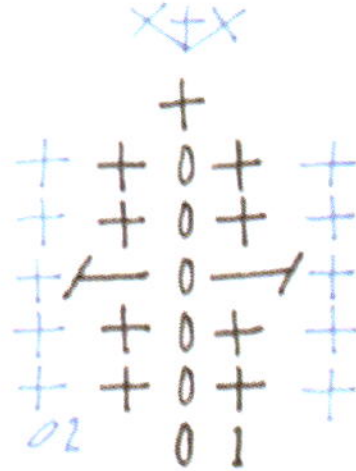

SMALL PLATE
ROW 1
JOIN PLATES
ROW 2
Insert hook into each stitch of both pieces at the same time to join

TAIL SPIKES

LARGE SPIKES (MAKE 2)

With 2.5mm hook and A, make 11 ch.
Row 1 (WS): 1 dc in second ch from hook, 1 dc in next 8 ch, 3 dc in end ch, 1 dc in opposite side of next 9 ch, turn (21 sts).
Row 2 (RS) (inc): 2 ch, 1 htr in next 3 dc, 1 dc in next 7 dc, dc2inc, 1 dc in next 7 dc, 1 htr in next 3 dc (22 sts).
Fasten off, leaving a long tail of yarn.

SMALL SPIKES (MAKE 2)

With 2.5mm hook and A, make 9 ch.
Row 1 (WS): 1 dc in second ch from hook, 1 dc in next 6 ch, 3 dc in end ch, 1 dc in opposite side of next 7 ch, turn (17 sts).
Row 2 (RS) (inc): 2 ch, 1 htr in next 2 dc, 1 dc in next 6 dc, dc2inc, 1 dc in next 6 dc, 1 htr in next 2 dc (18 sts).
Fasten off, leaving a long tail of yarn.

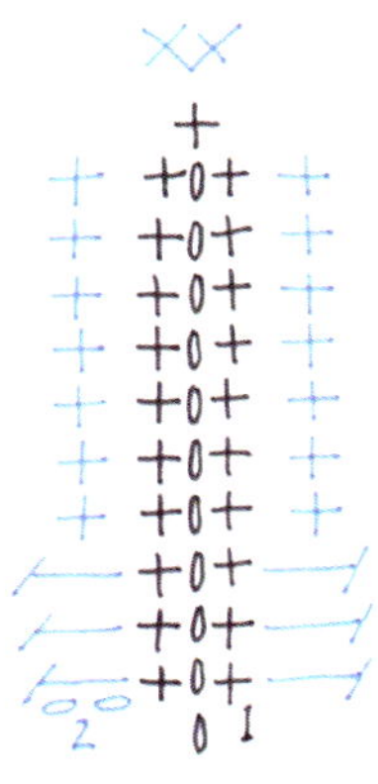

LARGE SPIKE
ROWS 1–2

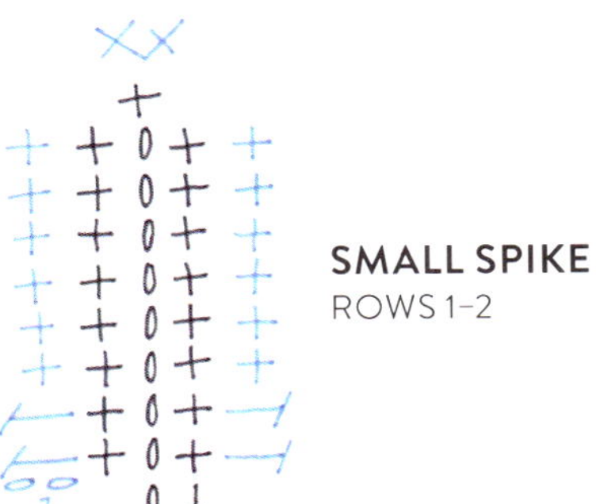

SMALL SPIKE
ROWS 1–2

MAKING UP

HEAD

Fold the tongue and sew together the 3 stitches on each side. Sew the end of the tongue securely to the centre of the mouth.

If using safety eyes, attach them before stuffing the head. Poke the post of the safety eye through the centre of the eye socket. Pull tightly on the short end of yarn to close the loop around the post of the safety eye, before attaching it to the head (see page 163).

Stuff the head, pushing the stuffing into the beak with the end of the hook and keeping the inside of the mouth flat. Use the tail of yarn B to neatly sew together the open edges of the head.

If using looped glass eyes, poke the loop of an eye through the centre of each eye socket before attaching each one to the head using 23⅝in (60cm) length of clear invisible or strong sewing thread (see page 163).

Embroider the nostrils in satin stitch (see page 164), using two strands of embroidery thread.

BACK PLATES

Lightly stuff each plate, keeping them flat. Embroider three lazy daisy stitches (see page 165) in yarn A on both sides of the large and medium plates. Sew the back plates, in two staggered rows down the centre of the back, positioning the largest ones in the middle and the smallest ones at the neck and tail end. Sew through the stitches around the open edges to attach them securely to the body.

TAIL SPIKES

Fold the spike lengthways, WS together, matching the stitches on each side. Use the tail of yarn left after fastening off to sew the stitches together. Stuff the spikes. Sew the spikes to the tail, placing the shorter pair nearest the tip of the tail and stitching all around the lower edges to attach them securely.

Weave in all the yarn ends.

LEGS

Follow the instructions on page 164 to attach the legs, using 63in (160cm) length of yarn A or strong thread for each pair of legs.

TYRANNOSAURUS REX

THIS T-REX HAS BOBBLE-STITCH MARKINGS OVER THE TOP OF ITS HEAD, WIDE, GAPING JAWS BARING ITS TEETH AND A CURLING TONGUE.

MATERIALS

- Drops Flora, 65% wool, 35% alpaca (230yd/210m per 50g ball):
  1 × 50g ball in 23 Misty Forest (A)
  1 × 50g ball in 30 Desert Rose (B)
- 2¼yd (2m) length of 4ply white yarn, such as 22 White Fog (C)
- 1 pair of 5⁄32–3⁄16in (4–5mm) looped glass teddy bear eyes or safety eyes
- Clear invisible or strong thread to attach the looped glass eyes
- Stranded embroidery thread in black, such as Anchor Stranded Cotton, shade 0403, for the nostrils
- 2.25mm (UK13:USB/1) and 2.5mm (UK12:US-) crochet hooks
- Stitch markers
- Blunt-ended yarn needle
- Toy stuffing
- 4 pipe cleaners, each measuring 12in (30cm) long to strengthen the legs (optional: not suitable for young children)

SIZE

Approximately 16⅜in (42cm) long and 8⅞in (22.5cm) tall

TENSION

27 sts and 33 rows to 4in (10cm) over double crochet using 2.5mm hook and yarn A. Use larger or smaller hook if necessary to obtain correct tension.

METHOD

The upper and lower jaws are worked in rows of double crochet with a line of bobble stitches decorating the top of the head. The pieces are joined to complete the back of the head. The mouth is crocheted in rows and joined to form the back of the throat. An edging of double crochet is worked around the mouth and jaws. The teeth and buccal flaps, worked in various stitches, are crocheted into the back loops of the edging of the mouth. The tongue is made in two pieces which are joined by crocheting into each stitch of both pieces at the same time. The tongue is stitched in place before joining the mouth to the jaw.

The first row of the neck is crocheted into unworked stitches of the lower jaw and around the edges of the rows at the back of the head. The neck, body and tail are crocheted in one piece, shaping the front of the body by working in short rows. The curl in the tail is formed by increasing and decreasing the stitches.

The arms and legs are crocheted in rounds. The bends in the limbs are produced by making a length of chain stitches and skipping a number of stitches of the previous row. The stitches of the following row are gathered together to form the joints. The skipped stitches and the opposite side of the chain stitches are then crocheted into to begin the other parts of the arms and legs. The arms and legs are attached to the body so they are movable.

The dinosaur is finished with looped glass or safety eyes attached to a crocheted disc and simple embroidery for the nostrils.

1 ch at beg of the row/round does not count as a st throughout.

HEAD

UPPER JAW

The bobbles appear on the reverse side of the work. This will be the right side. See page 158 for instructions to make bobble (mb).

With 2.5mm hook and A, make 5 ch.

Row 1 (RS): 1 dc in second ch from hook, 1 dc in next 3 ch, turn (4 sts).

Row 2 (WS) (inc): 1 ch, (dc2inc) 4 times, turn (8 sts).

Row 3 (inc): 1 ch, (dc2inc, 1dc) twice (1 dc, dc2inc) twice, turn (12 sts).

Rows 4–5: 1 ch, 1 dc in each st, turn.

Row 6: 1 ch, 1 dc in next 4 dc, mb, 1 dc in next 2 dc, mb, 1 dc in next 4 dc, turn.

Row 7: 1 ch, 1 dc in each st, turn.

Row 8: As row 6.

Row 9 (inc): 1 ch, 1 dc in next 4 dc, dc2inc, 1 dc in next 2 dc, dc2inc, 1 dc in next 4 dc, turn (14 sts).

KEY

- Magic loop
- Chain (ch)
- Slip stitch (sl st)
- Double crochet (dc)
- Dc2inc
- Dc2tog
- Half treble (htr)
- Treble (tr)
- Make bobble (mb)
- Work into back loop only

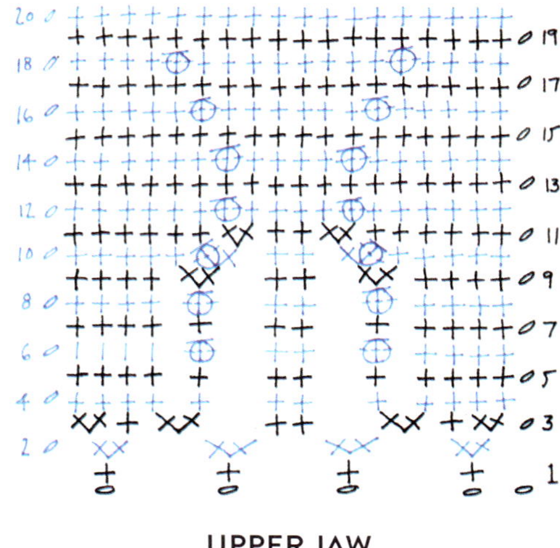

UPPER JAW
ROWS 1–20

Row 10 (inc): 1 ch, 1 dc in next 5 dc, (mb, 1 dc) in next dc, 1 dc in next 2 dc, (1 dc, mb) in next dc, 1 dc in next 5 dc, turn (16 sts).
Row 11 (inc): 1 ch, 1 dc in next 6 dc, dc2inc, 1 dc in next 2 dc, dc2inc, 1 dc in next 6 dc, turn (18 sts).
Row 12: 1 ch, 1 dc in next 6 dc, mb, 1 dc in next 4 dc, mb, 1 dc in next 6 dc, turn.
Row 13: 1 ch, 1 dc in each st, turn.
Row 14: As row 12.
Row 15: 1 ch, 1 dc in each st, turn.
Row 16: 1 ch, 1 dc in next 5 dc, mb, 1 dc in next 6 dc, mb, 1 dc in next 5 dc, turn.
Row 17: 1 ch, 1 dc in each st, turn.
Row 18: 1 ch, 1 dc in next 4 dc, mb, 1 dc in next 8 dc, mb, 1 dc in next 4 dc, turn.
Rows 19–20: 1 ch, 1 dc in each st, turn.
Place a marker at each end of the last row.
Fasten off.

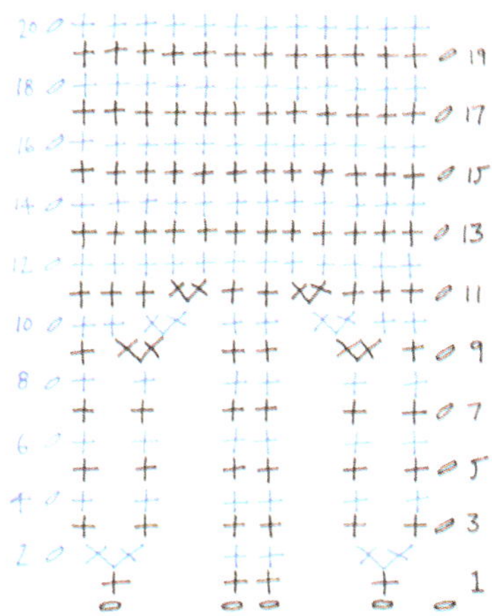

LOWER JAW
ROWS 1–20

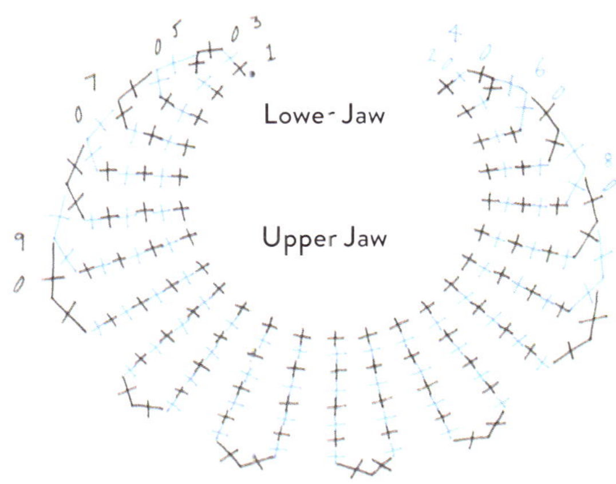

SHAPE BACK OF HEAD
ROWS 1–9

LOWER JAW

With 2.5mm hook and A, make 5 ch.
Row 1 (RS): 1 dc in second ch from hook, 1 dc in next 3 ch, turn (4 sts).
Row 2 (WS) (inc): 1 ch, dc2inc, 1 dc in next 2 dc, dc2inc, turn (6 sts).
Rows 3–8: 1 ch, 1 dc in each st, turn.
Row 9 (inc): 1 ch, (1 dc, dc2inc, 1 dc) twice, turn (8 sts).
Row 10 (inc): 1 ch, (2 dc, dc2inc) twice, 1 dc in next 2 dc, turn (10 sts).
Row 11 (inc): 1 ch, 1 dc in next 2 dc, (1 dc, dc2inc, 1 dc) twice, 1 dc in next 2 dc, turn (12 sts).
Rows 12–20: 1 ch, 1 dc in each st, turn.
Place a marker at each end of the last row.
Fasten off.

SHAPE BACK OF HEAD

With RS of lower jaw facing, skip the first 9 sts and join A with a sl st to the next dc.
Row 1 (RS): 1 dc in same st as sl st, 1 dc in next 2 dc; with RS facing, work 1 dc in each st of the upper jaw; with RS facing, work 1 dc in first 3 dc of lower jaw to join, turn, leaving the centre 6 sts of the lower jaw unworked.
Continue on these 24 sts.
Row 2 (WS): 1 ch, 1 dc in each st, turn.
Rows 3–8 (dec): 1 ch, dc2tog, 1 dc in each dc to last 2 sts, dc2tog, turn (12 sts).
Row 9 (dec): 1 ch, (dc2tog) 6 times (6 sts).
Fasten off and thread the tail of yarn through the last row of stitches.
Pull tightly on the end of yarn and fasten off.

MOUTH

With 2.5mm hook and B, make 5 ch.
Row 1 (RS): 1 dc in second ch from hook, 1 dc in next 3 ch, turn (4 sts).
Row 2 (WS): 1 ch, 1 dc in each st, turn.
Rows 3–6: As row 2.
Row 7 (inc): 1 ch, dc2inc, 1 dc in next 2 dc, dc2inc, turn (6 sts).
Rows 8–10: 1 ch, 1 dc in each st, turn.
Row 11 (inc): 1 ch, dc2inc, 1 dc in next 4 dc, dc2inc, turn (8 sts).
Rows 12–20: 1 ch, 1 dc in each dc, turn.
Place a marker at each end of the last row.
Fasten off.
Make one more mouth piece to match the first. Do not fasten off at the end.

JOIN MOUTH PIECES

Row 21 (RS): 1 ch, 1 dc in each dc; with RS of first mouth piece facing, 1 dc in each dc, sl st to the first dc to join the other end, turn (16 sts).

SHAPE THROAT

Row 22 (WS) (dec): (Dc2tog, 2 dc) 4 times (12 sts).
Row 23 (RS) (dec): 1 ch, (dc2tog) 6 times, sl st to first dc (6 sts).
Fasten off and thread tail of yarn through last round of stitches. Pull tightly on end of yarn to close and fasten off.

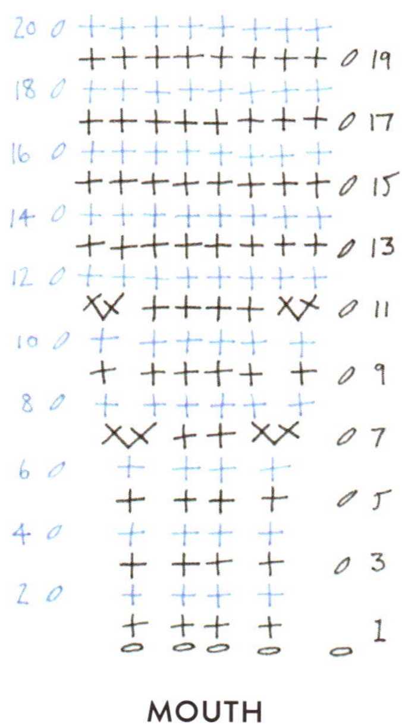

MOUTH
ROWS 1–20

JOIN MOUTH PIECES
ROW 21

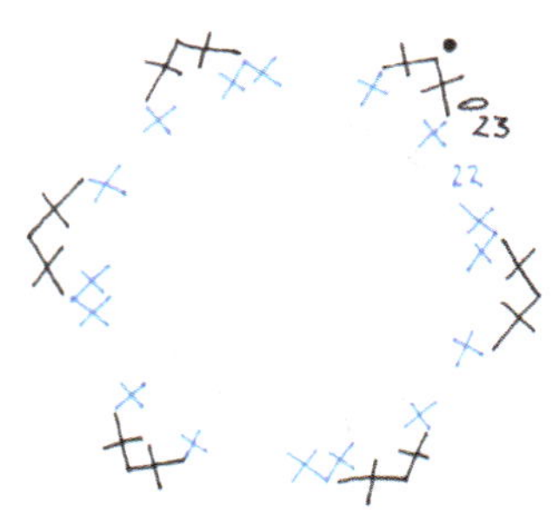

SHAPE THROAT
ROWS 22–23

MOUTH EDGING

With 2.5mm hook and RS facing, join B with a sl st to the st at the edge of row 20 of one mouth piece, indicated by the marker.

Round 1 (RS): Starting in the same st as the sl st, *work 1 dc into each stitch at the edge of the next 20 rows, 1 dc in the opposite side of next 4 ch, 1 dc into each stitch at the edge of the next 20 rows, finishing at the corner of the other side of the mouth, indicated by the marker*; rep from * to * to finish the edging on the other mouth piece (88 sts).

Fasten off.

TEETH

With 2.25mm hook and WS of the mouth facing, skip the first 8 edging sts.

Next: *With C, (sl st in back loop only of next dc, 3 ch, sl st in second ch from hook, 1 dc in next ch, sl st in back loop only of next dc) 14 times. Fasten off.*

Next: With WS of mouth facing, skip the next 16 edging sts from the last tooth made; rep from * to * to finish the other set of teeth.

BUCCAL FLAPS

*With 2.25mm hook and WS of the mouth facing, skip the first 8 edging stitches from the last tooth and join B with a sl st to the back loop only of the next dc.

Next: Working in back loops only, 1 dc in same st as sl st, 1 dc in next st, 1 htr in next 3 sts, 1 tr in next 3 sts. Fasten off, leaving a long tail of yarn* (8 sts).

Rotate the mouth and rep from * to * to make a second flap to match the first on the other mouth piece.

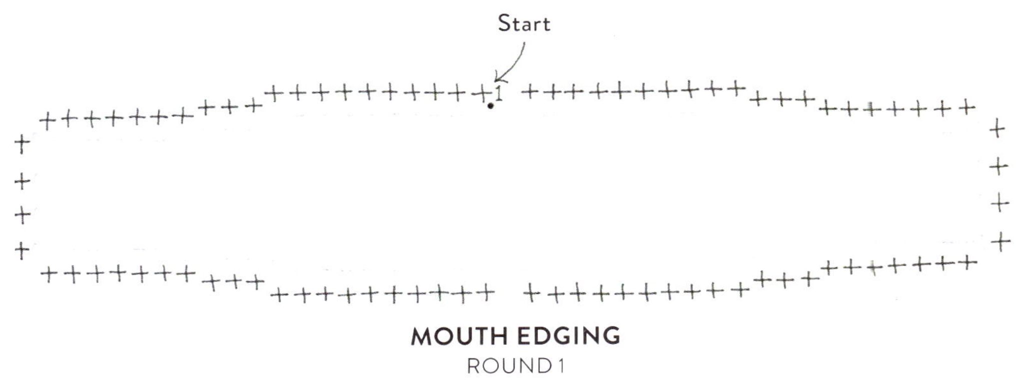

MOUTH EDGING
ROUND 1

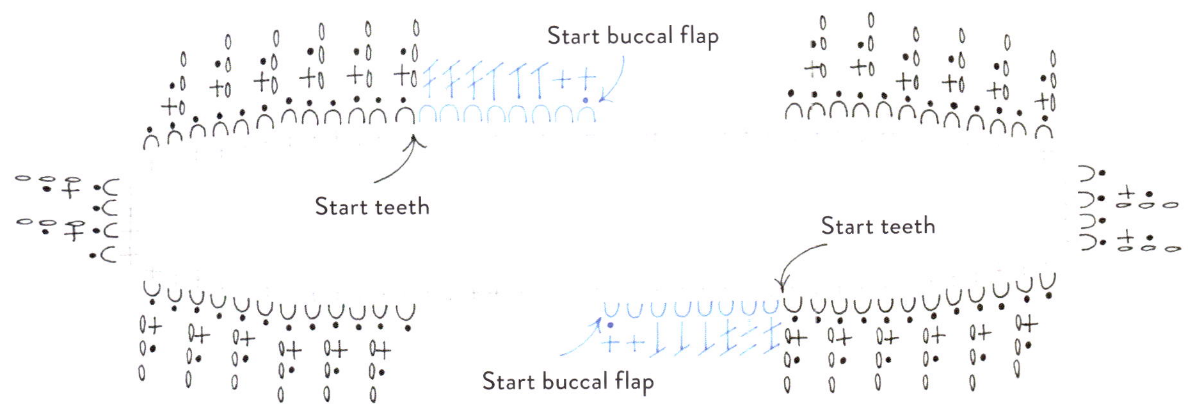

TEETH & BUCCAL FLAPS

TONGUE

With 2.5mm hook and B, make 19 ch.

Row 1: 1 dc in second ch from hook, 1 dc in next 16 ch, 3 dc in end ch, 1 dc in opposite side of each ch to end (37 sts).

Fasten off, leaving a long tail of yarn at the end.

Make a second piece to match the first. Turn at the end of row 1. Do not fasten off.

JOIN TONGUE PIECES

Hold the tongue pieces together, aligning the stitches.

Row 2 (inc): Working into each st of both pieces at the same time to join, 1 ch, 1 dc in next 18 dc, dc3inc, 1 dc in next 18 dc (39 sts).

Fasten off, leaving a long tail of yarn.

FINISH MOUTH

Use the tail of yarn to sew the open edges of the tongue to the back of one mouth piece, near the throat. This will be the floor of the mouth. Thread the yarn through to the inside of the tongue. Pull on the yarn to ripple the tongue and sew a few stitches at intervals to secure the tongue to the floor of the mouth, and to hold its shape.

Sew the tops of the buccal flaps to the back loops only of the corresponding 8 sts on the opposite side of the mouth to connect the top and bottom mouth pieces, leaving the front loops of the edging stitches unworked to join the mouth to the jaw.

Start

TONGUE
ROW 1

JOIN TONGUE PIECES
ROW 2
Insert hook into each stitch of both pieces at the same time to join

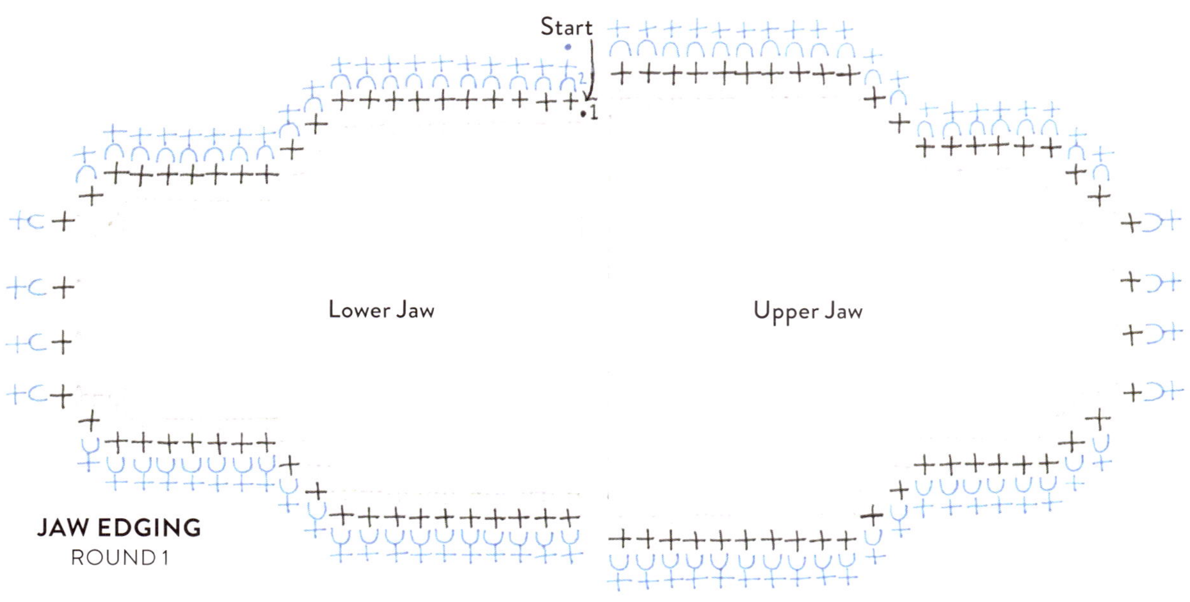

JAW EDGING
ROUND 1

JOIN MOUTH TO JAW
ROUND 2
Insert hook into each stitch of both pieces at the same time to join

JAW EDGING

With 2.5mm hook and RS facing, join A with a sl st to the st at the edge of row 20 of the lower jaw, indicated by the marker.

Round 1 (RS): Starting in the same st as the sl st, *work 1 dc into each stitch at the edge of the next 20 rows, 1 dc in the opposite side of next 4 ch, 1 dc into each stitch at the edge of the next 20 rows, finishing at the corner of the other side of the jaw, by the marker*; starting in the st at the edge of row 20 of the upper jaw, indicated by the marker; rep from * to * to finish the edging (88 sts).

Do not fasten off.

JOIN MOUTH TO JAW

Round 2 (RS): Insert the mouth into the head, ensuring the floor of the mouth is on the lower jaw and aligning the edging stitches of the jaw and mouth. With the jaw facing and working into the back loops only of each stitch of the jaws and the unworked loops of the mouth at the same time to join, 1 dc in the next 88 sts, sl st to next st and fasten off.

EYE SOCKET
(make 2)

With 2.25mm hook and A, make a magic loop.

Round 1 (RS): 3 ch, 9 tr into loop, sl st to third of 3 ch.

Fasten off, leaving a long tail of yarn. If using safety eyes, attach them at this stage. Poke the post of the safety eye through the centre of the eye socket. Pull tightly on the short end of yarn to close the loop around the post of the safety eye, before attaching it to the head (see page 163).

EYE SOCKET
ROUND 1

BODY

NECK

With 2.5mm hook and RS of head facing, join A with a sl st to first of unworked 6 dc of lower jaw.

Row 1 (RS): 1 dc in same dc as sl st, 1 dc in next 5 dc, work 9 dc evenly along the edge of rows of the first side of the head, work 9 dc evenly along the edge of rows down the other side of the head, sl st to first dc, turn (24 sts).

Row 2 (WS): 1 dc in each st, turn.

Row 3 (inc): 1 ch, 1 dc in next 6 dc, (1 dc, dc2inc, 1 dc) 6 times, sl st to first dc, turn (30 sts).

Row 4: 1 dc in each st, turn.

Row 5: 1 ch, 1 dc in each st, sl st to first dc, turn.

Rows 6–9: Rep rows 4–5 twice.

Row 10: 1 dc in next 30 dc, sl st in first dc, turn.

Before continuing, stuff the head to the beginning of the neck, keeping the inside of the mouth flat.

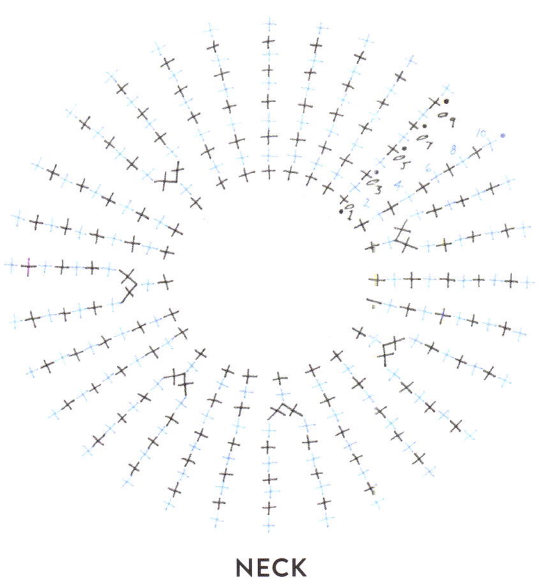

NECK
ROWS 1–10

SHAPE FRONT OF BODY

The following is worked in short rows.

Row 1 (RS) (inc): 1 dc in same dc as sl st, 1 dc in next 3 dc, (dc2inc) twice, 1 dc in next 4 dc, sl st in next dc, turn (32 sts).

Row 2 (WS): 1 dc in same dc as sl st, 1 dc in next 13 dc, sl st in next dc, turn.

Row 3 (inc): 1 dc in same dc as sl st, 1 dc in next 6 dc, (dc2inc) twice, 1 dc in next 7 dc, sl st in next dc, turn (34 sts).

Row 4: 1 dc in same dc as sl st, 1 dc in next 19 dc, sl st in next dc, turn.

Row 5 (inc): 1 dc in same dc as sl st, 1 dc in next 9 dc, (dc2inc) twice, 1 dc in next 10 dc, sl st in next dc, turn (36 sts).

Row 6: 1 dc in same dc as sl st, 1 dc in next 25 dc, sl st in next dc, turn.

Row 7 (inc): 1 dc in same dc as sl st, 1 dc in next 12 dc, (dc2inc) twice, 1 dc in next 13 dc, sl st in next dc, turn (38 sts).

Row 8: 1 dc in same dc as sl st, 1 dc in next 31 dc, sl st in next dc, turn.

Row 9 (inc): 1 dc in same dc as sl st, 1 dc in next 15 dc, (dc2inc) twice, 1 dc in next 16 dc, sl st in next dc, turn (40 sts).

Row 10: 1 dc in same dc as sl st, 1 dc in next 37 dc, sl st in next dc, turn.

Row 11 (inc): 1 dc in same dc as sl st, 1 dc in next 18 dc, (dc2inc) twice, 1 dc in next 19 dc, sl st in first dc, turn (42 sts).

Row 12: 1 dc in each st, turn.

SHAPE MIDDLE OF BODY

Row 13 (inc): 1 ch, (3 dc, dc2inc, 13 dc, dc2inc, 3 dc) twice, sl st to first dc, turn (46 sts).

Row 14: 1 dc in each st, turn.

Row 15 (inc): 1 ch, (3 dc, dc2inc, 15 dc, dc2inc, 3 dc) twice, sl st to first dc, turn (50 sts).

Row 16: 1 dc in each st, turn.

Row 17 (inc): 1 ch, (3 dc, dc2inc, 17 dc, dc2inc, 3 dc) twice, sl st to first dc, turn (54 sts).

Row 18: 1 dc in each st, turn.

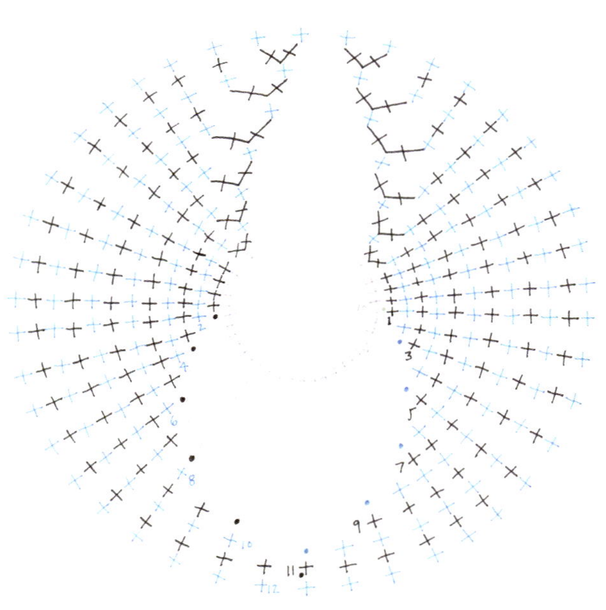

SHAPE FRONT OF BODY
ROWS 1–12

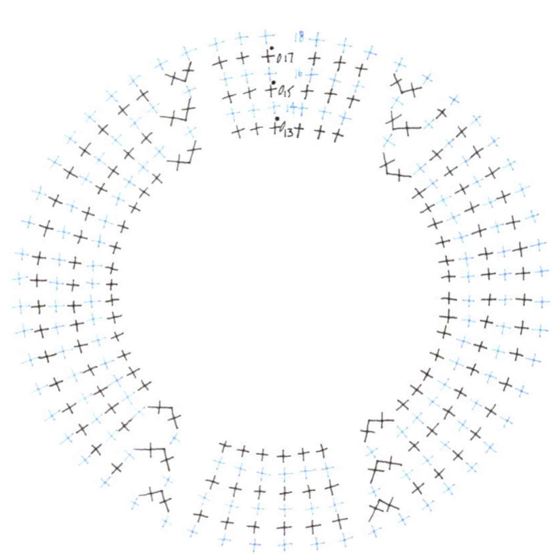

SHAPE MIDDLE OF BODY
ROWS 13–18

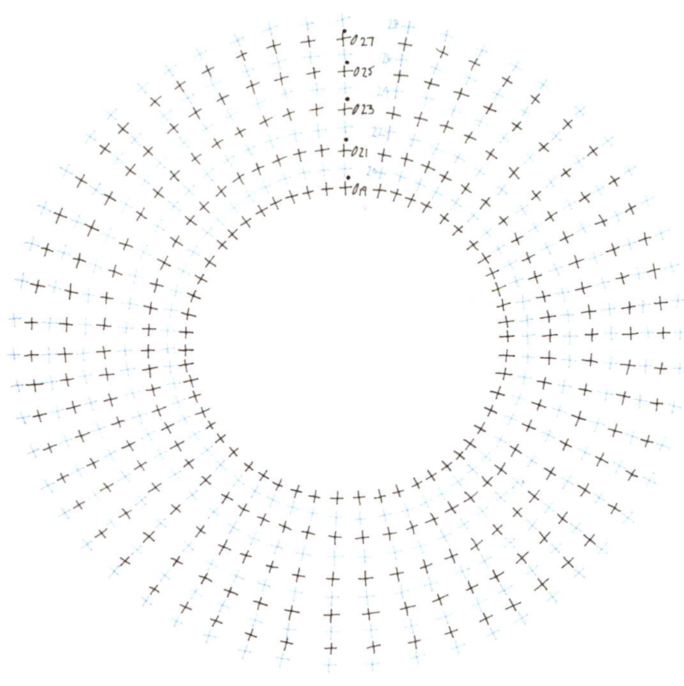

SHAPE MIDDLE OF BODY
ROWS 19–28

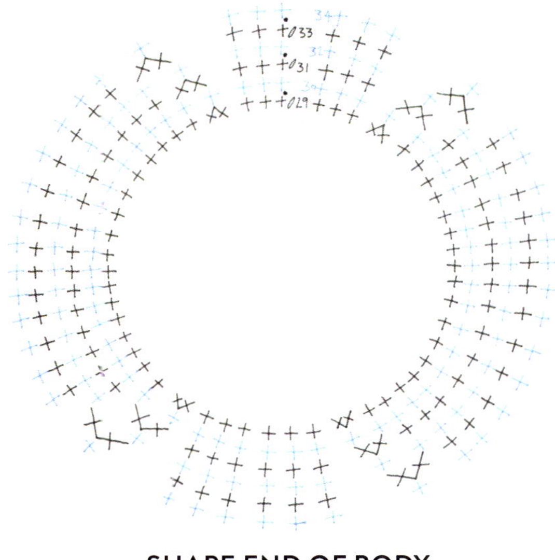

SHAPE END OF BODY
ROWS 29–34

Row 19: 1 ch, 1 dc in each st, sl st to first dc, turn.
Rows 20–27: Rep rows 18–19 4 times.
Row 28: As row 18.
Stuff the neck before continuing.

SHAPE END OF BODY

Row 29 (dec): 1 ch, (3 dc, dc2tog, 17 dc, dc2tog, 3 dc) twice, sl st to first dc, turn (50 sts).
Row 30: 1 dc in each st, turn.
Row 31 (dec): 1 ch, (3 dc, dc2tog, 15 dc, dc2tog, 3 dc) twice, sl st to first dc, turn (46 sts).
Row 32: 1 dc in each st, turn.
Row 33 (dec): 1 ch, (3 dc, dc2tog, 13 dc, dc2tog, 3 dc) twice, sl st to first dc, turn (42 sts).
Row 34: 1 dc in each st, turn.
Before continuing, stuff the body to within the last three rows.
Row 35 (dec): 1 ch, (3 dc, dc2tog, 11 dc, dc2tog, 3 dc) twice, sl st to first dc, turn (38 sts).
Row 36: 1 dc in each st, turn.
Row 37 (dec): 1 ch, (3 dc, dc2tog, 9 dc, dc2tog, 3 dc) twice, sl st to first dc, turn (34 sts).
Row 38: 1 dc in each st, turn.
Row 39 (dec): 1 ch, (3 dc, dc2tog, 7 dc, dc2tog, 3 dc) twice, sl st to first dc, turn (30 sts).
Row 40: 1 dc in each st, turn.
Row 41: 1 ch, 1 dc in each st, sl st to first dc, turn.
Row 42: 1 dc in each st, turn.
Insert more stuffing before continuing.

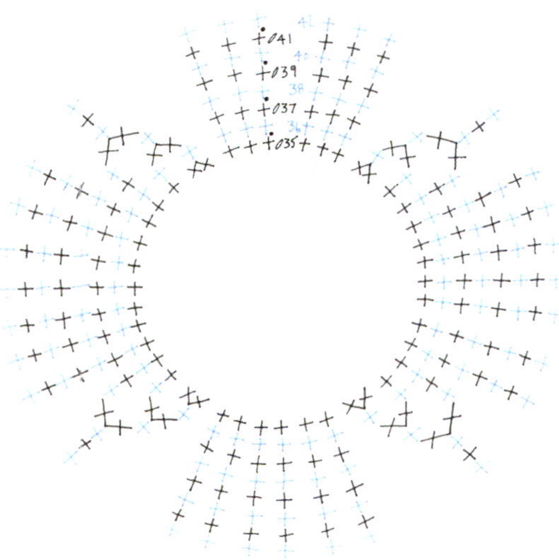

SHAPE END OF BODY
ROWS 35–42

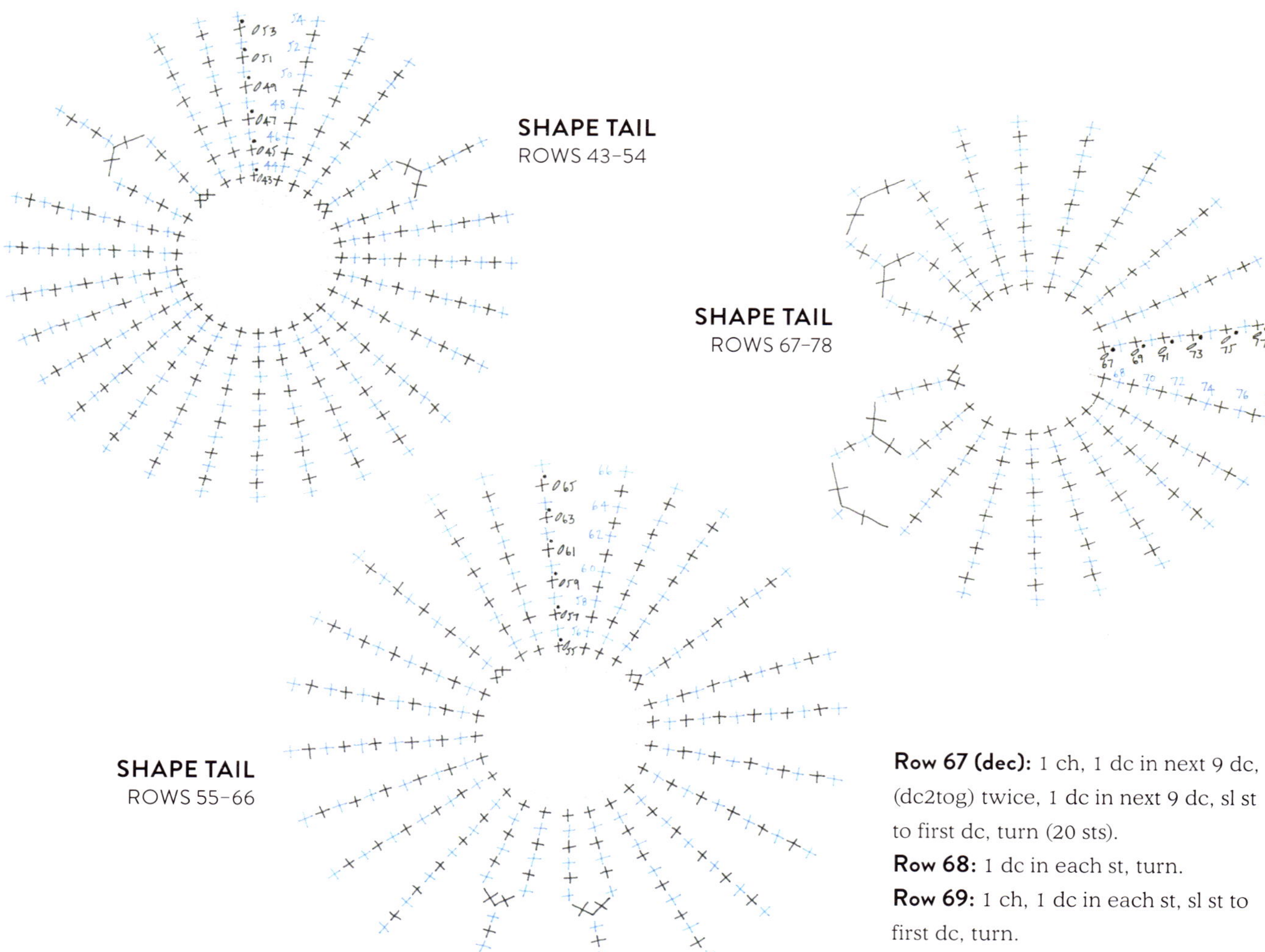

SHAPE TAIL

Row 43 (dec): 1 ch, 1 dc in next 3 dc, dc2tog, 1 dc in each dc to last 5 sts, dc2tog, 1 dc in next 3 dc, sl st to first dc, turn (28 sts).
Row 44: 1 dc in each st, turn.
Row 45: 1 ch, 1 dc in each st, sl st to first dc, turn.
Row 46: 1 dc in each st, turn.
Row 47: 1 ch, 1 dc in each st, sl st to first dc, turn.
Row 48: 1 dc in each st, turn.
Rows 49–60 (dec): As rows 43–48 twice (24 sts).
Stuff the tail to within the last three rows before continuing.
Row 61 (dec): 1 ch, 1 dc in next 10 dc, (dc2tog) twice, 1 dc in next 10 dc, sl st to first dc, turn (22 sts).
Row 62: 1 dc in each st, turn.
Row 63: 1 ch, 1 dc in each st, sl st to first dc, turn.
Rows 64–65: As rows 62–63.
Row 66: 1 dc in each st, turn.
Row 67 (dec): 1 ch, 1 dc in next 9 dc, (dc2tog) twice, 1 dc in next 9 dc, sl st to first dc, turn (20 sts).
Row 68: 1 dc in each st, turn.
Row 69: 1 ch, 1 dc in each st, sl st to first dc, turn.
Rows 70–71: As rows 68–69.
Row 72: 1 dc in each st, turn.
Insert more stuffing before continuing.
Row 73 (dec): 1 ch, 1 dc in next 8 dc, (dc2tog) twice, 1 dc in next 8 dc, sl st to first dc, turn (18 sts).
Row 74: 1 dc in each st, turn.
Row 75: 1 ch, 1 dc in each st, sl st to first dc, turn.
Row 76: 1 dc in each st, turn.
Row 77 (dec): 1 ch, 1 dc in next 7 dc, (dc2tog) twice, 1 dc in next 7 dc, sl st to first dc, turn (16 sts).
Row 78: 1 dc in each st, turn.

Row 79: 1 ch, 1 dc in next dc, dc2inc, 1 dc in next 4 dc, (dc2tog) twice, 1 dc in next 4 dc, dc2inc, 1 dc in next dc, sl st to first dc, turn.

Row 80: 1 dc in each st, turn.

Insert more stuffing before continuing.

Row 81 (dec): 1 ch, 1 dc in next 6 dc, (dc2tog) twice, 1 dc in next 6 dc, sl st to first dc, turn (14 sts).

Row 82: 1 dc in each st, turn.

Row 83: 1 ch, 1 dc in next dc, dc2inc, 1 dc in next 3 dc, (dc2tog) twice, 1 dc in next 3 dc, dc2inc, 1 dc in next dc, sl st to first dc, turn.

Row 84: 1 dc in each st, turn.

Row 85 (dec): 1 ch, 1 dc in next 5 dc, (dc2tog) twice, 1 dc in next 5 dc, sl st to first dc, turn (12 sts).

Row 86: 1 dc in each st, turn.

Row 87: 1 ch, 1 dc in each st, sl st to first dc, turn.

Row 88: 1 dc in each st, turn.

Row 89: 1 ch, 1 dc in next dc, dc2tog, 1 dc in next 2 dc, (dc2inc) twice, 1 dc in next 2 dc, dc2tog, 1 dc in next dc, sl st to first dc, turn.

Row 90: 1 dc in each st, turn.

Rows 91–94: Rep rows 89–90 twice.

Use the end of the crochet hook to push more stuffing into the tail before continuing.

SHAPE TIP OF TAIL

The following rows are not joined with a slip stitch at the end.

Row 95 (dec): 1 ch, 1 dc in next dc, dc2tog, 1 dc in each dc to last 3 sts, dc2tog, 1 dc in next dc, turn (10 sts).

Row 96: 1 ch, dc in each st, turn.

Rows 97–100 (dec): Rep rows 95–96 twice (6 sts).

Rows 101–104: 1 ch, dc in each st, turn.

Fasten off, leaving a long tail of yarn at the end. Thread the tail of yarn through the last round of stitches and pull tightly to gather the end. Sew the open edges together, inserting stuffing into the tip of the tail before closing the seam.

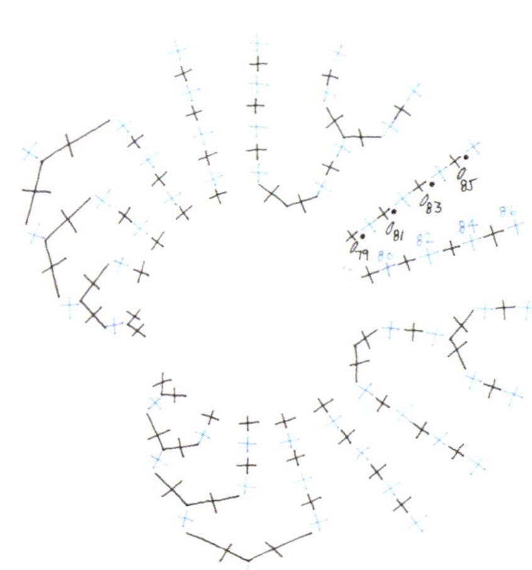

SHAPE TAIL
ROWS 79–86

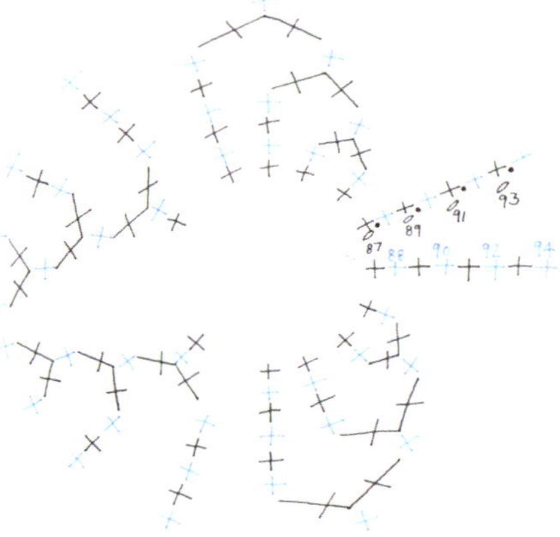

SHAPE TAIL
ROWS 87–94

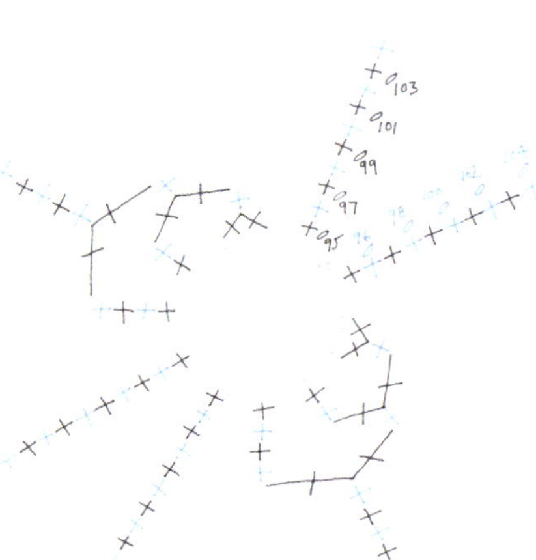

SHAPE TIP OF TAIL
ROWS 95–104

LEGS
(make 2)

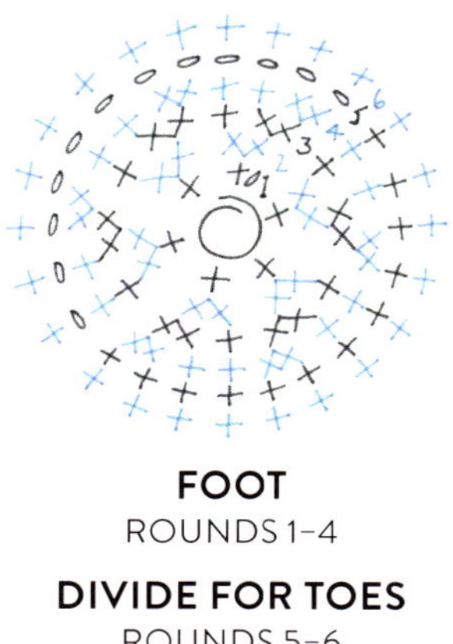

FOOT
ROUNDS 1–4

DIVIDE FOR TOES
ROUNDS 5–6

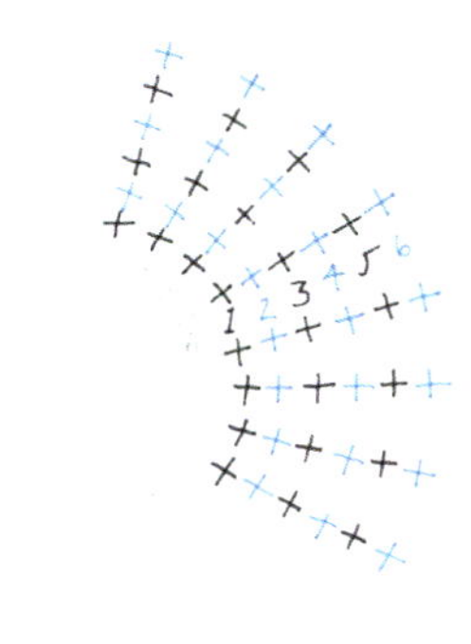

SHAPE FIRST TOE
ROUNDS 1–6

SHAPE MIDDLE TOE
ROUNDS 1–6

FOOT
With 2.5mm hook and A, make a magic loop.

Round 1: 1 ch, 6 dc into loop (6 sts).

Round 2 (inc): (Dc2inc) 6 times (12 sts).

Pull tightly on short end of yarn to close loop.

Round 3 (inc): (Dc2inc, 1 dc) 6 times (18 sts).

Round 4 (inc): (Dc2inc, 2 dc) 6 times (24 sts).

DIVIDE FOR TOES
Round 5: 12 ch, skip next 12 dc, 1 dc in next 12 dc.

Round 6: 1 dc in next 12 ch, 1 dc in next 12 dc.

Continue on these 24 sts.

SHAPE FIRST TOE
Round 1: 1 dc in next 4 dc, skip next 16 dc, 1 dc in next 4 dc.

Continue on these 8 sts.

Rounds 2–6: 1 dc in each st.

Fasten off and thread the tail of yarn through the last round of stitches. Pull tightly to close the end and fasten off.

SHAPE MIDDLE TOE
With RS facing, join A with a sl st to the first of the 16 skipped sts.

Round 1: 1 dc in the same dc as the sl st, 1 dc in next 3 dc, skip next 8 dc, 1 dc in next 4 dc.

Continue on these 8 sts.

Rounds 2–6: 1 dc in each st.

Fasten off and finish as for first toe.

SHAPE THIRD TOE
With RS facing, join A with a sl st to the first of the 8 skipped sts.

Round 1: 1 dc in the same dc as the sl st, 1 dc in next 7 dc (8 sts).

Rounds 2–6: 1 dc in each st.

Fasten off and finish as for first toe.

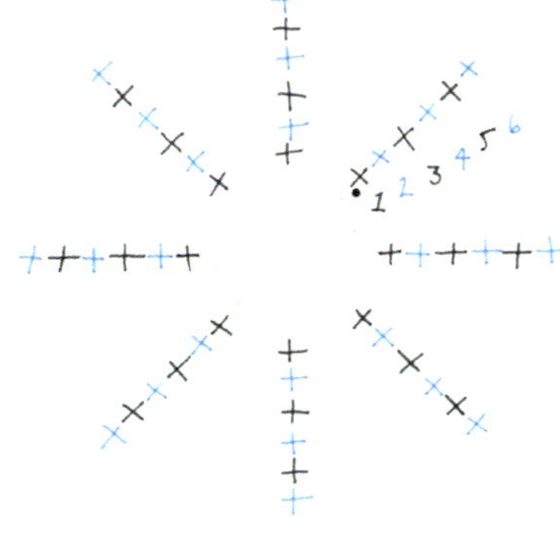

SHAPE THIRD TOE
ROUNDS 1–6

SHAPE FOOT

With RS facing, join A with a sl st to the first of the 12 skipped sts of the foot.

Round 1: 1 dc in same dc as sl st, 1 dc in next 11 dc, 1 dc in opposite side of next 12 ch (24 sts).

Round 2: 1 dc in each st.

Round 3 (dec): (Dc2tog, 2 dc) 6 times (18 sts).

Round 4 (dec): (Dc2tog, 1 dc) 6 times (12 sts).

Rounds 5–9: 1 dc in each st.

Round 10: 1 dc in next 8 dc, finishing at the side of the leg, 4 sts before the end of the round.

Stuff the toes before continuing.

ANKLE JOINT

Round 11: 6 ch, skip next 6 dc, 1 dc in next 6 dc.

Round 12: 1 dc in next 6 ch, 1 dc in next 6 dc (12 sts).

Fasten off and thread tail of yarn through last round of stitches. Pull tightly on end of yarn to close and fasten off.

SHAPE LOWER LEG

With RS facing, join A with a sl st to the first of the 6 skipped sts of the foot.

Round 1: 1 dc in same dc as sl st, 1 dc in next 5 dc, 1 dc in opposite side of next 6 ch of ankle joint (12 sts).

Rounds 2–5: 1 dc in each st.

Round 6 (inc): (Dc2inc, 1 dc) 6 times (18 sts).

Rounds 7–9: 1 dc in each st.

Round 10: 1 dc in next 11 dc, finishing at the side of the leg, 7 sts before the end of the round.

ANKLE JOINT
ROUNDS 11–12

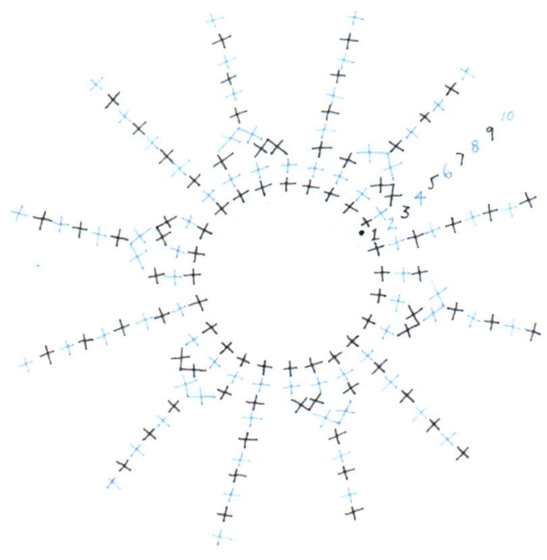

SHAPE FOOT
ROUNDS 1–10

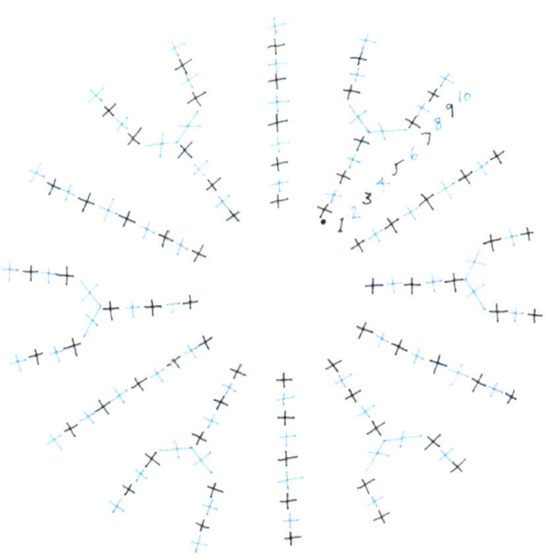

SHAPE LOWER LEG
ROUNDS 1–10

KNEE JOINT

Round 11: 6 ch, skip next 12 dc, 1 dc in next 6 dc at the front of the leg.

Round 12: 1 dc in next 6 ch, 1 dc in next 6 dc (12 sts).

Fasten off and thread tail of yarn through last round of stitches. Pull tightly on end of yarn to close and fasten off.

Hold two pipe cleaners together and make a bend in the middle. Twist the four lengths together, keeping a small loop at the bend. Bend back the sharp ends. Insert the twisted pipe cleaners into the leg, pushing the looped end into the foot. Push stuffing into the lower leg and foot, around the pipe cleaner.

SHAPE THIGH

With RS facing, join A with a sl st to the first of the 12 skipped sts of the lower leg.

Round 1: 1 dc in same dc as sl st, 1 dc in next 11 dc, 1 dc in opposite side of next 6 ch of the knee joint (18 sts).

Round 2 (inc): (Dc2inc, 1 dc) 6 times, 1 dc in next 6 dc (24 sts).

Rounds 3–4: 1 dc in each st.

Round 5 (inc): (Dc2inc, 3 dc) 6 times (30 sts).

Rounds 6–7: 1 dc in each st.

Round 8 (inc): (Dc2inc, 4 dc) 6 times (36 sts).

Rounds 9–18: 1 dc in each st.

Round 19 (dec): (Dc2tog, 4 dc) 6 times (30 sts).

Round 20 (dec): (Dc2tog, 3 dc) 6 times (24 sts).

Stuff the thigh before continuing, keeping the twisted pipe cleaners in the middle of the leg. Bend back any excess pipe cleaner and cover the top with stuffing.

Round 21 (dec): (Dc2tog, 2 dc) 6 times (18 sts).

Round 22 (dec): (Dc2tog, 1 dc) 6 times (12 sts).

Round 23 (dec): (Dc2tog) 6 times (6 sts).

Fasten off and thread the tail of yarn through the last round of stitches. Pull tightly on the end of yarn to close and fasten off.

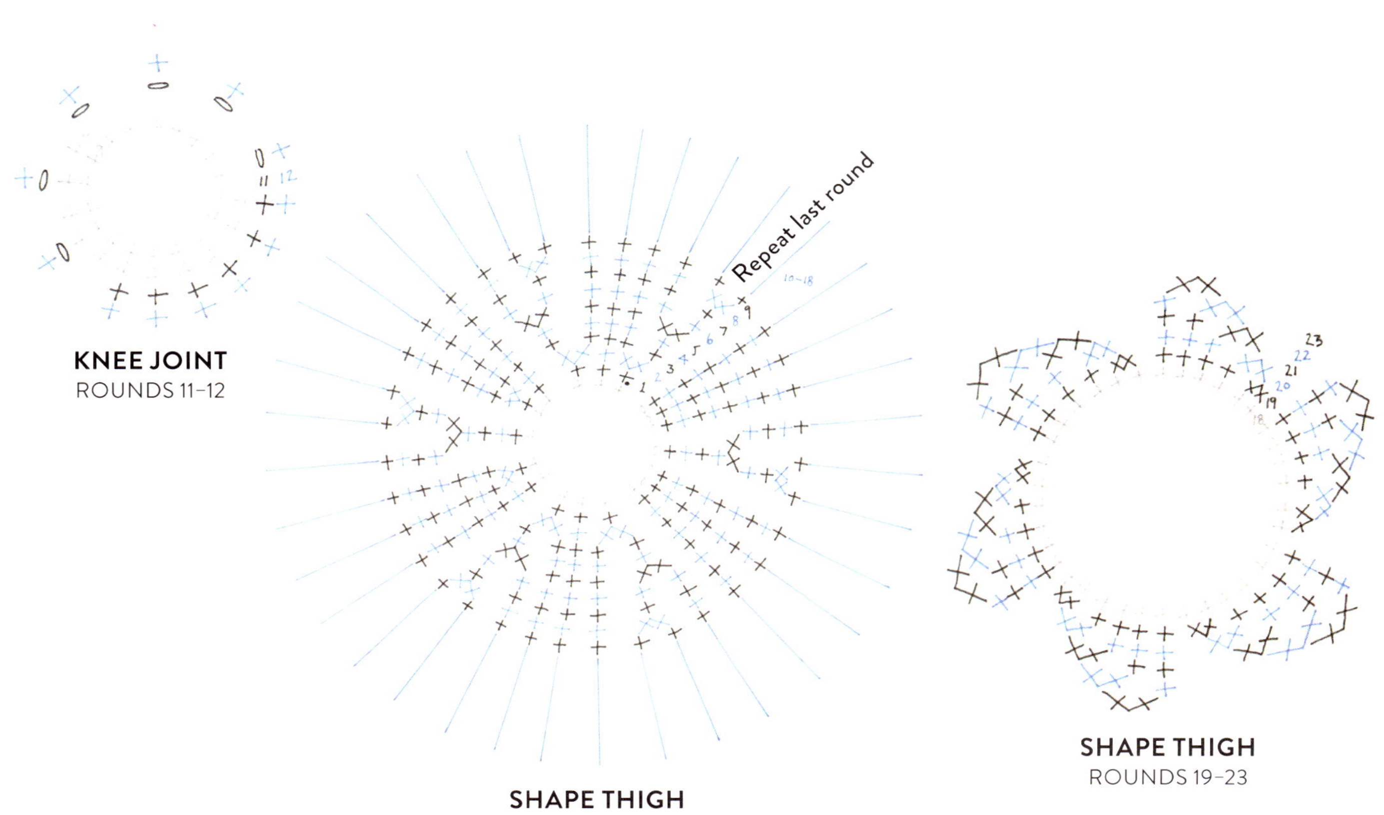

KNEE JOINT
ROUNDS 11–12

SHAPE THIGH
ROUNDS 1–18

SHAPE THIGH
ROUNDS 19–23

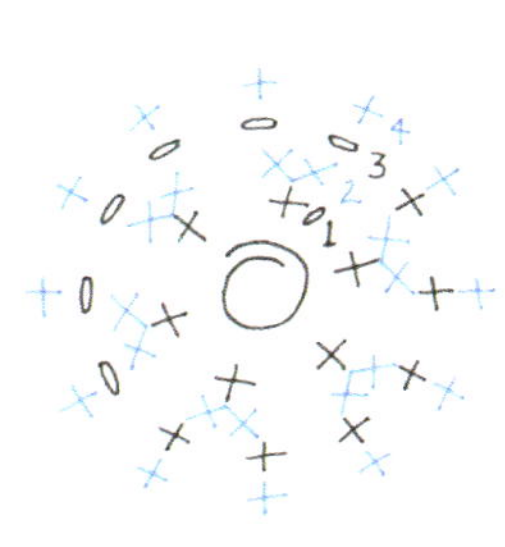

WRIST JOINT
ROUNDS 1–2

DIVIDE FOR FINGERS
ROUNDS 3–4

ARMS
(make 2)

WRIST JOINT

With 2.5mm hook and A, make a magic loop.

Round 1: 1 ch, 6 dc into loop (6 sts).

Round 2 (inc): (Dc2inc) 6 times (12 sts).

Pull tightly on short end of yarn to close loop.

DIVIDE FOR FINGERS

Round 3: 6 ch, skip next 6 dc, 1 dc in next 6 dc.

Round 4: 1 dc in next 6 ch, 1 dc in next 6 dc.

Continue on these 12 sts.

SHAPE FIRST FINGER

Round 1: 1 dc in next 3 dc, skip next 6 dc, 1 dc in next 3 dc.

Continue on these 6 sts.

Rounds 2–4: 1 dc in each st.

Fasten off and thread the tail of yarn through the last round of stitches. Pull tightly to close the end and fasten off.

SHAPE SECOND FINGER

With RS facing, join A with a sl st to the first of the 6 skipped sts.

Round 1: 1 dc in the same dc as the sl st, 1 dc in next 5 dc (6 sts).

Rounds 2–4: 1 dc in each st.

Fasten off and finish as for first finger.

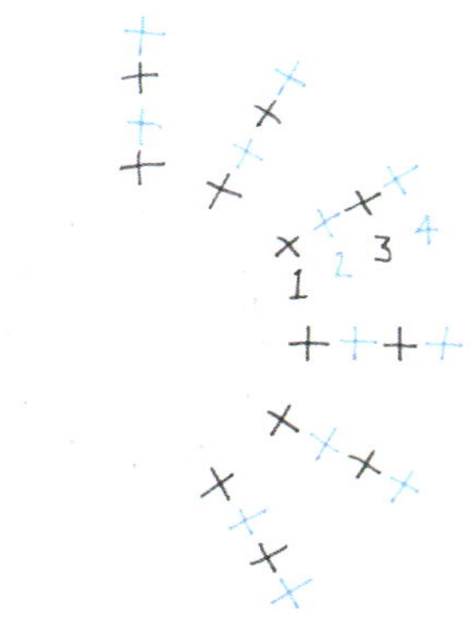

SHAPE FIRST FINGER
ROUNDS 1–4

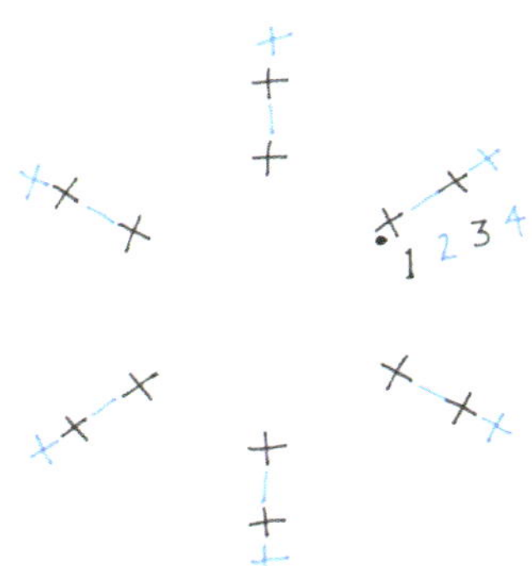

SHAPE SECOND FINGER
ROUNDS 1–4

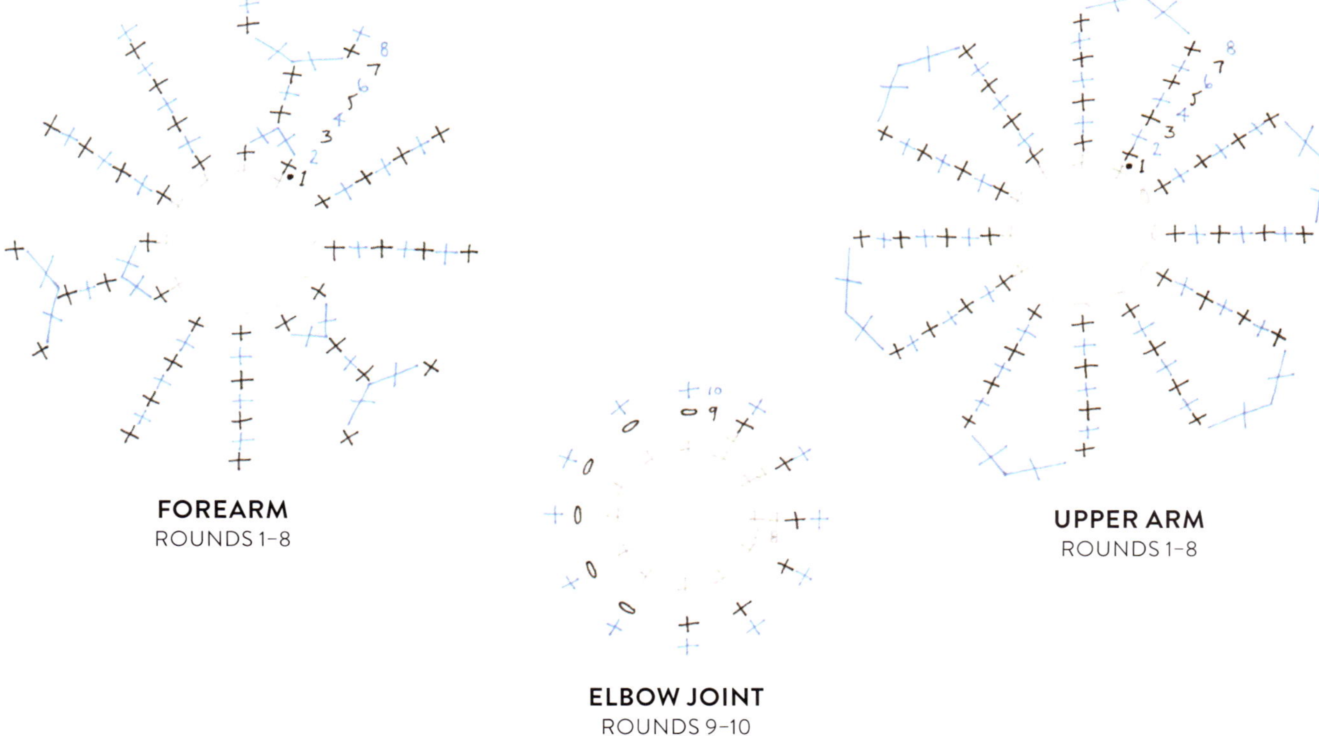

FOREARM
ROUNDS 1–8

UPPER ARM
ROUNDS 1–8

ELBOW JOINT
ROUNDS 9–10

FOREARM

With RS facing, join A with a sl st to the first of the 6 skipped sts of the wrist joint.

Round 1: 1 dc in same dc as sl st, 1 dc in next 5 dc, 1 dc in opposite side of next 6 ch (12 sts).

Round 2 (dec): (Dc2tog, 2 dc) 3 times (9 sts).

Rounds 3–5: 1 dc in each st.

Round 6 (inc): (Dc2inc, 2 dc) 3 times (12 sts).

Round 7: 1 dc in each st.

Round 8: 1 dc in next 3 dc, finishing at the side of the hand, 9 sts before the end of the round.

Stuff the fingers before continuing.

ELBOW JOINT

Round 9: 6 ch, skip next 6 dc, 1 dc in next 6 dc.

Round 10: 1 dc in next 6 ch, 1 dc in next 6 dc (12 sts).

Fasten off and thread tail of yarn through last round of stitches. Pull tightly on end of yarn to close and fasten off.

UPPER ARM

With RS facing, join A with a sl st to the first of the 6 skipped sts of the forearm.

Round 1: 1 dc in same dc as sl st, 1 dc in next 5 dc, 1 dc in opposite side of next 6 ch of the elbow joint (12 sts).

Rounds 2–7: 1 dc in each st.

Stuff the arm before continuing.

Round 8 (dec): (Dc2tog) 6 times (6 sts).

Fasten off and thread tail of yarn through last round of stitches. Pull tightly on end of yarn to close and fasten off.

MAKING UP

HEAD

If using looped glass eyes, poke the loop of an eye through the centre of each eye socket before attaching each one to the head using 23⅝in (60cm) length of clear invisible or strong sewing thread (see page 163). Use the tail of yarn left after fastening off the sockets to neatly sew the edges to the head.

Embroider the nostrils in satin stitch (see page 164), using two strands of embroidery thread.

ARMS AND LEGS

Sew together the gaps between the fingers and toes.

Follow the instructions on page 164 to attach the limbs, using a 55¼in (140cm) length of yarn A or strong thread for the arms and 63in (160cm) length for the legs.

Weave in all the yarn ends.

PTERODACTYL

THE PTERODACTYL IS SHAPED WITH SIMPLE INCREASES, DECREASES AND VARIOUS STITCHES. LIMB SECTIONS ARE WORKED ALONG THE EDGES OF THE WINGS, WITH OPTIONAL CRAFT WIRE FOR ADDED STRUCTURAL SUPPORT.

MATERIALS

- DMC Natura, 100% cotton (170yd/155m per 50g ball), or any 4ply yarn:
  1 × 50g ball in N18 Coral (A)
  1 × 50g ball in N81 Acanthe (B)
  1 × 50g ball in N47 Safran (C)
- 1 pair of 5/32–3/16in (4–5mm) looped glass teddy bear eyes or safety eyes
- Clear invisible or strong thread to attach the looped glass eyes
- Stranded embroidery thread in black, such as Anchor Stranded Cotton, shade 0403, for the nostrils
- 2.25mm (UK13:USB/1) and 2.5mm (UK12:US-) crochet hooks
- Stitch markers
- Blunt-ended yarn needle
- Toy stuffing
- 14½in (37cm) length of 18-gauge (1mm) craft wire for the arms (optional: not suitable for young children)
- Long-nose pliers to bend and trim the wire

SIZE

Approximately 12¼in (31cm) wingspan

TENSION

26 sts and 26 rows to 4in (10cm) over double crochet using 2.5mm hook and yarn A. Use larger or smaller hook if necessary to obtain correct tension.

METHOD

The beak, head and crest are worked in rows of double crochet. The first row of the neck is crocheted along the edges of the rows of the head and into unworked stitches under the beak. The front and back of the body and tail are crocheted separately.

Each wing is worked in rows of double crochet, from a single length of chain stitches running down the centre and crocheted outwards, finishing at the wing-tip.

The arms, elongated fourth finger and the thighs are crocheted in rows along the edges of the wings. The limbs are folded over, and the stitches of the last row are sewn to unworked loops of the first row. Craft wire can be inserted, if desired. The other three fingers, and the lower legs and toes, are crocheted separately and sewn in place.

The wings are inserted between the front and back of the body. The edges of the body are sewn to the wings.

The pterodactyl is finished with glass eyes attached to crocheted eye sockets and simple embroidered nostrils.

1 ch at beg of the row/round does not count as a st throughout.

KEY

- Magic loop
- Chain (ch)
- Slip stitch (sl st)
- Double crochet (dc)
- Dc2inc
- Dc2tog
- Half treble (htr)
- Treble (tr)
- Htr2tog
- Tr2tog
- Work into back loop only
- Work into front loop only

COLOUR

 A

 B

HEAD

BEAK

Starting at the tip of the beak, with 2.5mm hook and A, make 3 ch.

Row 1 (RS): 1 dc in second ch from hook, 1 dc in next ch, turn (2 sts).

Row 2 (WS) (inc): 1 ch, (dc2inc) twice, turn (4 sts).

Rows 3–4: 1 ch, 1 dc in each st, turn.

Row 5 (inc): 1 ch, 1 dc in next dc, (dc2inc) twice, 1 dc in next dc, turn (6 sts).

Rows 6–7: 1 ch, 1 dc in each st, turn.

Row 8 (inc): 1 ch, 1 dc in next 2 dc, (dc2inc) twice, 1 dc in next 2 dc, turn (8 sts).

Rows 9–10: 1 ch, 1 dc in each st, turn.

Row 11 (inc): 1 ch, (dc2inc, 2 dc, dc2inc) twice, turn (12 sts).

Rows 12: 1 ch, 1 dc in each st.

Fasten off, leaving a long tail of yarn.

SHAPE BACK OF HEAD

With RS of head facing and 2.5mm hook, skip the first 2 sts of the last row and join A with a sl st to the next st.

Row 1 (RS): Starting in same dc as sl st, (dc2inc, 2 dc, dc2inc) twice, turn, finishing 2 sts before the end of the row.

Continue on these 12 sts.

Rows 2–3: 1 ch, 1 dc in each st to end, turn.

Place a marker at each end of the last row.

CREST

Rows 4–5 (dec): 1 ch, dc2tog, 1 dc in each dc to last 2 sts, dc2tog, turn (8 sts).

Row 6: 1 ch, 1 dc in each st to end, turn.

Rows 7–10: Rep rows 5–6 twice (4 sts).

Row 11 (dec): 1 ch, (dc2tog) twice, turn (2 sts).

Row 12: 1 ch, 1 dc in each st to end, turn.

Fasten off, leaving a long tail of yarn.

Use the tails of yarn left after fastening off the beak and crest to sew together the edges, matching the rows.

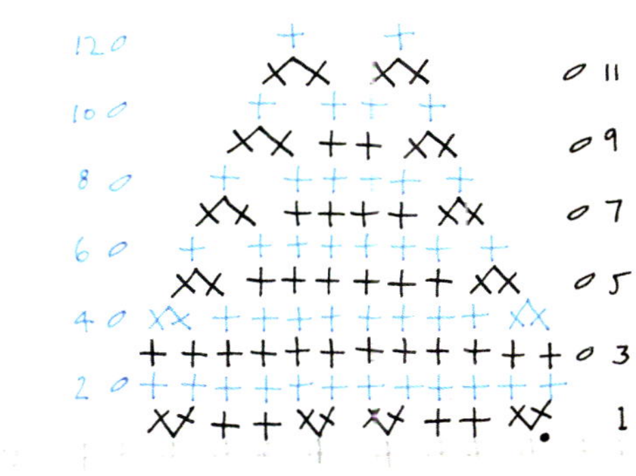

SHAPE BACK OF HEAD
ROWS 1–3

CREST
ROWS 4–12

BEAK
ROWS 1–12

EYE SOCKET
(make 2)

With 2.25mm hook and A, make a magic loop.
Round 1 (RS): 1 ch, 6 dc into loop, sl st to first dc.
Fasten off.
If using safety eyes, attach them at this stage. Poke the post of the safety eye through the centre of the eye socket. Pull tightly on the short end of yarn to close the loop around the post of the safety eye, before attaching it to the head (see page 163).

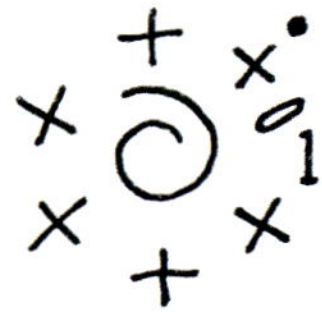

EYE SOCKET
ROUND 1

BODY

NECK
With 2.5mm hook and RS of head facing, join A with a sl st to the stitch at the edge of row 3 of the head, indicated by the marker.
Row 1 (RS): 1 dc in same dc as sl st, 1 dc in the edge of the next 2 rows, 1 dc in next 2 unworked sts of one side of the beak, 1 dc in next 2 unworked sts on the opposite side of the beak to join the edges, 1 dc in the edge of the next 3 rows on the other side of the head, finishing at the marker, turn (10 sts).
Row 2 (WS): 1 ch, 1 dc in each st to end, turn.
Row 3 (dec): 1 ch, 1 dc in next dc, dc2tog, join B in last dc and carry unused yarn on WS of work, 1 dc in next 4 dc with B, dc2tog with A, 1 dc in next dc, turn (8 sts).
Rows 4–6: 1 ch, 1 dc in next 2 dc with A, 1 dc in next 4 dc with B, 1 dc in next 2 dc with A, turn.
Row 7 (inc): 1 ch, 1 dc in next dc, dc2inc with A, with B, dc2inc, 1 dc in next 2 dc, dc2inc; with A, dc2inc, 1 dc in next dc, turn (12 sts).
Row 8: 1 ch, 1 dc in next 3 dc with A, 1 dc in next 6 dc with B, 1 dc in next 3 dc with A, sl st to first dc to join the edges, turn.
Do not fasten off B.
Fasten off A, leaving a long tail of yarn.
Stuff the beak, crest and head before continuing.

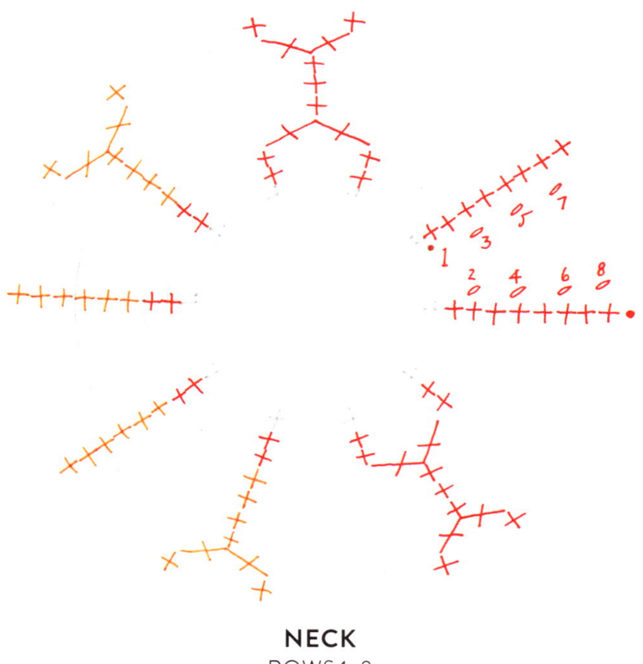

NECK
ROWS 1–8

SHAPE FRONT

With RS facing, 2.5mm hook and B, skip the first 3 sts and sl st in the first of the 6 dc worked in B at the front of the neck.

Row 1 (RS) (inc): 2 dc in same st as sl st, 1 dc in next 4 dc, dc2inc, turn, finishing 3 sts before the end of the row (8 sts).

Row 2 (WS) (inc): 1 ch, dc2inc, 1 dc in each dc to last st, dc2inc, turn (10 sts)

Row 3 (inc): As row 2 (12 sts).

Rows 4–6: 1 ch, 1 dc in each dc to end, turn.

Row 7 (dec): 1 ch, dc2tog, 1 dc in each dc to last 2 sts, dc2tog, turn (10 sts).

Row 8: 1 ch, 1 dc in each dc to end, turn.

Rows 9–11 (dec): 1 ch, dc2tog, 1 dc in each dc to last 2 sts, dc2tog, turn (4 sts).

FRONT OF TAIL

Row 12: 1 ch, (dc2tog) twice (2 sts).

Row 13: 1 ch, 1 dc in each dc to end, turn.

Row 14: 1 ch, (dc2tog) (1 st).

Fasten off, leaving a long tail of yarn.

SHAPE BACK

With RS facing and 2.5mm hook, join A with a sl st to the first of the 6 dc unworked sts at the back of the neck.

Rows 1–11: Work rows 1–11 as for shape front with A.

BACK OF TAIL

Rows 12–14: Work rows 12–14 as for front of tail.

Fasten off, leaving a long tail of yarn. Sew the edges of the neck together using the tail of yarn left after fastening off. Stuff the neck.

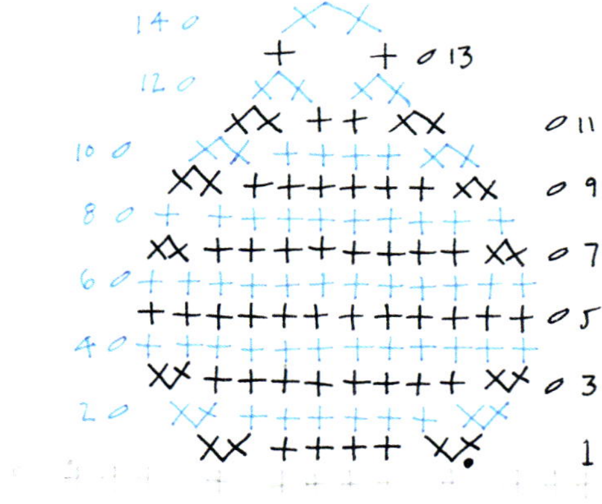

SHAPE FRONT
ROWS 1–11

FRONT OF TAIL
ROWS 12–14

WINGS

Shape each wing separately.

FIRST WING

With 2.25mm hook and C, make 9 ch.

Row 1 (RS): 1 dc in second ch from hook, 1 dc in each ch to end, turn (8 sts).

Row 2 (WS) (dec): 1 ch, dc2tog, 1 dc in each dc to end, turn (7 sts).

Row 3 (inc): 1 ch, dc2inc, 1 dc in each dc to end, turn (8 sts).

Row 4: 1 ch, dc2tog, 1 dc in each dc to last st, dc2inc, turn.

Row 5 (inc): 1 ch, dc2inc, 1 dc in each dc to end, turn (9 sts).

Row 6: 1 ch, dc2tog, 1 dc in each dc to last st, dc2inc, turn. Place a marker in the last dc.

Place a marker between rows 5 and 6, in the middle of the stitches.

Row 7 (dec): 1 ch, dc2tog, 1 dc in each st to end, turn (8 sts).

Row 8 (dec): 1 ch, 1 dc in each dc to last 2 sts, dc2tog, turn (7 sts).

Row 9: 1 ch, dc2tog, 1 dc in each dc to last st, dc2inc, turn.

Row 10 (inc): 1 ch, dc2inc, 1 dc in each st to end, turn (8 sts).

Row 11 (inc): 1 ch, 1 dc in each dc to last st, dc2inc, turn (9 sts).

Row 12 (inc): 1 ch, dc2inc, 1 dc in each st to end, turn (10 sts).

Row 13 (inc): 1 ch, 1 dc in each dc to last st, dc2inc, turn (11 sts).

Row 14–20: 1 ch, 1 dc in each st to end, turn. Place a marker in the first dc of rows 14 and 20.

Row 21 (dec): 1 ch, 1 dc in each dc to last 2 sts, dc2tog, turn (10 sts).

Row 22: 1 ch, 1 dc in each st to end, turn.

Row 23–28 (dec): Rep rows 21–22 3 times (7 sts).

Row 29 (dec): 1 ch, 1 dc in each dc to last 2 sts, dc2tog, turn (6 sts).

Row 30: 1 ch, dc2tog, 1 dc in each dc to last 2 sts, dc2inc, 1 dc in next st, turn.

Row 31 (dec): 1 ch, 1 dc in each dc to last 2 sts, dc2tog, turn (5 sts).

Row 32: 1 ch, 1 dc in each st to end, turn.

Row 33 (dec): 1 ch, 1 dc in each dc to last 2 sts, dc2tog, turn (4 sts).

Row 34: 1 ch, dc2tog, dc2inc, 1 dc in next st, turn.

Row 35 (dec): 1 ch, 1 dc in next 2 sts, dc2tog, turn (3 sts).

Row 36: 1 ch, 1 dc in each st to end, turn.

Row 37 (dec): 1 ch, 1 dc in next dc, dc2tog, turn (2 sts).

Row 38: 1 ch, 1 dc in each st to end, turn.

Row 39 (dec): 1 ch, dc2tog, turn (1 st).

Row 40: 1 ch, 1 dc in next st.

Fasten off.

SECOND WING

With 2.25mm hook, starting at the lower edge of the wing, join C with a sl st to the opposite side of the first ch.

Row 1 (WS): 1 dc in same ch as sl st, 1 dc in each ch to end, turn (8 sts).

Row 2 (RS) (dec): 1 ch, dc2tog, 1 dc in each dc to end, turn (7 sts).

Rows 3–40: Work rows 3–40 as for first wing. Turn at the end of the last row. Do not fasten off.

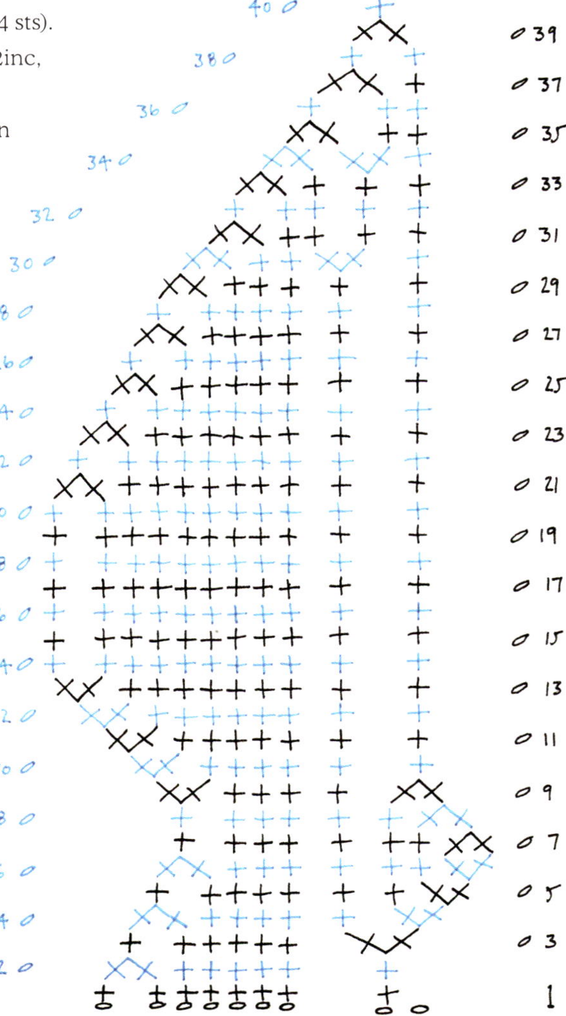

FIRST WING
ROWS 1–40

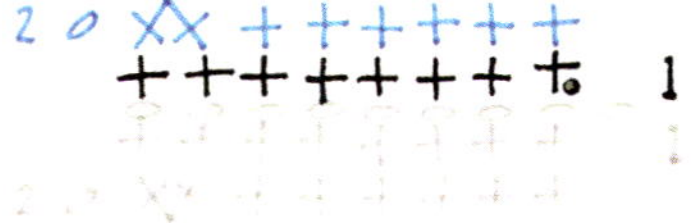

SECOND WING
ROWS 1–2

FOR ROWS 3–40, FOLLOW CHART FOR FIRST WING

ARMS AND FOURTH FINGER

Row 1 (WS): 1 ch, dc2inc, work 1 dc in the edge of the next 19 rows at the top of the wing, *2 dc in the edge of the next row with the marker, 1 dc in the edge of the next 5 rows, 2 dc in the edge of the next row with the marker,* 1 dc in the edge of the next 13 rows, 2 dc in the ch between the wings, 1 dc in the edge of the next 13 rows; rep from * to *, 1 dc in the edge of the next 19 rows, 2 dc in the dc at the tip of the wing. Join A in last dc, turn (88 sts).

Continue with A.

Row 2 (inc): 1 ch, working into the back loop only of each st, (2 dc, dc2inc, 2 dc) 4 times, 1 dc in next 2 dc, dc2inc, 1 dc in next 5 sts, dc2inc, 1 dc in next 30 sts, dc2inc, 1 dc in next 5 sts, dc2inc, 1 dc in next 2 dc, (2 dc, dc2inc, 2 dc) 4 times, turn (100 sts).

Row 3 (dec): 1 ch, (2 dc, dc2tog, 2 dc) 4 times, 1 dc in next 2 dc, dc2tog, 1 dc in next 5 sts, dc2tog, 1 dc in back loop only of next 30 sts; continuing in both loops of each st, dc2tog, 1 dc in next 5 sts, dc2tog, 1 dc in next 2 dc, (2 dc, dc2tog, 2 dc) 4 times, turn (88 sts).

Fasten off, leaving a long tail of yarn.

SHAPE TOP OF WINGS

With RS of wings facing and 2.25mm hook, join C with a sl st to the first of the 30 unworked front loops of row 1 of the arms.

Row 1 (RS): Working into the remaining 29 unworked front loops, 1 dc in next 3 sts, *1 htr in next 2 sts, htr2tog, 1 htr in next 2 sts*, 1 dc in next 10 sts; rep from * to *, 1 dc in next 3 sts, sl st in next st (26 sts).

Fasten off.

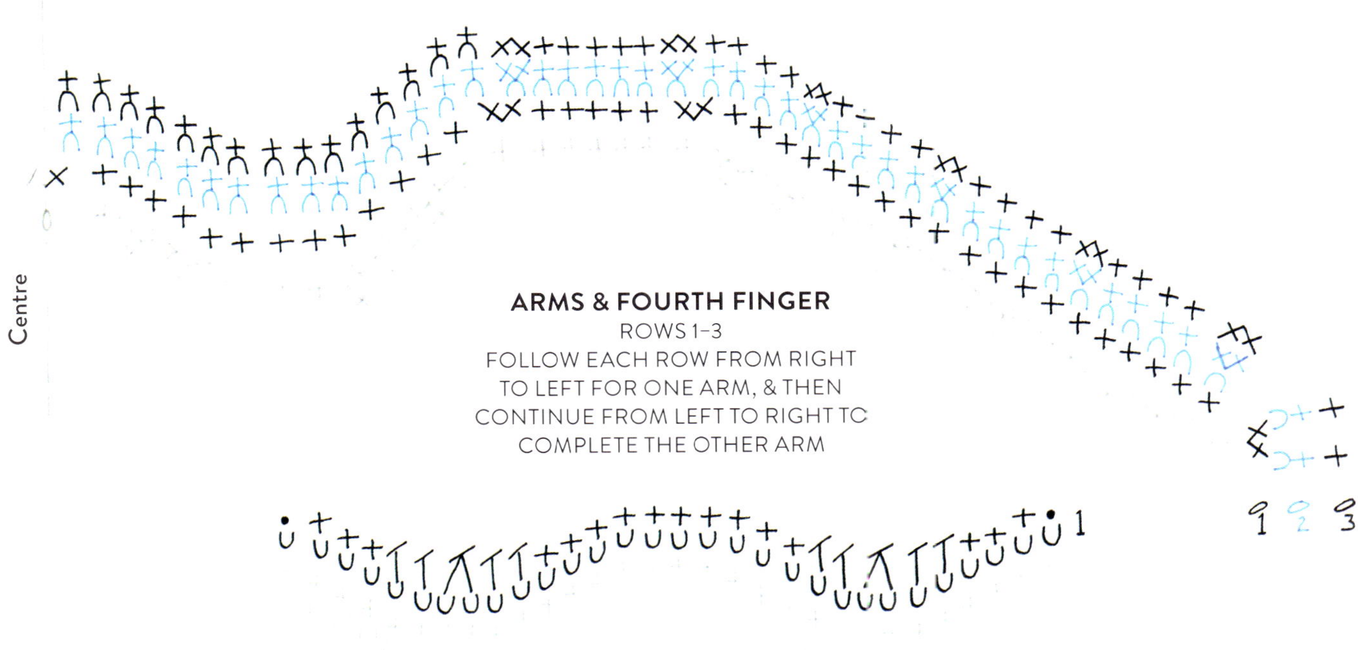

HANDS
(make 2)

With 2.25mm hook and A, make 2 ch.
Row 1 (WS): 3 dc in second ch from hook, turn (3 sts).

FINGERS

Row 2 (RS): (4 ch, sl st in second ch from hook, sl st in next 2 ch, sl st in next dc) 3 times.
Fasten off, leaving a long tail of yarn.

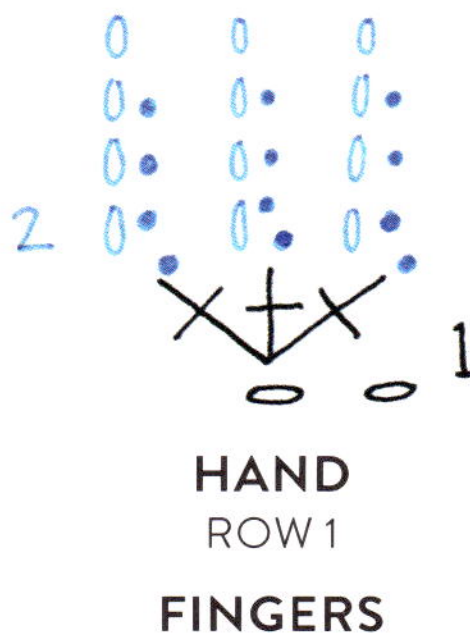

HAND
ROW 1
FINGERS
ROW 2

THIGHS

With 2.25mm hook and WS of wings facing, join C with a sl st to the marked stitch at the lower edge of row 6 of the wing.
Row 1 (RS): 1 dc in the same dc as the sl st, 1 dc in the edge of the next 5 rows, 1 dc in the ch between the wings, 1 dc in the edge of the next 6 rows, finishing in the marked stitch at the lower edge of the other wing. Join A in last dc, turn (13 sts).
Row 2 (RS): With A, 1 ch, 1 dc into the back loop only of each st, turn.
Row 3: As row 2.
Fasten off A, leaving a long tail of yarn.

THIGHS
ROWS 1–3

SHAPE LOWER EDGE OF WINGS

With RS facing, 2.25mm hook and C, sl st into the first of the 13 unworked front loops of row 2 of the legs.
Row 1: 1 dc in the same st as the sl st, dc2tog, 1 htr in next st, tr2tog, 1 tr in next st, tr2tog, 1 htr in next st, dc2tog, 1 dc in next st (9 sts).
Fasten off.

SHAPE LOWER EDGE OF WINGS
ROW 1

LOWER LEGS AND FEET
(make 2)

With 2.25mm hook and A, make 6 ch.
Row 1 (WS): 1 dc in second ch from hook, 1 dc in next 3 ch, 4 dc in end ch, 1 dc in opposite side of next 4 ch, do not turn (12 sts).

TOES
Next: (4 ch, sl st in second ch from hook, sl st in next 2 ch, sl st in end ch of leg) 3 times.
Fasten off, leaving a long tail of yarn.

LOWER LEGS & FEET
ROW 1

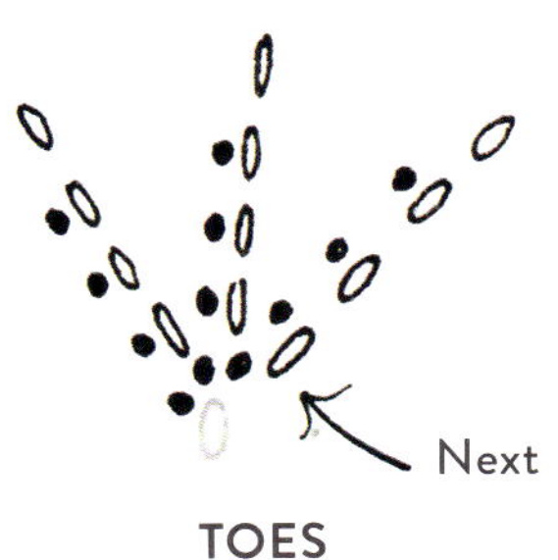

TOES

MAKING UP

ARMS AND LEGS
Place the craft wire, if using, on the second row of the arms, on the right side of the wings, and make bends in the wire, following the shaping of the arms. Bend the excess wire at each end. Squeeze or twist the wire together with the pliers to prevent the sharp ends poking through the crocheted fabric when the edges of the arms have been sewn in place.

Fold the third row of the arms to the RS of the wings and use the tail of yarn, left after fastening off, to sew each stitch to the corresponding unworked loops of row 1. Use the tail of yarn left after fastening off the hands to sew each one to the base of the elongated fourth finger, at the first bend from the tip of the wing.

Fold the third row of the thighs towards the top of the wings and use the tail of yarn to sew each stitch to the corresponding unworked loops of row 1. Sew together the 6 stitches on each side of the lower legs, using the tail of yarn left after fastening off. Sew the tops of the lower legs to the thighs.

BODY
Slip the wings between the front and back of the body. With the tail of yarn left after fastening off the front of the body, sew together the stitches at the tip of the front and back of the tail together, to join them just below the lower edge of the wings. Sew each side of the front of the body neatly to the wings, keeping the widest part of the body within the stitch markers and taking care not to catch the back of the body in the stitches. Leave a gap for stuffing.

Use the tail of yarn left after fastening off to sew the side edges of the back of the body to the wings, to match the front, leaving a gap at the lower edge. Push a small amount of stuffing into the opening at the front and back of the body, keeping the wings flat. Sew the open ends of the front and back body to the wings.

HEAD
If using looped glass eyes, poke the loop of an eye through the centre of each eye socket before attaching each one to the head using 23⅝in (60cm) length of clear invisible or strong sewing thread (see page 163). Embroider the nostrils in satin stitch (see page 164), using two strands of embroidery thread.

Weave in all the yarn ends.

PLESIOSAURUS

THIS PREHISTORIC MARINE REPTILE FEATURES SIMPLE COLOUR CHANGES AND SHAPING. FINE CROCHET THREAD IS USED TO CREATE THE JAGGED TEETH IN ITS OPEN MOUTH.

MATERIALS

- Scheepjes Catona, 100% mercerized cotton (137yd/125m per 50g ball):
  1 × 50g ball in 401 Dark Teal (A)
  1 × 50g ball in 528 Silver Blue (B)
  1 × 10g ball in 518 Marshmallow (C)
- Scheepjes Maxi Sweet Treat, 100% mercerized cotton (153yd/140m per 25g ball):
  1 × 25g ball in 105 Bridal White (D)
- 1 pair of 5/32–3/16in (4–5mm) looped glass teddy bear eyes or safety eyes
- Clear invisible or strong sewing thread to attach the looped glass eyes
- Stranded metallic embroidery thread in black, such as DMC Light Effects, shade E310, for the nostrils
- 1.25mm (UK5½:US10), 2.25mm (UK13:USB/1) and 2.5mm (UK12:US-) crochet hooks
- Stitch markers
- Blunt-ended yarn needle
- Toy stuffing

SIZE

Approximately 15¼in (39cm) long

TENSION

25 sts and 25 rows to 4in (10cm) over double crochet using 2.5mm hook and yarn A. Use larger or smaller hook if necessary to obtain correct tension.

METHOD

The jaws are worked separately in rows of double crochet and are joined together in the last two rows. Double crochet and half treble stitches form the shaping of the roof and floor of the mouth, which are worked in one piece. The teeth are crocheted into the back loops of the mouth before joining the mouth to the jaws.

The neck is worked in two colours, continuing from the last row of stitches of the head. The neck, body and tail are crocheted in one piece. Increasing and decreasing an equal amount of stitches on the same row forms the curve in the neck, and the front of the body is shaped by working short rows.

KEY

- Magic loop
- Chain (ch)
- Slip stitch (sl st)
- Double crochet (dc)
- Dc2inc
- Dc2tog
- Half treble (htr)
- Htr2inc
- Work into back loop only
- Slip stitch together back loops on each side to join

COLOUR

A

B

The flippers are crocheted in rows using various stitches, increasing and decreasing to create the shape. The pieces are folded and the stitches on each side of the last row are joined together. The flippers are lightly stuffed before sewing in place.

Finishing touches include looped glass or safety eyes attached to a crocheted eye socket and simple embroidery in metallic thread for the nostrils.

1 ch at beg of the row/round does not count as a st throughout.

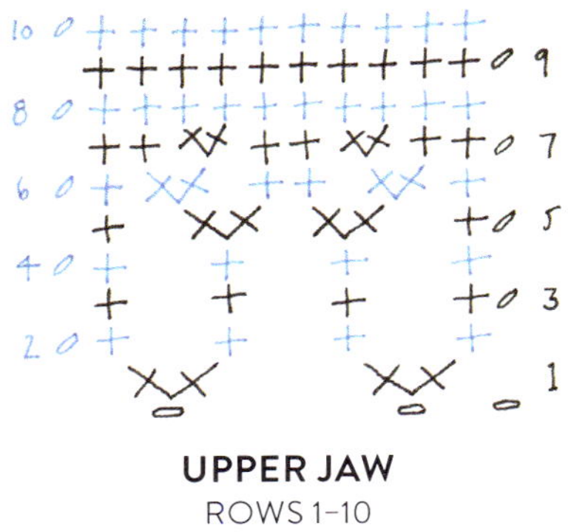

UPPER JAW
ROWS 1–10

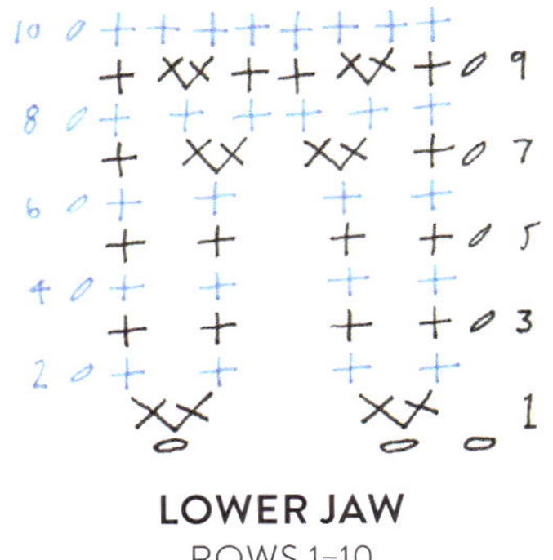

LOWER JAW
ROWS 1–10

HEAD

UPPER JAW

With 2.5mm hook and A, make 3 ch.

Row 1 (RS): 2 dc in second ch from hook, 2 dc in next ch, turn (4 sts).

Row 2 (WS): 1 ch, 1 dc in each st, turn.

Rows 3–4: As row 2.

Row 5 (inc): 1 ch, 1 dc in next dc, (dc2inc) twice, 1 dc in next dc, turn (6 sts).

Row 6 (inc): 1 ch, (1 dc, dc2inc, 1 dc) twice, turn (8 sts).

Row 7 (inc): 1 ch, 1 dc in next 2 dc, (dc2inc, 2 dc) twice, turn (10 sts).

Rows 8–10: 1 ch, 1 dc in each st. Place a marker at each end of the last row.

Fasten off.

LOWER JAW

With 2.5mm hook and B, make 3 ch.

Row 1 (RS): 2 dc in second ch from hook, 2 dc in next ch, turn (4 sts).

Row 2 (WS): 1 ch, 1 dc in each st, turn.

Rows 3–6: As row 2.

Row 7 (inc): 1 ch, 1 dc in next dc, (dc2inc) twice, 1 dc in next dc, turn (6 sts).

Row 8: 1 ch, 1 dc in each st, turn.

Row 9: 1 ch, (1 dc, dc2inc, 1 dc) twice, turn (8 sts).

Row 10: 1 ch, 1 dc in each st, turn.

Place a marker at each end of the last row. Do not fasten off.

JOIN JAW PIECES

Row 11 (RS): 1 ch, 1 dc in each dc. Join A in last dc. With RS of upper jaw facing, 1 dc in each dc, sl st to the first dc of the lower jaw to join the other end, turn (18 sts).

Row 12 (WS): 1 dc in next 10 sts with A, 1 dc in next 8 sts with B.

Fasten off.

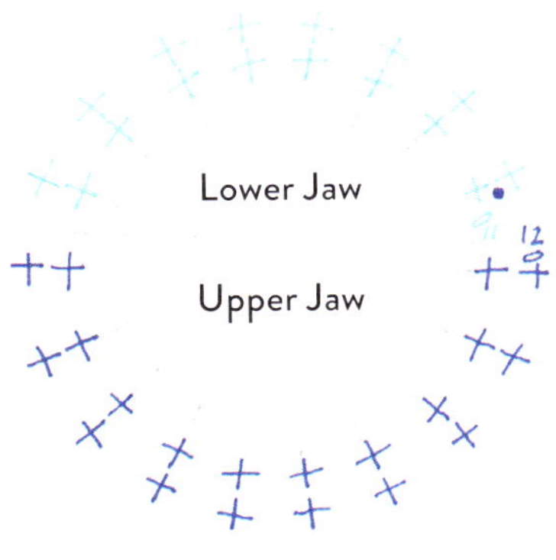

JOIN JAW PIECES
ROWS 11–12

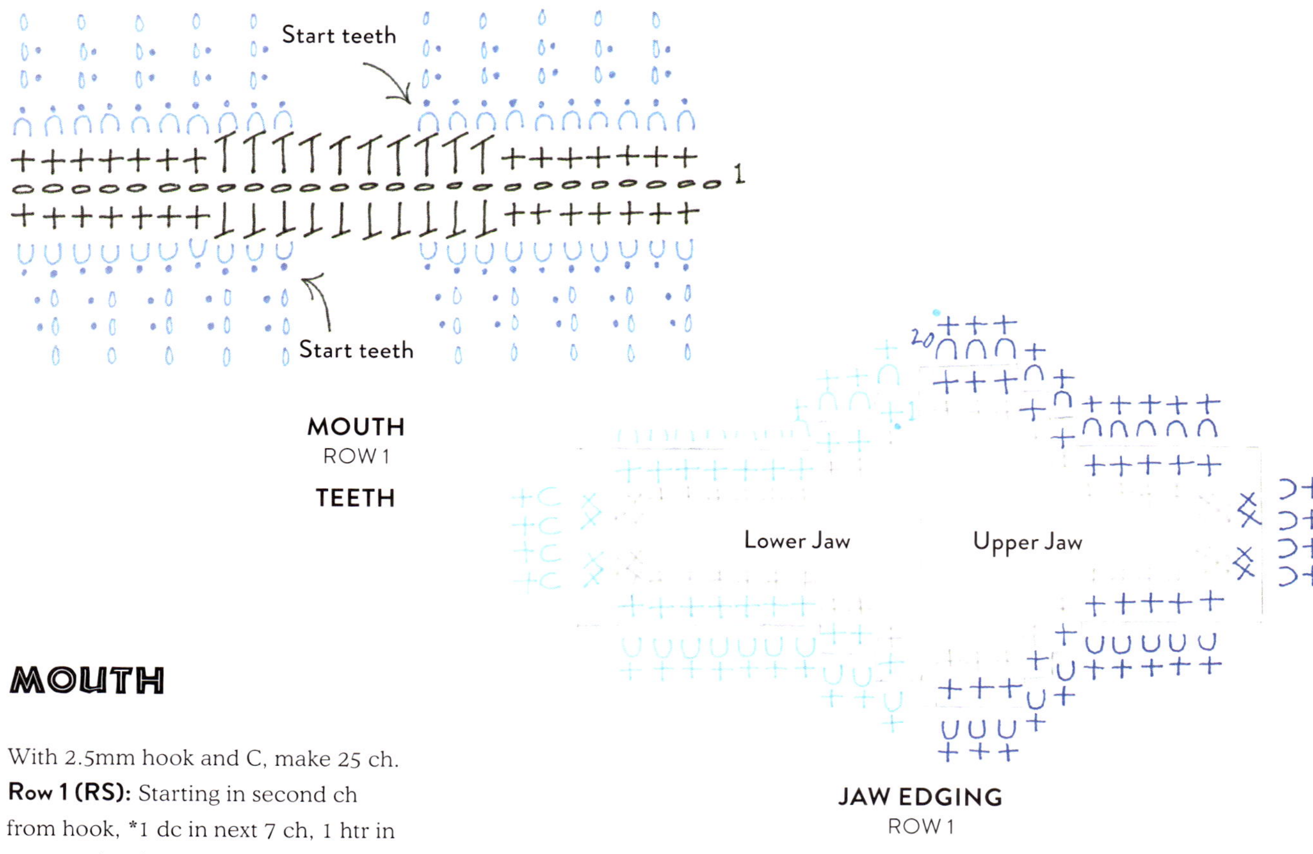

MOUTH

With 2.5mm hook and C, make 25 ch.

Row 1 (RS): Starting in second ch from hook, *1 dc in next 7 ch, 1 htr in next 10 ch, place a marker between the fifth and sixth htr sts, 1 dc in next 7 ch*; working in opposite side of each ch; rep from * to * (48 sts).

Fasten off.

TEETH

With 1.25mm hook and WS of the mouth facing, skip the first 2 htr sts from the marker.

Next: *With D, (sl st in back loop only of next dc, 3 ch, sl st in second and third ch from hook, sl st in back loop only of next dc) 10 times. Fasten off.*

Next: With WS of mouth facing, skip the next 4 sts from the last tooth made; rep from * to * to finish the other set of teeth.

JAW EDGING

With 2.5mm hook and WS facing, join B with a sl st to the st at the edge of row 10 of the lower jaw, indicated by the marker.

Row 1 (WS): Starting in the same st as the sl st, *work 1 dc into each stitch at the edge of the next 10 rows, dc2inc in the opposite side of each of the next 2 ch, 1 dc into each stitch at the edge of the next 10 rows, finishing at the corner of the other side of the jaw, indicated by the marker*; join A in the last dc and rep from * to * to finish the edging on the upper jaw, turn (48 sts).

JOIN MOUTH TO JAW

Row 2 (RS): Insert the mouth into the head, with WS together, aligning the markers and the stitches around the edges of the mouth and jaws. With the upper jaw facing and working into the back loops only of each stitch of the jaws and the corresponding and unworked loops of the mouth at the same time to join, 1 ch, 1 dc in the next 24 sts with A, 1 dc in the next 24 sts with B, sl st to next st and fasten off.

EYE SOCKET
(make 2)

With 2.5mm hook and A, make a magic loop.

Round 1 (RS): 1 ch, 6 dc into loop, sl st to first dc.

Fasten off.

If using safety eyes, attach them at this stage. Poke the post of the safety eye through the centre of the eye socket. Pull tightly on the short end of yarn to close the loop around the post of the safety eye, before attaching it to the head (see page 163).

BODY

NECK

With 2.5mm hook and RS of head facing, join A with a sl st to first of 10 dc of upper jaw.

Row 1 (RS): 1 dc in same dc as sl st, 1 dc in next 9 dc, join B in last dc, work 1 dc in next 8 dc of lower jaw with B, sl st to first dc, turn (18 sts).

Row 2 (WS): 1 dc in next 8 dc with B, 1 dc in next 10 dc with A, turn.

Row 3: With A, 1 ch, dc2inc, 1 dc in next 2 dc, (dc2tog) twice, 1 dc in next 2 dc, dc2inc; with B, dc2tog, 1 dc in next dc, (dc2inc) twice, 1 dc in next dc, dc2tog, sl st to first dc, turn.

Row 4: 1 dc in next 8 dc with B, 1 dc in next 10 dc with A, turn.

Before continuing, stuff the head to the beginning of the neck, keeping the inside of the mouth flat.

Rows 5–24: Rep rows 3–4 10 times.

Stuff the neck to within the last three rows before continuing.

EYE SOCKET
ROUND 1

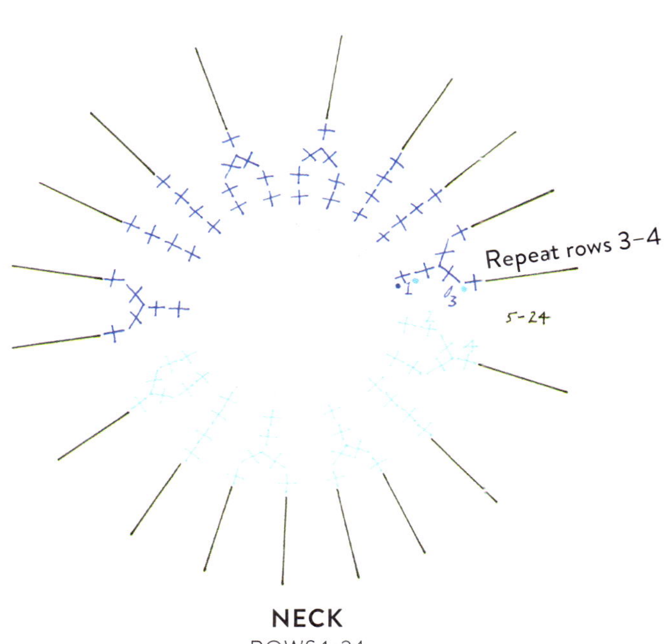

NECK
ROWS 1–24

Row 25 (inc): With A, 1 ch, 1 dc in next 10 dc; with B, 1 dc in next 2 dc, (dc2inc, 2 dc), twice, sl st to first dc, turn (20 sts).
Row 26: 1 dc in next 10 sts with B, 1 dc in next 10 sts with A, turn.
Row 27: 1 ch, 1 dc in next 10 dc with A, 1 dc in next 10 dc with B, sl st to first dc, turn.
Row 28: 1 dc in next 10 sts with B, 1 dc in next 10 sts with A, turn.
Row 29 (inc): 1 ch, 1 dc in next 10 dc with A; with B, 1 dc in next 3 dc, dc2inc, 1 dc in next 2 dc, dc2inc, 1 dc in next 3 dc, sl st to first dc, turn (22 sts).
Row 30: 1 dc in next 12 sts with B, 1 dc in next 10 sts with A, turn.

SHAPE BASE OF NECK

The following is worked in short rows.
Row 31 (RS): 1 ch, 1 dc in next 10 dc with A, 1 dc in next 8 dc with B, sl st in next dc, turn, finishing 3 sts before the end of the row.
Row 32 (WS): With B, 1 dc in same dc as sl st, 1 dc in next 5 dc, sl st in next dc, turn.
Row 33 (inc): 1 dc in same dc as sl st, (1 dc, dc2inc, 1 dc) twice, 1 dc in next dc, sl st in next dc, turn (24 sts).
Row 34: 1 dc in same dc as sl st, 1 dc in next 11 dc, sl st in next dc, turn.
Row 35: 1 dc in same dc as sl st, 1 dc in next 13 dc, sl st to next dc, turn.
Row 36: 1 dc in next 14 sts with B, 1 dc in next 10 sts with A, turn.
Row 37 (inc): With A, 1 ch, dc2inc, (2 dc, dc2inc) 3 times; with B, 1 dc in next 5 dc, dc2inc, 1 dc in next 2 dc, dc2inc, 1 dc in next dc, sl st in next dc turn, finishing 3 sts before the end of the row (30 sts).
Row 38: With B, 1 dc in same dc as sl st, 1 dc in next 9 dc, sl st in next dc, turn.
Row 39: 1 dc in same dc as sl st, 1 dc in next 11 dc, sl st in next dc, turn.
Row 40: 1 dc in same dc as sl st, 1 dc in next 13 dc, sl st in next dc, turn.
Row 41 (inc): 1 dc in same dc as sl st, 1 dc in next 5 dc, dc2inc, 1 dc in next 2 dc, dc2inc, 1 dc in next 6 dc, sl st to next dc, turn (32 sts).
Row 42: 1 dc in next 18 sts with B, 1 dc in next 14 sts with A, turn.

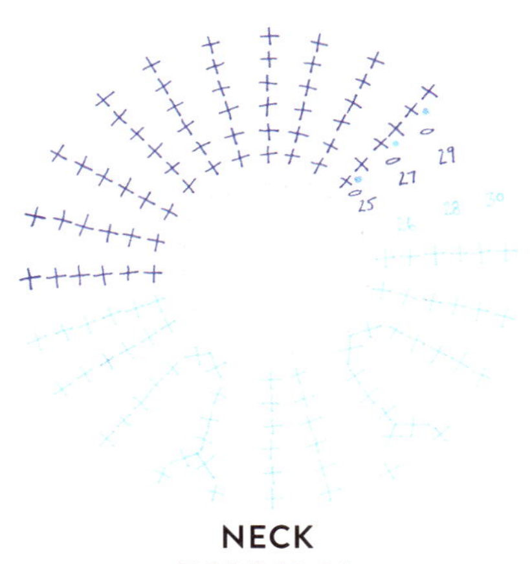

NECK
ROWS 25–30

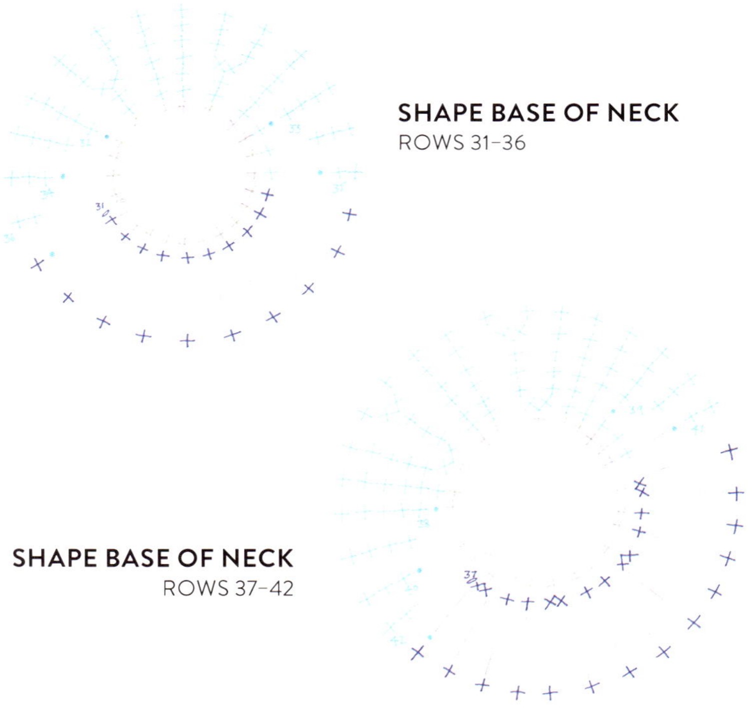

SHAPE BASE OF NECK
ROWS 31–36

SHAPE BASE OF NECK
ROWS 37–42

SHAPE FRONT OF BODY

Row 43 (RS) (inc): With A, 1 ch, dc2inc, 1 dc in next 4 dc, dc2inc, 1 dc in next 2 dc, dc2inc, 1 dc in next 4 dc, dc2inc, 1 dc in next 18 dc with B, sl st to first dc, turn (36 sts).

Row 44: 1 dc in next 18 sts with B, 1 dc in next 18 sts with A, turn.

Row 45 (inc): With A, 1 ch, 1 dc in next 7 dc, dc2inc, 1 dc in next 2 dc, dc2inc, 1 dc in next 7 dc; with B, dc2inc, 1 dc in each dc to last st, dc2inc, sl st to first dc, turn (40 sts).

Row 46: 1 dc in next 20 sts with B, 1 dc in next 20 sts with A, turn.

Row 47 (inc): With A, 1 ch, dc2inc, 1 dc in next 7 dc, dc2inc, 1 dc in next 2 dc, dc2inc, 1 dc in next 7 dc, dc2inc, 1 dc in next 20 dc with B, sl st to first dc, turn (44 sts).

Row 48: 1 dc in next 20 sts with B, 1 dc in next 24 sts with A, turn.

Row 49 (inc): With A, 1 ch, 1 dc in next 10 dc, dc2inc, 1 dc in next 2 dc, dc2inc, 1 dc in next 10 dc; with B, dc2inc, 1 dc in each dc to last st, dc2inc, sl st to first dc, turn (48 sts).

Row 50: 1 dc in next 22 sts with B, 1 dc in next 26 sts with A, turn.

Row 51 (inc): With A, 1 ch, dc2inc, 1 dc in next 10 dc, dc2inc, 1 dc in next 2 dc, dc2inc, 1 dc in next 10 dc, dc2inc, 1 dc in next 22 dc with B, sl st to first dc, turn (52 sts).

Row 52: 1 dc in next 22 sts with B, 1 dc in next 30 sts with A, turn.

Row 53 (inc): With A, 1 ch, 1 dc in next 13 dc, dc2inc, 1 dc in next 2 dc, dc2inc, 1 dc in next 13 dc; with B, dc2inc, 1 dc in each dc to last st, dc2inc, sl st to first dc, turn (56 sts).

Row 54: 1 dc in next 24 sts with B, 1 dc in next 32 sts with A, turn.

Row 55 (inc): With A, 1 ch, dc2inc, 1 dc in next 13 dc, dc2inc, 1 dc in next 2 dc, dc2inc, 1 dc in next 13 dc, dc2inc, 1 dc in next 24 dc with B, sl st to first dc, turn (60 sts).

Row 56: 1 dc in next 24 sts with B, 1 dc in next 36 sts with A, turn.

Row 57: 1 ch, 1 dc in next 36 sts with A, 1 dc in next 24 dc with B, sl st to first dc, turn.

Rows 58–61: Rep rows 56–57 twice.

Row 62: As row 56.

Stuff the base of the neck before continuing.

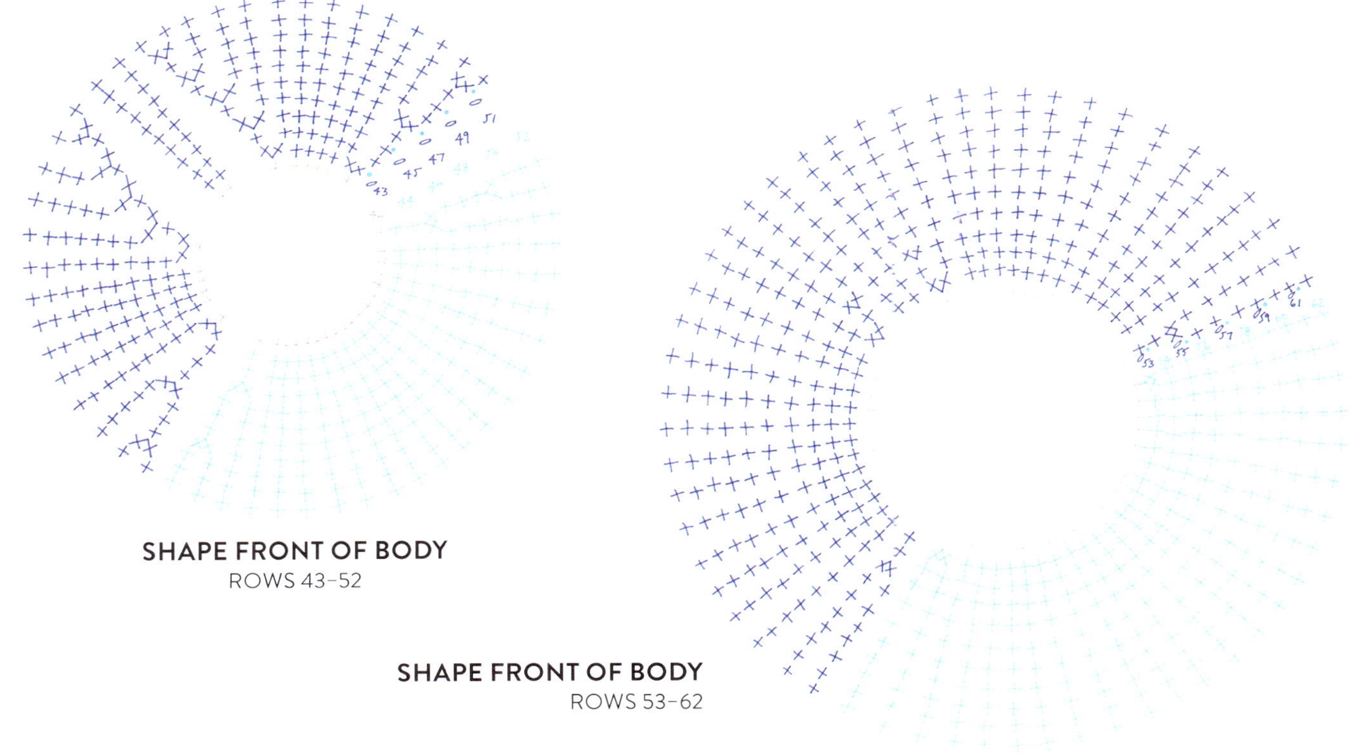

SHAPE FRONT OF BODY
ROWS 43–52

SHAPE FRONT OF BODY
ROWS 53–62

SHAPE END OF BODY

Row 63 (RS) (dec): With A, 1 ch, dc2tog, 1 dc in next 13 dc, dc2tog, 1 dc in next 2 dc, dc2tog, 1 dc in next 13 dc, dc2tog, 1 dc in next 24 dc with B, sl st to first dc, turn (56 sts).

Row 64: 1 dc in next 24 sts with B, 1 dc in next 32 sts with A, turn.

Row 65 (dec): With A, 1 ch, 1 dc in next 13 dc, dc2tog, 1 dc in next 2 dc, dc2tog, 1 dc in next 13 dc; with B, dc2tog, 1 dc in each dc to last st, dc2tog, sl st to first dc, turn (52 sts).

Row 66: 1 dc in next 22 sts with B, 1 dc in next 30 sts with A, turn.

Row 67 (dec): With A, 1 ch, dc2tog, 1 dc in next 10 dc, dc2tog, 1 dc in next 2 dc, dc2tog, 1 dc in next 10 dc, dc2tog, 1 dc in next 22 dc with B, sl st to first dc, turn (48 sts).

Row 68: 1 dc in next 22 sts with B, 1 dc in next 26 sts with A, turn.

Row 69 (dec): With A, 1 ch, 1 dc in next 10 dc, dc2tog, 1 dc in next 2 dc, dc2tog, 1 dc in next 10 dc; with B, dc2tog, 1 dc in each dc to last st, dc2tog, sl st to first dc, turn (44 sts).

Row 70: 1 dc in next 20 sts with B, 1 dc in next 24 sts with A, turn.

Row 71 (dec): With A, 1 ch, dc2tog, 1 dc in next 7 dc, dc2tog, 1 dc in next 2 dc, dc2tog, 1 dc in next 7 dc, dc2tog, 1 dc in next 20 dc with B, sl st to first dc, turn (40 sts).

Row 72: 1 dc in next 20 sts with B, 1 dc in next 20 sts with A, turn.

Row 73 (dec): With A, 1 ch, 1 dc in next 7 dc, dc2tog, 1 dc in next 2 dc, dc2tog, 1 dc in next 7 dc; with B, dc2tog, 1 dc in each dc to last st, dc2tog, sl st to first dc, turn (36 sts).

Row 74: 1 dc in next 18 sts with B, 1 dc in next 18 sts with A, turn.

Stuff the body to within the last three rows before continuing.

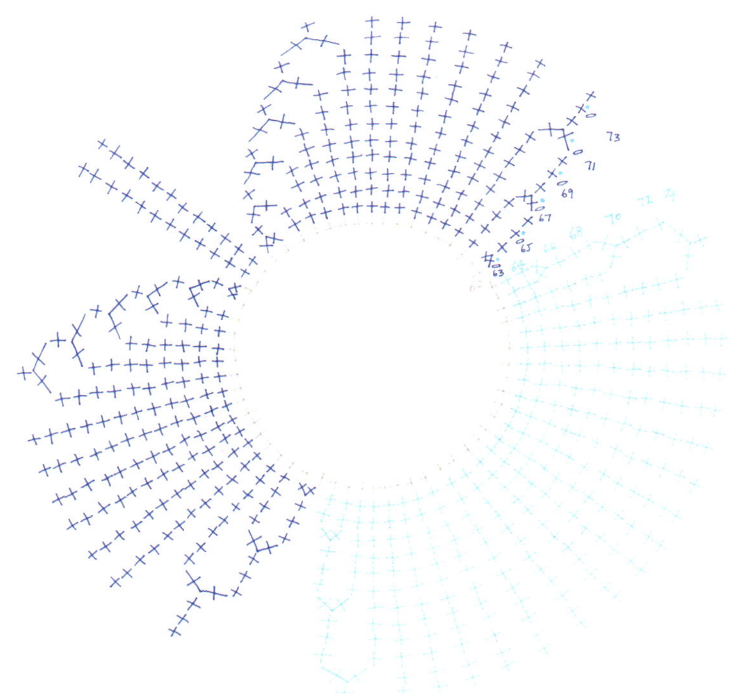

SHAPE END OF BODY
ROWS 63–74

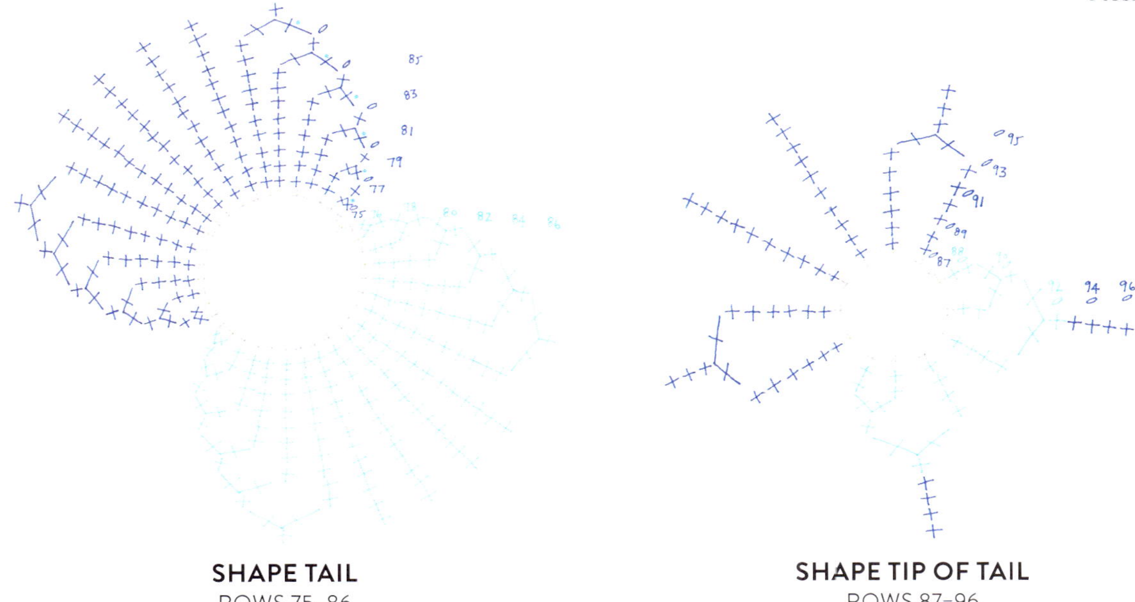

SHAPE TAIL
ROWS 75–86

SHAPE TIP OF TAIL
ROWS 87–96

SHAPE TAIL

Row 75 (dec): With A, 1 ch, *dc2tog, 1 dc in next 14 dc, dc2tog*; rep from * to * with B, sl st to first dc, turn (32 sts).

Row 76: 1 dc in next 16 sts with B, 1 dc in next 16 sts with A, turn.

Row 77 (dec): With A, 1 ch, *dc2tog, 1 dc in next 12 dc, dc2tog*; rep from * to * with B, sl st to first dc, turn (28 sts).

Row 78: 1 dc in next 14 sts with B, 1 dc in next 14 sts with A, turn.

Row 79 (dec): With A, 1 ch, *dc2tog, 1 dc in next 10 dc, dc2tog*; rep from * to * with B, sl st to first dc, turn (24 sts).

Row 80: 1 dc in next 12 sts with B, 1 dc in next 12 sts with A, turn.

Stuff the tail before continuing.

Row 81 (dec): With A, 1 ch, *dc2tog, 1 dc in next 8 dc, dc2tog*; rep from * to * with B, sl st to first dc, turn (20 sts).

Row 82: 1 dc in next 10 sts with B, 1 dc in next 10 sts with A, turn.

Row 83 (dec): With A, 1 ch, *dc2tog, 1 dc in next 6 dc, dc2tog*; rep from * to * with B, sl st to first dc, turn (16 sts).

Row 84: 1 dc in next 8 sts with B, 1 dc in next 8 sts with A, turn.

Row 85 (dec): With A, 1 ch, *dc2tog, 1 dc in next 4 dc, dc2tog*; rep from * to * with B, sl st to first dc, turn (12 sts).

Row 86: 1 dc in next 6 sts with B, 1 dc in next 6 sts with A, turn.

Use the end of the crochet hook to push more stuffing into the tail before continuing.

SHAPE TIP OF TAIL

The following rows are not joined with a slip stitch at the end.

Row 87: 1 ch, 1 dc in next 6 sts with A, 1 dc in next 6 sts with B, turn.

Row 88: 1 ch, 1 dc in next 6 sts with B, 1 dc in next 6 sts with A, turn.

Row 89 (dec): With A, 1 ch, 1 dc in next 6 dc; with B, dc2tog, 1 dc in next 2 dc, dc2tog, turn (10 sts).

Row 90: 1 ch, 1 dc in next 4 sts with B, 1 dc in next 6 sts with A, turn.

Row 91 (dec): With A, 1 ch, 1 dc in next 6 dc; with B, (dc2tog) twice, turn (8 sts).

Row 92: 1 ch, 1 dc in next 2 sts with B, 1 dc in next 6 sts with A, turn.

Continue with A.

Row 93 (dec): 1 ch, dc2tog, 1 dc in next 2 dc, dc2tog, 1 dc in next 2 dc, turn (6 sts).

Rows 94–96: 1 ch, 1 dc in each dc, turn.

Fasten off, leaving a long tail of yarn at the end. Thread the tail of yarn through the last round of stitches and pull tightly to gather the end. Sew the open edges together, inserting stuffing into the tip of the tail before closing the seam.

FLIPPERS
(make 4)

With 2.25mm hook and A, make 23 ch.

Row 1 (WS): 1 dc in second ch from hook, 1 dc in next 20 ch, 3 dc in end ch, 1 dc in opposite side of next 21 ch, turn (45 sts).

Row 2 (RS) (inc): 1 ch, 1 dc in next 22 dc, dc2inc, 1 dc in next 22 dc, turn (46 sts).

Row 3 (dec): 1 ch, 1 dc in next 9 dc, *(dc2tog, 2 dc) twice, dc2tog, 1 dc in next 3 dc*, (dc2inc) twice, 1 dc in next 3 dc; rep from * to *, sl st in next dc, turn, finishing 5 sts before the end of the row (42 sts).

Row 4 (inc): 1 dc in same dc as sl st, 1 dc in next 2 dc, (1 htr, htr2inc, 1 htr) twice, 1 dc in next 6 dc, (dc2inc) twice, 1 dc in next 6 dc, (1 htr, htr2inc, 1 htr) twice, 1 dc in next 3 dc, sl st in next dc, turn, finishing 4 sts before the end of the row (48 sts).

Row 5 (inc): 1 dc in same dc as sl st, 1 dc in next 4 sts, (1 htr, htr2inc, 1 htr) twice, 1 dc in next 8 dc, (dc2inc) twice, 1 dc in next 8 dc, (1 htr, htr2inc, 1 htr) twice, 1 dc in next 9 sts. Join B in last dc, turn (54 sts).

Row 6: With B, 1 ch, 1 dc in each st to end, do not turn.

JOIN FLIPPER EDGES

Fold the flipper, WS together and matching the stitches on each side.

Next: 1 ch, sl st together the back loops only of the next 27 sts on each side to join.

Fasten off, leaving a long tail of A to sew the flipper to the body.

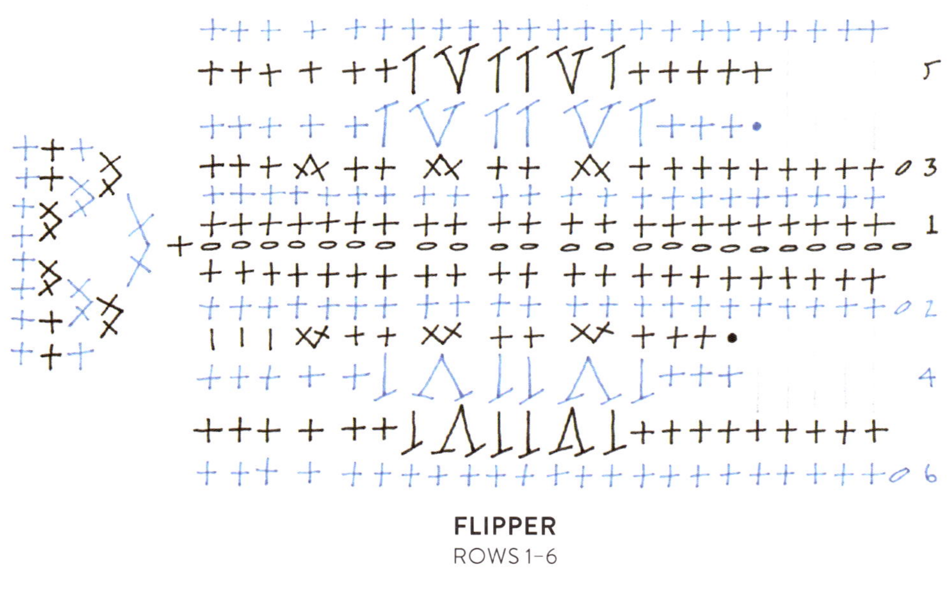

FLIPPER
ROWS 1–6

JOIN FLIPPER EDGES

MAKING UP

HEAD

Sew together the gaps at the side of the mouth. If using looped glass eyes, poke the loop of an eye through the centre of each eye socket before attaching each one to the head using 23⅝in (60cm) length of clear invisible or strong sewing thread (see page 163).

Embroider the nostrils in satin stitch (see page 164), using two strands of embroidery thread.

FLIPPERS

Lightly stuff the flippers, keeping them flattened in shape. Sew together the stitches at the open end to form a straight seam. Sew the flippers to the body.

Weave in all the yarn ends.

DIPLODOCUS

THE WHIP-LIKE TIP OF THIS DIPLODOCUS'S TAIL IS CROCHETED TO PRODUCE A GENTLE CURVE AND, WITH THE OPTIONAL ADDITION OF A PIPE CLEANER, IT CAN BE SHAPED INTO VARIOUS POSITIONS.

MATERIALS

- Jamieson & Smith 2ply jumper weight (4ply equivalent), 100% Shetland wool (114yd/105m per 25g ball):
  3 × 25g balls in FC11 Mix (A)
  1 × 25g ball in FC24 Mix (B)
  1 × 25g ball in 34 Green (C)
- 1 pair of 5/32–3/16in (4–5mm) looped glass teddy bear eyes or safety eyes
- Clear invisible or strong sewing thread to attach the looped glass eyes
- Stranded metallic embroidery thread in black, such as DMC Light Effects, shade E310, for the nostrils
- 2.5mm (UK12:US-) crochet hook
- 1 pipe cleaner, measuring 12in (30cm) long, for the tail (optional: not suitable for young children)
- Blunt-ended yarn needle
- Toy stuffing

SIZE

Approximately 28 3/8in (72cm) long, with tail extended

TENSION

26 sts and 28 rows to 4in (10cm) over double crochet using 2.5mm hook and yarn A. Use larger or smaller hook if necessary to obtain correct tension.

METHOD

The head is worked in rounds and rows of double crochet. The mouth is formed by working into the front loops only of the previous row and shaped with double crochet and half treble stitches. The unworked back loops are crocheted to continue the shaping of the head. The neck, body and tail are crocheted in one piece and worked in two colours. The first row of the neck is crocheted into unworked stitches of the head and around the edges of the last few rows that shape the back of the head. The base of the neck is shaped by working short rows. The rest of the body is shaped by increasing and decreasing stitches, including the curve in the tip of the tail. There is the option of adding a pipe cleaner so it can be posed in different positions. Puff stitches are used to create the spikes that run down the back of the neck, body and tail. The body is stuffed at intervals as it is crocheted.

The legs are crocheted in rounds of double crochet. Bobble stitches form the toes. The bends in the legs are made by working a length of chain stitches and skipping a number of stitches of the previous row. The stitches of the following row are gathered together to form the joints. The first round of the tops of the legs are crocheted into the skipped stitches and the opposite side of the chain stitches. The legs are attached to the body so that they are movable.

Looped glass or safety eyes are attached to a crocheted eye socket, and the nostrils are added with simple embroidery in metallic thread.

1 ch at beg of the row/round does not count as a st throughout.

KEY

- Magic loop
- Chain (ch)
- Slip stitch (sl st)
- Double crochet (dc)
- Dc2inc
- Dc2tog
- Half treble (htr)
- 2-htr puff
- Make bobble (mb)
- Work into back loop only
- Work into front loop only

COLOUR

 A

 B

 C

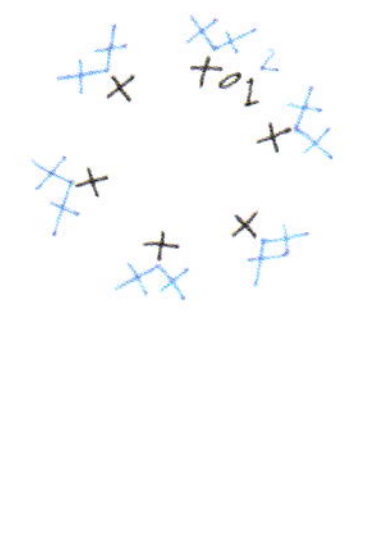

SNOUT
ROUNDS 1–2

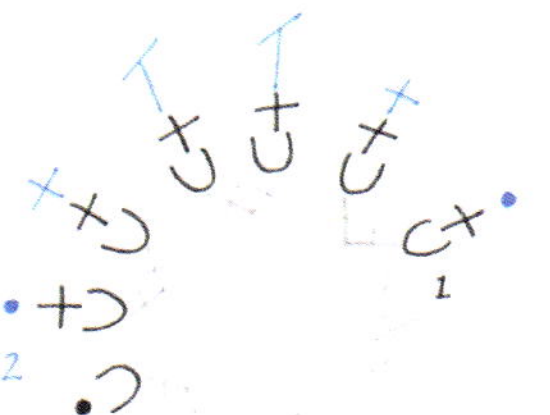

SHAPE MOUTH
ROWS 1–2

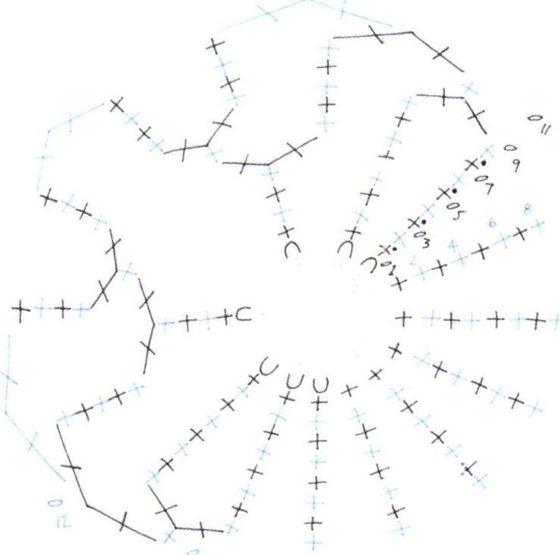

SHAPE HEAD
ROWS 1–12

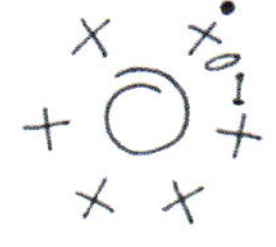

EYE SOCKET
ROUND 1

HEAD

SNOUT

Starting at the front of the snout, with 2.5mm hook and A, make a magic loop.

Round 1: 1 ch, 6 dc into loop (6 sts).

Round 2 (inc): (Dc2inc) 6 times (12 sts). Pull tightly on short end of yarn to close loop.

SHAPE MOUTH

The following is worked in rows.

Row 1: 1 dc in front loop only of next 6 dc, sl st in front loop of next dc, turn.

Row 2: Sl st in first dc, 1 dc in next dc, 1 htr in next 2 dc, 1 dc in next dc, sl st in next dc, turn.

SHAPE HEAD

Row 1 (RS): 1 ch, 1 dc in unworked back loops of next 7 dc of round 2 of snout, 1 dc in both loops of next 5 dc, sl st to first dc, turn.

Row 2 (WS): 1 dc in each st to end, turn.

Row 3: 1 ch, 1 dc in each st to end, sl st to first dc, turn.

Row 4: 1 dc in each st to end, turn.

Row 5 (inc): 1 ch, 1 dc in next 2 dc, (dc2inc) twice, 1 dc in next 8 dc, sl st to first dc, turn (14 sts).

Row 6: 1 dc in each st to end, turn.

Row 7 (inc): 1 ch, 1 dc in next 3 dc, (dc2inc) twice, 1 dc in next 9 dc, sl st to first dc, turn (16 sts).

Row 8: 1 dc in each st to end, turn.

Row 9 (dec): 1 ch, dc2tog, 1 dc in next 6 dc, dc2tog, turn, leaving the remaining 6 sts unworked (8 sts).

Row 10: 1 ch, 1 dc in each st to end, turn.

Row 11 (dec): 1 ch, dc2tog, 1 dc in next 4 dc, dc2tog, turn (6 sts).

Row 12 (dec): 1 ch, (dc2tog) 3 times (3 sts).

Fasten off.

EYE SOCKET
(make 2)

With 2.5mm hook and A, make a magic loop.

Round 1 (RS): 1 ch, 6 dc into loop, sl st to first dc.

Fasten off.

If using safety eyes, attach them at this stage. Poke the post of the safety eye through the centre of the eye socket. Pull tightly on the short end of yarn to close the loop around the post of the safety eye, before attaching it to the head (see page 163).

BODY

The puff stitches are crocheted on the wrong side of the work, as they will appear on the reverse side.
See page 159 for instructions to make a 2-htr puff.

NECK

With 2.5mm hook and RS of head facing, join B with a sl st to first of unworked 6 dc of head.

Row 1 (RS): 1 dc in same dc as sl st, 1 dc in next 5 dc, join A in last dc, work 3 dc evenly along the edge of rows of the first side of the head, 1 dc in next 3 dc of last row of head, work 3 dc evenly along the edge of rows down the other side of the head, sl st to first dc, turn (15 sts).

Row 2 (WS): 1 dc in next 9 dc with A, 1 dc in next 6 dc with B, turn.

Row 3: 1 ch, 1 dc in next 6 dc with B, 1 dc in next 9 dc with A, sl st to first dc, turn.

Row 4: 1 dc in next 4 dc with A, join C in last dc and work 2-htr puff, 1 dc in next 4 dc with A, 1 dc in next 6 dc with B, turn.

Row 5: 1 ch, 1 dc in next 6 dc with B, 1 dc in next 9 sts with A, sl st to first dc, turn.

Row 6: 1 dc in next 4 dc with A, 2-htr puff with C, 1 dc in next 4 dc with A, 1 dc in next 6 dc with B, turn.

Rows 7–10: Rep rows 5–6 twice.

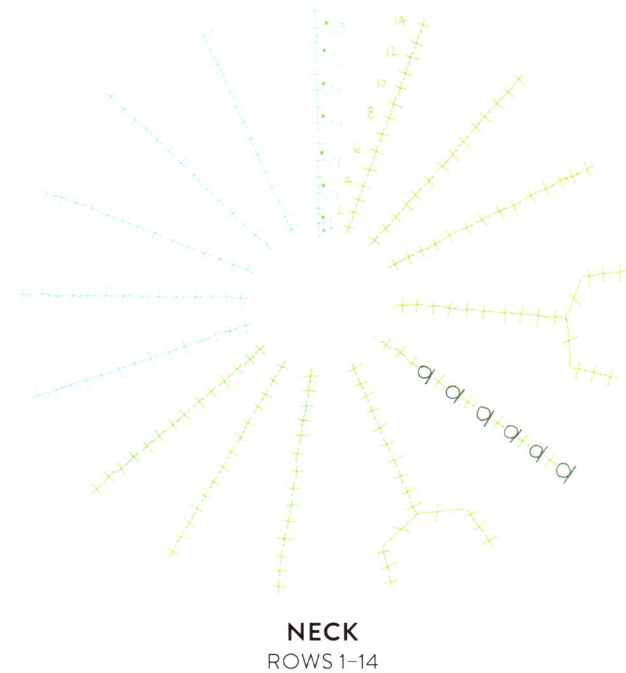

NECK
ROWS 1–14

Row 11 (inc): 1 ch, 1 dc in next 6 dc with B, 1 dc in next 3 dc with A, dc2inc, 1 dc in next st, dc2inc, 1 dc in next 3 dc, sl st to first dc, turn (17 sts).

Row 12: 1 dc in next 5 dc with A, 2-htr puff with C, 1 dc in next 5 dc with A, 1 dc in next 6 dc with B, turn.

Row 13: 1 ch, 1 dc in next 6 dc with B, 1 dc in next 11 sts with A, sl st to first dc, turn.

Row 14: As row 12.

Stuff the head and neck to within the last three rows before continuing.

Row 15 (inc): With B, 1 ch, dc2inc, 1 dc in next 4 dc with B, dc2inc; with A, 1 dc in next 11 sts, sl st to first dc, turn (19 sts).

Row 16: 1 dc in next 5 dc with A, 2-htr puff with C, 1 dc in next 5 dc with A, 1 dc in next 8 dc with B, turn.

Row 17: 1 ch, 1 dc in next 8 dc with B, 1 dc in next 11 sts with A, sl st to first dc, turn.

Row 18: As row 16.

Row 19 (inc): 1 ch, 1 dc in next 8 dc with B, 1 dc in next 4 dc with A, dc2inc, 1 dc in next st, dc2inc, 1 dc in next 4 dc, sl st to first dc, turn (21 sts).

Row 20: 1 dc in next 6 dc with A, 2-htr puff with C, 1 dc in next 6 dc with A, 1 dc in next 8 dc with B, turn.

Row 21: 1 ch, 1 dc in next 8 dc with B, 1 dc in next 13 sts with A, sl st to first dc, turn.

Row 22: As row 20.
Row 23 (inc): 1 ch, 1 dc in next 8 dc with B, 1 dc in next 5 dc with A, dc2inc, 1 dc in next st, dc2inc, 1 dc in next 5 dc, sl st to first dc, turn (23 sts).
Row 24: 1 dc in next 7 dc with A, 2-htr puff with C, 1 dc in next 7 dc with A, 1 dc in next 8 dc with B, turn.
Row 25: 1 ch, 1 dc in next 8 dc with B, 1 dc in next 15 sts with A, sl st to first dc, turn.
Row 26: As row 24.
Row 27 (inc): 1 ch, 1 dc in next 8 dc with B, 1 dc in next 6 dc with A, dc2inc, 1 dc in next st, dc2inc, 1 dc in next 6 dc, sl st to first dc, turn (25 sts).
Row 28: 1 dc in next 8 dc with A, 2-htr puff with C, 1 dc in next 8 dc with A, 1 dc in next 8 dc with B, turn.
Row 29: 1 ch, 1 dc in next 8 dc with B, 1 dc in next 17 sts with A, sl st to first dc, turn.
Row 30: As row 28.
Row 31 (inc): 1 ch, 1 dc in next 8 dc with B, 1 dc in next 7 dc with A, dc2inc, 1 dc in next st, dc2inc, 1 dc in next 7 dc, sl st to first dc, turn (27 sts).
Row 32: 1 dc in next 9 dc with A, 2-htr puff with C, 1 dc in next 9 dc with A, 1 dc in next 8 dc with B, turn.
Row 33: 1 ch, 1 dc in next 8 dc with B, 1 dc in next 19 sts with A, sl st to first dc, turn.
Row 34: As row 32.
Row 35 (inc): 1 ch, 1 dc in next 8 dc with B, 1 dc in next 8 dc with A, dc2inc, 1 dc in next st, dc2inc, 1 dc in next 8 dc, sl st to first dc, turn (29 sts).
Row 36: 1 dc in next 10 dc with A, 2-htr puff with C, 1 dc in next 10 dc with A, 1 dc in next 8 dc with B, turn.
Row 37: 1 ch, 1 dc in next 8 dc with B, 1 dc in next 21 sts with A, sl st to first dc, turn.
Row 38: 1 dc in next 10 dc with A, 2-htr puff with C, 1 dc in next 10 dc with A, 1 dc in next 7 dc with B, sl st in next dc, turn.
Stuff the neck to within the last three rows before continuing.

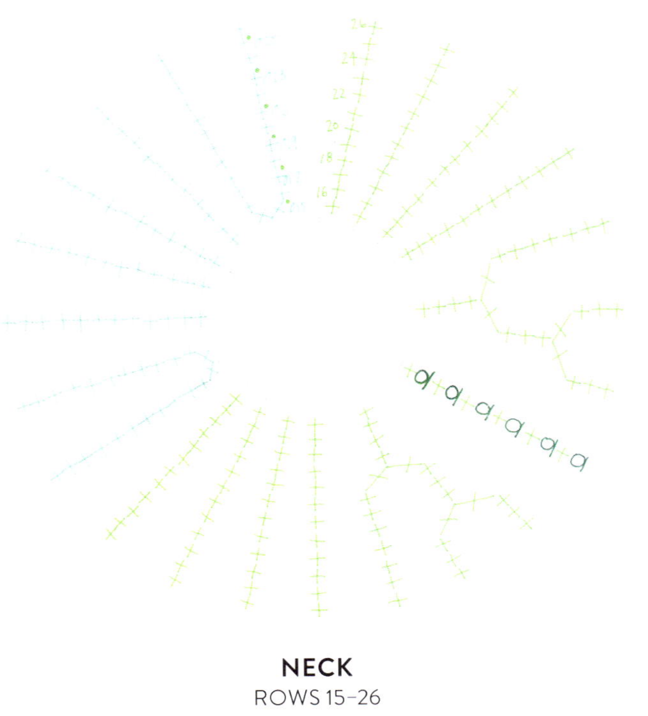

NECK
ROWS 15–26

NECK
ROWS 27–38

SHAPE BASE OF NECK

The following is worked in short rows.

Row 39 (RS) (inc): With B, 1 dc in same dc as sl st, (1 dc, dc2inc, 1 dc) twice, 1 dc in next dc; with A, 1 dc in next 4 dc, sl st in next dc, turn (31 sts). Carry unused yarn on WS of the work.

Row 40 (WS): 1 dc in same dc as sl st, 1 dc in next 4 dc with A, 1 dc in next 10 sts with B, 1 dc in next 5 dc with A, sl st in next dc, turn.

Row 41 (inc): 1 dc in same dc as sl st, 1 dc in next 5 dc with A, 1 dc in next 2 dc with B, (1 dc, dc2inc, 1 dc) twice, 1 in next 2 dc; with A, 1 dc in next 6 dc, sl st in next dc, turn (33 sts).

Row 42: 1 dc in same dc as sl st, 1 dc in next 6 dc with A, 1 dc in next 12 sts with B, 1 dc in next 7 dc with A, sl st in next dc, turn.

Row 43 (inc): 1 dc in same dc as sl st, 1 dc in next 7 dc with A, 1 dc in next 3 dc with B, (1 dc, dc2inc, 1 dc) twice, 1 in next 3 dc; with A, 1 dc in next 8 dc, sl st in next dc, turn (35 sts).

Row 44: 1 dc in same dc as sl st, 1 dc in next 8 dc with A, 1 dc in next 14 sts with B, 1 dc in next 9 dc with A, sl st in next dc, turn.

Row 45 (inc): 2 dc in same dc as sl st, 1 dc in next 9 dc with A, 1 dc in next 4 dc with B, (1 dc, dc2inc, 1 dc) twice, 1 in next 4 dc; with A, 1 dc in next 9 dc, dc2inc, 1 dc in next dc; with C, sl st to first dc, turn (39 sts).

Row 46: 2-htr puff with C, 1 dc in next 11 dc with A, 1 dc in next 16 dc with B, turn, finishing 11 sts before the end of the row.

SHAPE FRONT OF BODY

Row 47 (inc): 1 ch, 1 dc in next 16 dc with B, 1 dc in next 7 dc with A, (dc2inc, 1 dc) twice, 1 dc in next st, (1 dc, dc2inc) twice, 1 dc in next 7 dc, sl st to first dc, turn (43 sts).

Row 48: 1 dc in next 13 dc with A, 2-htr puff with C, 1 dc in next 13 dc with A, 1 dc in next 16 dc with B, turn.

Row 49 (inc): 1 ch, 1 dc in next 16 dc with B, 1 dc in next 7 dc with A, (dc2inc, 2 dc) twice, 1 dc in next st, (2 dc, dc2inc) twice, 1 dc in next 7 dc, sl st to first dc, turn (47 sts).

Row 50: 1 dc in next 15 dc with A, 2-htr puff with C, 1 dc in next 15 dc with A, 1 dc in next 16 dc with B, turn.

Row 51 (inc): 1 ch, 1 dc in next 16 dc with B, 1 dc in next 7 dc with A, (dc2inc, 3 dc) twice, 1 dc in next st, (3 dc, dc2inc) twice, 1 dc in next 7 dc, sl st to first dc, turn (51 sts).

Row 52: 1 dc in next 17 dc with A, 2-htr puff with C, 1 dc in next 17 dc with A, 1 dc in next 16 dc with B, turn.

Row 53 (inc): 1 ch, 1 dc in next 16 dc with B, 1 dc in next 7 dc with A, (dc2inc, 4 dc) twice, 1 dc in next st, (4 dc, dc2inc) twice, 1 dc in next 7 dc, sl st to first dc, turn (55 sts).

Row 54: 1 dc in next 19 dc with A, 2-htr puff with C, 1 dc in next 19 dc with A, 1 dc in next 16 dc with B, turn.

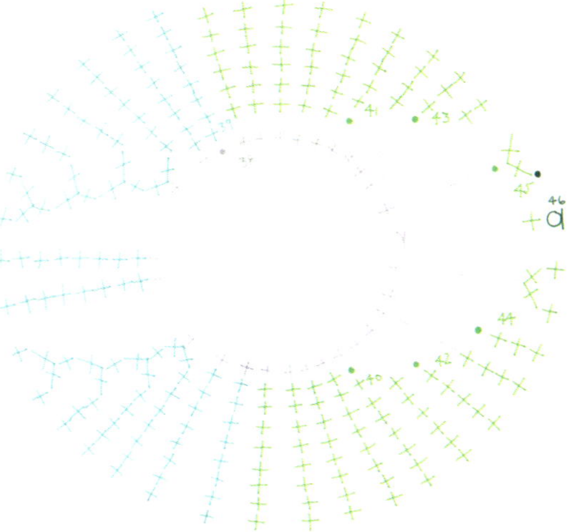

SHAPE BASE OF NECK
ROWS 39–46

Row 55 (inc): 1 ch, 1 dc in next 16 dc with B, 1 dc in next 7 dc with A, (dc2inc, 5 dc) twice, 1 dc in next st, (5 dc, dc2inc) twice, 1 dc in next 7 dc, sl st to first dc, turn (59 sts).
Row 56: 1 dc in next 21 dc with A, 2-htr puff with C, 1 dc in next 21 dc with A, 1 dc in next 16 dc with B, turn.
Row 57 (inc): 1 ch, 1 dc in next 16 dc with B, 1 dc in next 7 dc with A, (dc2inc, 6 dc) twice, 1 dc in next st, (6 dc, dc2inc) twice, 1 dc in next 7 dc, sl st to first dc, turn (63 sts).
Row 58: 1 dc in next 23 dc with A, 2-htr puff with C, 1 dc in next 23 dc with A, 1 dc in next 16 dc with B, turn.
Row 59 (inc): 1 ch, 1 dc in next 16 dc with B, 1 dc in next 7 dc with A, (dc2inc, 7 dc) twice, 1 dc in next st, (7 dc, dc2inc) twice, 1 dc in next 7 dc, sl st to first dc, turn (67 sts).
Row 60: 1 dc in next 25 dc with A, 2-htr puff with C, 1 dc in next 25 dc with A, 1 dc in next 16 dc with B, turn.

SHAPE MIDDLE OF BODY

Row 61: 1 ch, 1 dc in next 16 dc with B, 1 dc in next 51 sts with A, sl st to first dc, turn.
Row 62: 1 dc in next 25 dc with A, 2-htr puff with C, 1 dc in next 25 dc with A, 1 dc in next 16 dc with B, turn.
Rows 63–76: Rep rows 61–62 7 times.
Stuff the base of the neck and the front of the body before continuing.

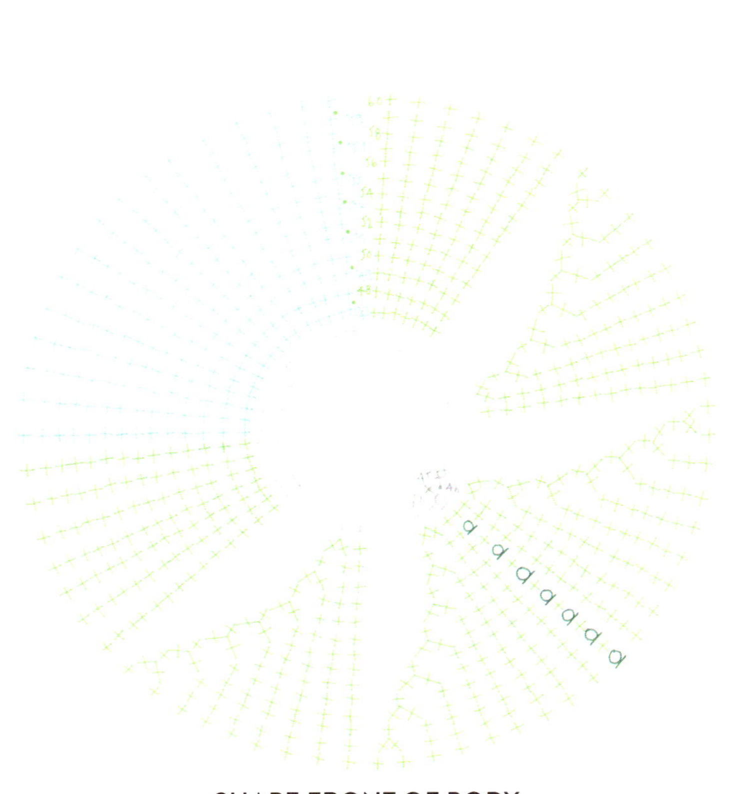

SHAPE FRONT OF BODY
ROWS 47–60

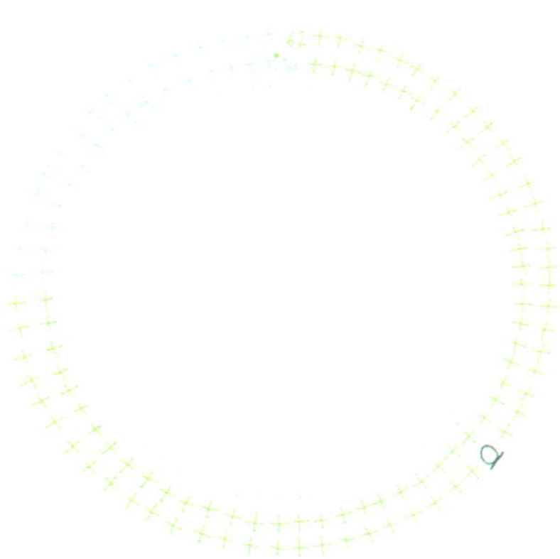

SHAPE MIDDLE OF BODY
ROWS 61–62
FOR ROWS 63–76, REPEAT ROWS 61–62

SHAPE END OF BODY

Row 77 (dec): 1 ch, dc2tog, 1 dc in next 12 dc, dc2tog with B, 1 dc in next 7 dc with A, (dc2tog, 7 dc) twice, 1 dc in next st, (7 dc, dc2tog) twice, 1 dc in next 7 dc, sl st to first dc, turn (61 sts).

Row 78: 1 dc in next 23 dc with A, 2-htr puff with C, 1 dc in next 23 dc with A, 1 dc in next 14 dc with B, turn.

Row 79 (dec): 1 ch, dc2tog, 1 dc in next 10 dc, dc2tog with B, 1 dc in next 7 dc with A, (dc2tog, 6 dc) twice, 1 dc in next st, (6 dc, dc2tog) twice, 1 dc in next 7 dc, sl st to first dc, turn (55 sts).

Row 80: 1 dc in next 21 dc with A, 2-htr puff with C, 1 dc in next 21 dc with A, 1 dc in next 12 dc with B, turn.

Row 81 (dec): 1 ch, dc2tog, 1 dc in next 8 dc, dc2tog with B, dc2tog with A, 1 dc in next 39 sts, dc2tog, sl st to first dc, turn (51 sts).

Row 82: 1 dc in next 20 dc with A, 2-htr puff with C, 1 dc in next 20 dc with A, 1 dc in next 10 dc with B, turn.

Row 83 (dec): 1 ch, dc2tog, 1 dc in next 6 dc, dc2tog with B, dc2tog with A, 1 dc in next 37 sts, dc2tog, sl st to first dc, turn (47 sts).

Row 84: 1 dc in next 19 dc with A, 2-htr puff with C, 1 dc in next 19 dc with A, 1 dc in next 8 dc with B, turn.

Row 85 (dec): 1 ch, dc2tog, 1 dc in next 4 dc, dc2tog with B, dc2tog with A, 1 dc in next 35 sts, dc2tog, sl st to first dc, turn (43 sts).

Row 86: 1 dc in next 18 dc with A, 2-htr puff with C, 1 dc in next 18 dc with A, 1 dc in next 6 dc with B, turn.

Stuff the body to within the last three rows before continuing.

SHAPE TOP OF TAIL

Row 87 (dec): 1 ch, 1 dc in next 6 dc with B, dc2tog with A, 1 dc in next 33 sts, dc2tog, sl st to first dc, turn (41 sts).

Row 88 (dec): Dc2tog, 1 dc in next 15 dc with A, 2-htr puff with C, 1 dc in next 15 dc with A, dc2tog; with B, 1 dc in next 6 dc, turn (39 sts).

Row 89 (dec): 1 ch, 1 dc in next 6 dc with B, dc2tog with A, 1 dc in next 29 sts, dc2tog, sl st to first dc, turn (37 sts).

Row 90 (dec): Dc2tog, 1 dc in next 13 dc with A, 2-htr puff with C, 1 dc in next 13 dc with A, dc2tog; with B, 1 dc in next 6 dc, turn (35 sts).

Row 91 (dec): 1 ch, 1 dc in next 6 dc with B, dc2tog with A, 1 dc in next 25 sts, dc2tog, sl st to first dc, turn (33 sts).

Row 92 (dec): Dc2tog, 1 dc in next 11 dc with A, 2-htr puff with C, 1 dc in next 11 dc with A, dc2tog; with B, 1 dc in next 6 dc, turn (31 sts).

Stuff the tail before continuing.

Row 93 (dec): 1 ch, 1 dc in next 6 dc with B, dc2tog with A, 1 dc in next 21 sts, dc2tog, sl st to first dc, turn (29 sts).

Row 94 (dec): Dc2tog, 1 dc in next 9 dc with A, 2-htr puff with C, 1 dc in next 9 dc with A, dc2tog; with B, 1 dc in next 6 dc, turn (27 sts).

Row 95 (dec): 1 ch, 1 dc in next 6 dc with B, dc2tog with A, 1 dc in next 17 sts, dc2tog, sl st to first dc, turn (25 sts).

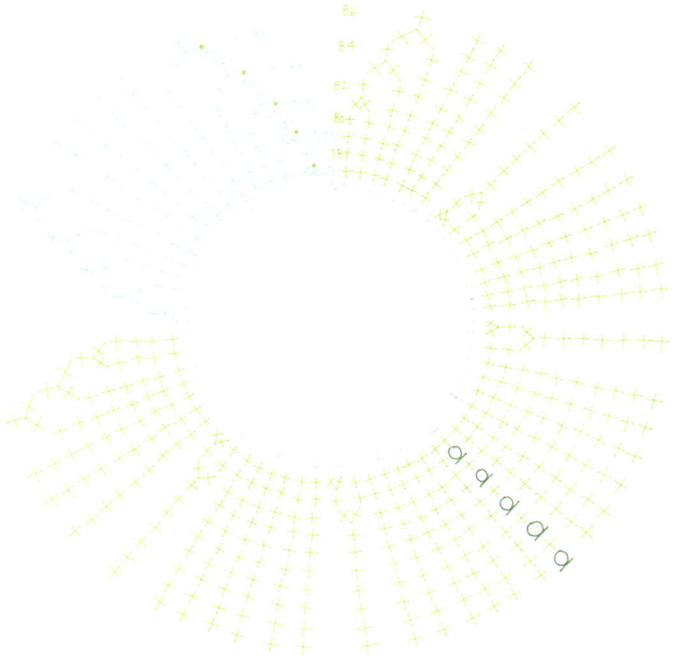

SHAPE END OF BODY
ROWS 77–86

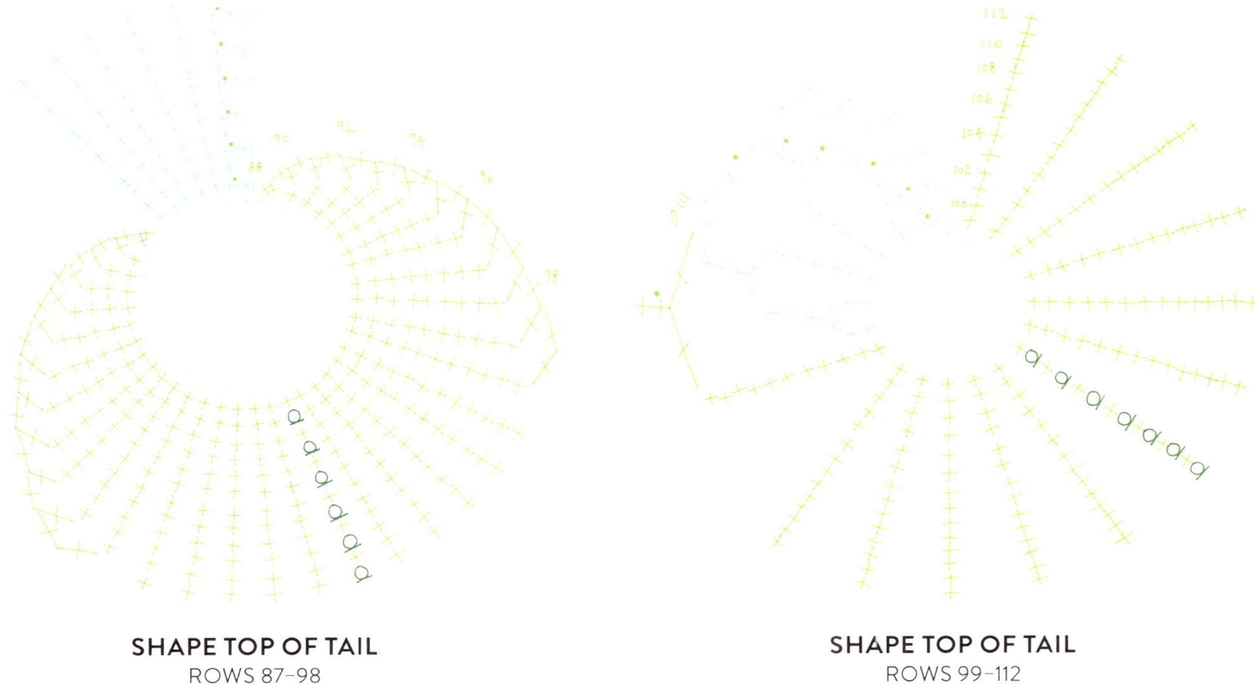

SHAPE TOP OF TAIL
ROWS 87–98

SHAPE TOP OF TAIL
ROWS 99–112
FOR ROWS 113–122, REPEAT ROWS 111–112

Row 96 (dec): Dc2tog, 1 dc in next 7 dc with A, 2-htr puff with C, 1 dc in next 7 dc with A, dc2tog; with B, 1 dc in next 6 dc, turn (23 sts).

Row 97 (dec): 1 ch, 1 dc in next 6 dc with B, dc2tog with A, 1 dc in next 13 sts, dc2tog, sl st to first dc, turn (21 sts).

Row 98 (dec): Dc2tog, 1 dc in next 5 dc with A, 2-htr puff with C, 1 dc in next 5 dc with A, dc2tog; with B, 1 dc in next 6 dc, turn (19 sts).

Insert more stuffing into the tail before continuing.

Row 99: 1 ch, 1 dc in next 6 dc with B, 1 dc in next 13 sts with A, sl st to first dc, turn.

Row 100: 1 dc in next 6 dc with A, 2-htr puff with C, 1 dc in next 6 dc with A, 1 dc in next 6 dc with B, turn.

Row 101 (dec): 1 ch, dc2tog, 1 dc in next 2 dc, dc2tog with B, 1 dc in next 13 sts with A, sl st to first dc, turn (17 sts).

Row 102: 1 dc in next 6 dc with A, 2-htr puff with C, 1 dc in next 6 dc with A, 1 dc in next 4 dc with B, turn.

Row 103: 1 ch, 1 dc in next 4 dc with B, 1 dc in next 13 sts with A, sl st to first dc, turn.

Row 104: As row 102.

Row 105 (dec): 1 ch, (dc2tog) twice with B, 1 dc in next 13 sts with A, sl st to first dc, turn (15 sts).

Row 106: 1 dc in next 6 dc with A, 2-htr puff with C, 1 dc in next 6 dc with A, 1 dc in next 2 dc with B, turn.

Row 107: 1 ch, 1 dc in next 2 dc with B, 1 dc in next 13 sts with A, sl st to first dc, turn.

Row 108: As row 106.

Use the end of the crochet hook to push more stuffing into the tail before continuing.

Row 109 (dec): 1 ch, dc2tog with B, 1 dc in next 13 sts with A, sl st to first dc, turn (14 sts).

Row 110 (dec): 1 dc in next 6 dc with A, 2-htr puff with C, 1 dc in next 5 dc with A, dc2tog, turn (13 sts).

Row 111: 1 ch, 1 dc in each st with A, sl st to first dc, turn.

Row 112: 1 dc in next 6 dc with A, 2-htr puff with C, 1 dc in next 6 dc with A, turn.

Rows 113–122: Rep rows 111–112 5 times.

Insert more stuffing before continuing.

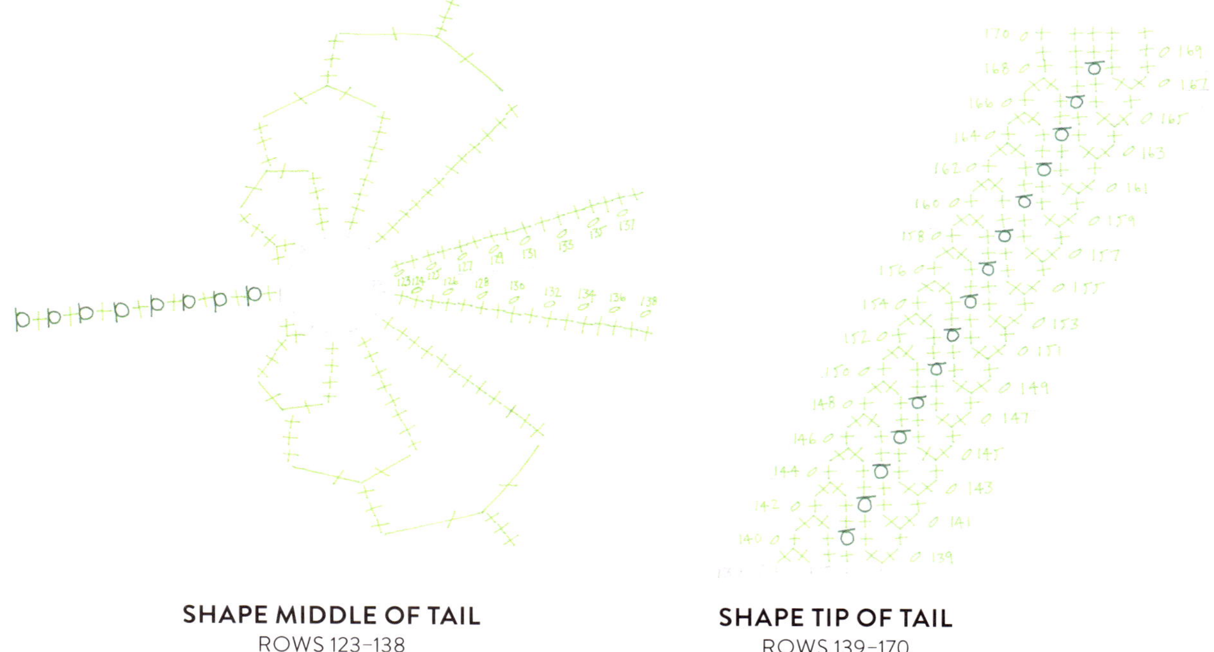

SHAPE MIDDLE OF TAIL
ROWS 123–138

SHAPE TIP OF TAIL
ROWS 139–170

SHAPE MIDDLE OF TAIL

The following rows are not joined with a slip stitch at the end.

Row 123 (dec): 1 ch, 1 dc in next 4 dc with A, dc2tog, 1 dc in next st, dc2tog, 1 dc in next 4 dc, turn (11 sts).

Row 124: 1 ch, 1 dc in next 5 dc with A, 2-htr puff with C, 1 dc in next 5 dc with A, turn.

Row 125: 1 ch, 1 dc in each st with A, turn.

Row 126: As row 124.

Row 127 (dec): 1 ch, 1 dc in next 3 dc with A, dc2tog, 1 dc in next st, dc2tog, 1 dc in next 3 dc, turn (9 sts).

Row 128: 1 ch, 1 dc in next 4 dc with A, 2-htr puff with C, 1 dc in next 4 dc with A, turn.

Row 129: 1 ch, 1 dc in each st with A, turn.

Row 130: As row 128.

Row 131 (dec): 1 ch, 1 dc in next 2 dc with A, dc2tog, 1 dc in next st, dc2tog, 1 dc in next 2 dc, turn (7 sts).

Row 132: 1 ch, 1 dc in next 3 dc with A, 2-htr puff with C, 1 dc in next 3 dc with A, turn.

Row 133: 1 ch, 1 dc in each st with A, turn.

Row 134: As row 132.

Row 135 (dec): 1 ch, 1 dc in next dc with A, (dc2tog, 1 dc) twice, turn (5 sts).

Row 136: 1 ch, 1 dc in next 2 dc with A, 2-htr puff with C, 1 dc in next 2 dc with A, turn.

Row 137: 1 ch, 1 dc in each st with A, turn.

Row 138: As row 136.

SHAPE TIP OF TAIL

Row 139: 1 ch, dc2inc with A, 1 dc in next 2 sts, dc2tog, turn (5 sts).

Row 140: 1 ch, 1 dc in next 2 dc with A, 2-htr puff with C, 1 dc in next 2 dc with A, turn.

Rows 141–168: Rep rows 139–140 14 times.

Rows 169–170: 1 ch, 1 dc in each st with A, turn.

Fasten off, leaving a long tail of yarn at the end. Thread the tail of yarn through the last row of stitches and pull tightly to gather the end.

If using a pipe cleaner, turn under ¼in (6mm) at both ends to prevent the wire poking through the tail. Insert one end of the pipe cleaner into the tip of the tail and push excess wire inside the other end, towards the body. Sew the edges of the tail together, matching the rows and encasing the pipe cleaner. Add small amounts of stuffing at regular intervals as the tail gets wider. Bend the tail into shape.

If not using a pipe cleaner, sew the edges of the tail together, matching the rows. Use the end of the crochet hook to push small amounts of stuffing into the tail at regular intervals.

BACK LEGS
(make 2)

FOOT

The bobbles that form the toes appear on the reverse side of the work. This will be the right side. See page 158 for instructions to make bobble (mb). Starting at the base of the foot, with 2.5mm hook and A, make a magic loop.

Round 1 (WS): 1 ch, 6 dc into loop (6 sts).

Round 2 (inc): (Dc2inc) 6 times (12 sts). Pull tightly on short end of yarn to close loop.

Round 3 (inc): (Dc2inc, 1 dc) 6 times (18 sts).

Join B and carry unused yarn on the WS of the work.

Round 4: (Mb with C, 1 dc in next dc with A) 4 times, mb with C, 1 dc in next 9 dc with B, turn.

Continue with A.

Round 5 (RS): 1 ch, 1 dc in each st.

Round 6: 1 dc in each st.

Round 7 (dec): 1 dc in next 11 dc, (dc2tog, 1 dc) twice, 1 dc in next dc (16 sts).

Round 8 (dec): 1 dc in next 10 dc, (dc2tog, 1 dc) twice (14 sts).

SHAPE LOWER BACK LEG

Rounds 9–10: 1 dc in each dc.

Round 11 (inc): (Dc2inc, 2 dc) 4 times, 1 dc in next 2 dc (18 sts).

Rounds 12–15: 1 dc in each dc.

Round 16: 1 dc in next 3 dc, finishing in line with the stitch between the first two toes and 15 sts before the end of the round.

KNEE JOINT

Round 17: 6 ch, skip next 12 dc, 1 dc in next 6 dc.

Round 18: 1 dc in next 6 ch, 1 dc in next 6 dc (12 sts).

Fasten off and thread tail of yarn through last round of stitches. Pull tightly on end of yarn to close and fasten off.

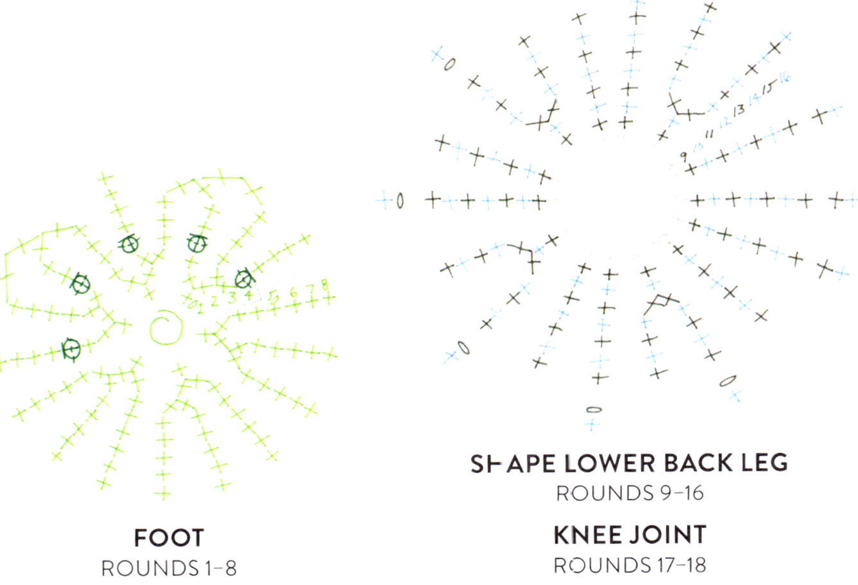

FOOT
ROUNDS 1–8

SHAPE LOWER BACK LEG
ROUNDS 9–16

KNEE JOINT
ROUNDS 17–18

SHAPE THIGH

With RS facing, join A with a sl st to the first of the 12 skipped sts of the lower back leg.

Round 1: 1 dc in same dc as sl st, 1 dc in next 11 dc, 1 dc in opposite side of next 6 ch of the knee joint (18 sts).

Round 2 (inc): (1 dc, dc2inc) 3 times, (dc2inc, 1 dc) 3 times, 1 dc in next 6 dc (24 sts).

Rounds 3–4: 1 dc in each dc.

Round 5 (inc): (2 dc, dc2inc) 6 times, 1 dc in next 6 dc (30 sts).

Rounds 6–7: 1 dc in each dc.

Round 8 (inc): (2 dc, dc2inc, 2 dc) 6 times (36 sts).

Rounds 9–13: 1 dc in each dc.

Round 14 (dec): (Dc2tog, 4 dc) 6 times (30 sts).

Round 15 (dec): (Dc2tog, 3 dc) 6 times (24 sts).

Stuff the leg before continuing.

Round 16 (dec): (Dc2tog, 2 dc) 6 times (18 sts).

Round 17 (dec): (Dc2tog, 1 dc) 6 times (12 sts).

Round 18 (dec): (Dc2tog) 6 times (6 sts).

Fasten off and thread the tail of yarn through the last round of stitches. Pull tightly on the end of yarn to close and fasten off.

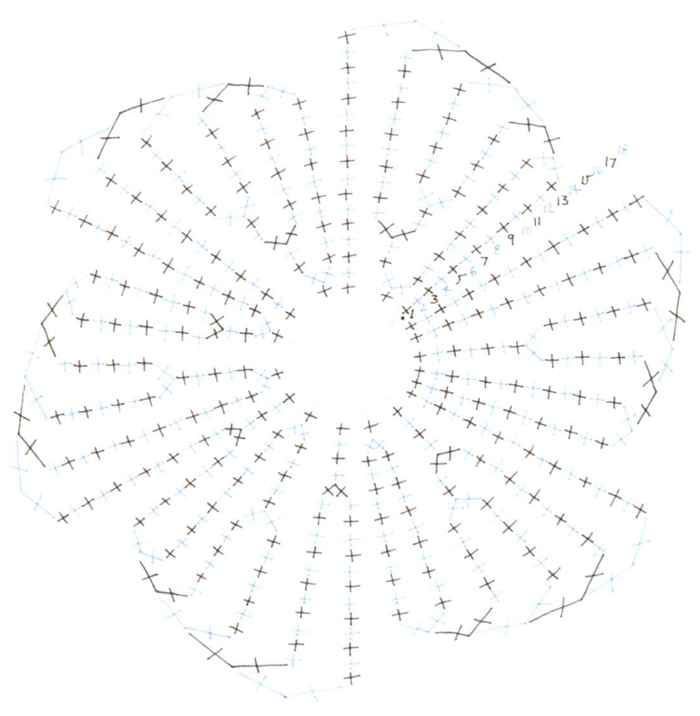

SHAPE THIGH
ROUNDS 1–18

FRONT LEGS
(make 2)

FOOT

Starting at the base of the foot, with 2.5mm hook and A, make a magic loop.

Rounds 1–8: As for Rounds 1–8 of back foot (see page 75).

SHAPE LOWER FRONT LEG

Rounds 9–13: 1 dc in each dc.

Round 14: 1 dc in next 10 dc, finishing at the side of the leg, 4 sts before the end of the round.

ELBOW JOINT

Round 15: 6 ch, skip next 8 dc, 1 dc in next 6 dc.

Round 16: 1 dc in next 6 ch, 1 dc in next 6 dc (12 sts).

Fasten off and thread tail of yarn through last round of stitches. Pull tightly on end of yarn to close and fasten off.

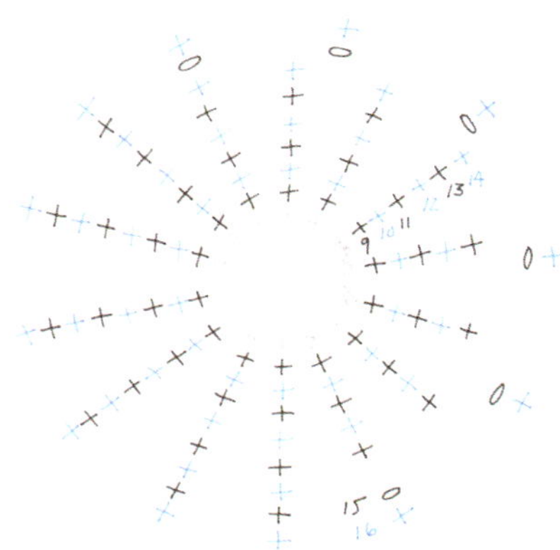

SHAPE LOWER FRONT LEG
ROUNDS 9–14

ELBOW JOINT
ROUNDS 15–16

SHAPE SHOULDER

With RS facing, join A with a sl st to the first of the 8 skipped sts of the lower front leg.

Round 1: 1 dc in same dc as sl st, 1 dc in next 7 dc, 1 dc in opposite side of next 6 ch of the elbow joint (14 sts).

Round 2 (inc): 1 dc in next dc, dc2inc, 1 dc in next 4 dc, (dc2inc, 2 dc) twice, dc2inc, 1 dc in next dc (18 sts).

Rounds 3–12: 1 dc in each dc.

Stuff the leg before continuing.

Round 13 (dec): (Dc2tog, 1 dc) 6 times (12 sts).

Round 14 (dec): (Dc2tog) 6 times (6 sts).

Fasten off and thread the tail of yarn through the last round of stitches. Pull tightly on the end of yarn to close and fasten off.

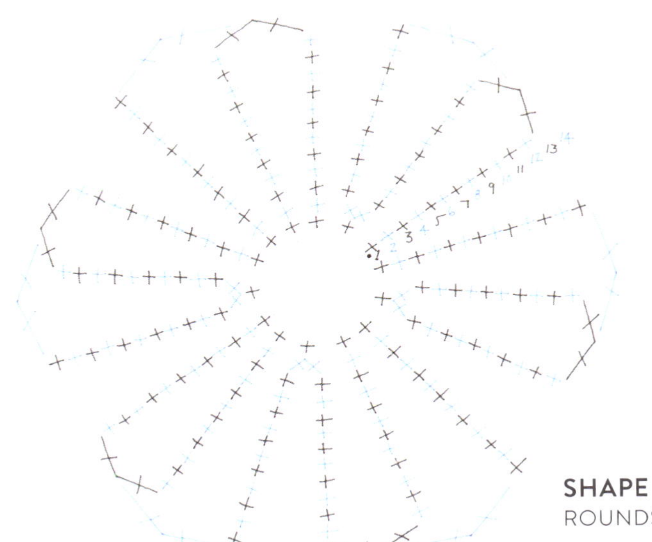

SHAPE SHOULDER
ROUNDS 1–14

MAKING UP

HEAD

If using looped glass eyes, poke the loop of an eye through the centre of each eye socket before attaching each one to the head using $23\frac{5}{8}$in (60cm) length of clear invisible or strong sewing thread (see page 163).

Embroider the nostrils in satin stitch (see page 164), using two strands of embroidery thread.

LEGS

Follow the instructions on page 164 to attach the legs, using 71in (180cm) length of yarn A or strong thread for each pair of legs.

Weave in all the yarn ends.

TRICERATOPS

SHORT ROWS FORM THE SHAPING OF THE TRICERATOPS, WHILE VARIOUS STITCHES ARE USED TO PRODUCE THE BONES ALONG THE TOP OF THE FRILL AND THE TEXTURED SURFACE OF THE BODY.

MATERIALS

- Drops Nord, 45% alpaca, 30% polyamide, 25% wool (186yd/170m per 50g ball):
  2 × 50g balls in 11 Rust Mix (A)
  1 × 50g ball in 07 Light Beige Mix (B)
- 52in (132cm) length of 4ply yarn in pink, such as Drops Nord 20 Blush, for the mouth (C)
- 1 pair of 5/32–3/16in (4–5mm) looped glass teddy bear eyes or safety eyes
- Clear invisible or strong thread to attach the looped glass eyes
- Stranded embroidery thread in black, such as Anchor Stranded Cotton, shade 0403, for the nostrils
- 2.25mm (UK13:USB/1) and 2.5mm (UK12:US-) crochet hooks
- Stitch marker
- Blunt-ended yarn needle
- Toy stuffing

SIZE

Approximately 12in (30cm) long

TENSION

27 sts and 30 rows to 4in (10cm) over double crochet using 2.5mm hook and yarn A. Use larger or smaller hook if necessary to obtain correct tension.

METHOD

The Triceratops' body is crocheted from the tail up. The tip of the tail is crocheted in continuous rounds and continued in rows of double crochet to finish the body, neck and head. Short rows form the shaping of the body, frill and beak, working into a few stitches of the previous row and then crocheting into an unworked stitch at the end of each subsequent row. Puff stitches produce a textured pattern over the body. The mouth is attached to the beak by working into each stitch of both pieces at the same time to join. The body is stuffed as it is crocheted.

KEY

- Magic loop
- Chain (ch)
- Slip stitch (sl st)
- Double crochet (dc)
- Dc2inc
- Dc2tog
- Half treble (htr)
- Treble (tr)
- Htr2inc
- 3-htr puff
- Make bobble (mb)
- Work into back loop only
- Work into front loop only

COLOUR

 A

 B

The legs are crocheted in rounds of double crochet. Bobble stitches form the claws on the feet. The bends in the legs are made by working a length of chain stitches and skipping a number of stitches of the previous row. The stitches of the following row are gathered together to form the elbow and knee joints. The first round of the tops of the legs are crocheted into the skipped stitches and the opposite side of the chain stitches. The legs are attached to the body so they are movable.

Looped glass or safety eyes are attached to a crocheted eye socket. Simple embroidery for the nostrils and three crocheted horns complete the finishing touches of the Triceratops.

1 ch and 2 ch at beg of the row/round do not count as a st throughout.

FRILL

With 2.5mm hook and A, make 25 ch.

Row 1 (WS): Starting in second ch from hook, (dc2inc, 3 dc) 3 times, (3 dc, dc2inc) 3 times, turn (30 sts).

Row 2 (RS): 1 ch, 1 dc in next 21 dc, sl st in next dc, turn, finishing 8 sts before the end.

Row 3 (inc): 1 dc in same dc as sl st, 1 dc in next 2 dc, dc2inc, 1 dc in next 6 dc, dc2inc, 1 dc in next 3 dc, sl st in next dc, turn (32 sts).

Row 4 (inc): 1 dc in same dc as sl st, 1 dc in next 4 dc, dc2inc, 1 dc in next 6 dc, dc2inc, 1 dc in next 5 dc, sl st in next dc, turn (34 sts).

Row 5 (inc): 1 dc in same dc as sl st, (6 dc, dc2inc) twice, 1 dc in next 7 dc, sl st in next dc, turn (36 sts).

Row 6 (inc): 1 dc in same dc as sl st, 1 dc in next 8 dc, dc2inc, 1 dc in next 6 dc, dc2inc, 1 dc in next 9 dc, sl st in next dc, turn (38 sts).

Row 7 (inc): 1 dc in same dc as sl st, 1 dc in next 10 dc, dc2inc, 1 dc in next 6 dc, dc2inc, 1 dc in next 11 dc, sl st in next dc, turn (40 sts).

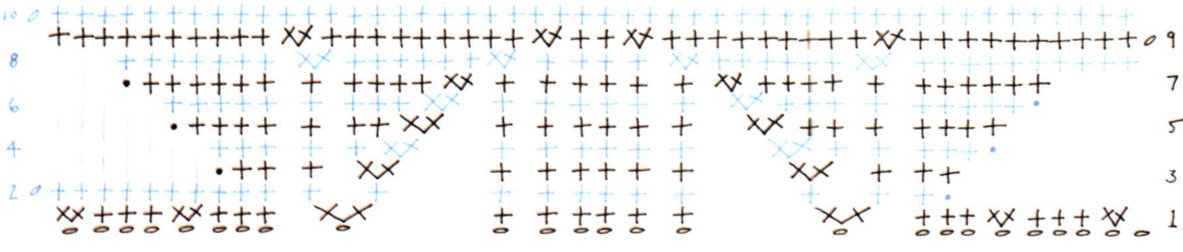

FRILL
ROWS 1–9

JOIN FRILL PIECES
ROW 10
Insert hook into each stitch of both pieces at the same time to join

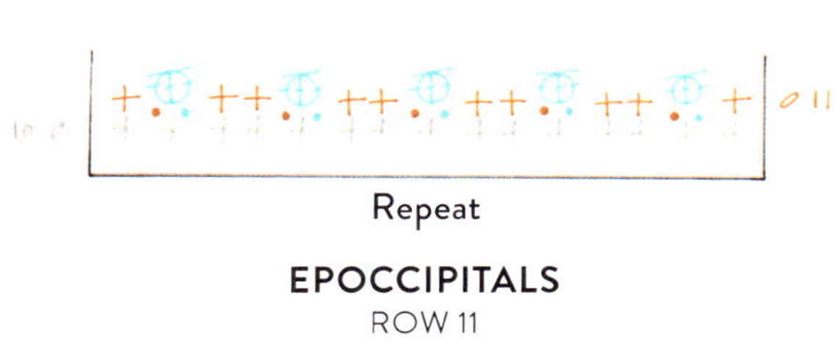

Repeat

EPOCCIPITALS
ROW 11

FRILL
JOIN LOWER EDGES
ROW 1

FRILL
JOIN LOWER EDGES
ROW 2
Insert hook into each stitch of both pieces at the same time to join

Row 8 (inc): 1 dc in same dc as sl st, (6 dc, dc2inc) twice, 1 dc in next 4 dc, dc2inc, 1 dc in next 6 dc, dc2inc, 1 dc in next 10 dc, turn (44 sts).
Row 9 (inc): 1 ch, 1 dc in next 10 dc, dc2inc, 1 dc in next 9 dc, dc2inc, 1 dc in next 2 dc, dc2inc, 1 dc in next 9 dc, dc2inc, 1 dc in next 10 dc, turn (48 sts).
Fasten off.
Make one more piece to match the first. Do not fasten off.

JOIN FRILL PIECES

Hold two pieces with WS together and aligning the stitches of the last row.
Row 10: 1 ch, 1 dc into each of the next 48 sts of both pieces at the same time to join, turn.

EPOCCIPITALS

The bobbles appear on the reverse side of the work. This will be the front of the frill. See page 158 for instructions to make bobble (mb).
Carry unused yarn along the line of stitches.
Row 11: 1 ch, *1 dc in next dc with A, (sl st with B, mb with B, sl st with A) in next dc, 1 dc in next dc with A*; rep from * 15 more times.
Fasten off, leaving a long tail of A.

JOIN LOWER EDGES

With RS facing of the back of the frill facing, join A with a sl st to the opposite side of the first ch.
Row 1: 1 dc in the same ch as the sl st, 1 dc in the opposite side of the next 23 ch; with RS of the front piece facing, 1 dc in the opposite side of the next 24 ch, turn (48 sts).
Before continuing, add a thin layer of stuffing to the frill, keeping it flat.
Hold the lower edges, WS together and aligning the 24 sts on each side.
Row 2: With back of frill facing, 1 ch, 1 dc into each of the 24 sts on both sides at the same time to join (24 sts).
Fasten off, leaving a long tail of A.

BODY

TAIL

With 2.5mm hook and A, make a magic loop.

Round 1: 1 ch, 6 dc into loop (6 sts).

Round 2: 1 dc in each st.

Pull tightly on the short end of yarn to close the loop.

Rounds 3–4: 1 dc in each st.

Round 5 (inc): (Dc2inc, 1 dc) 3 times (9 sts).

Rounds 6–8: 1 dc in each st.

TAIL
ROUNDS 1–8

SHAPE TAIL

The following is worked in rows.

Row 1 (RS) (inc): (1 dc, dc2inc, 1 dc) 3 times, sl st to first dc, turn (12 sts).

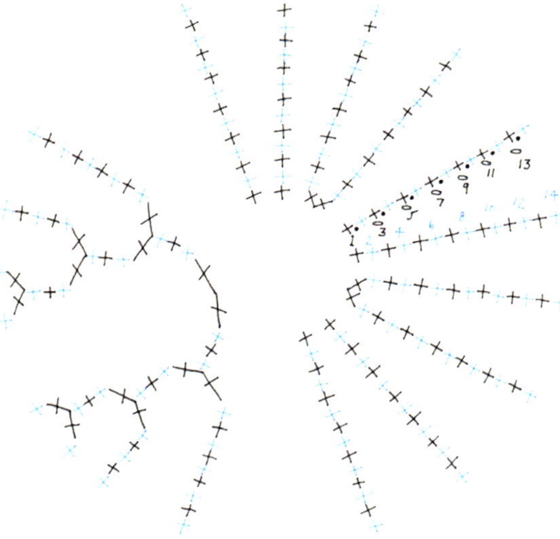

SHAPE TAIL
ROWS 1–14

Row 2: 1 dc in each st, turn.

Row 3: 1 ch, 1 dc in each st, sl st to first dc, turn.

Row 4: 1 dc in each st, turn.

Row 5 (inc): 1 ch, 1 dc in next 5 sts, (dc2inc) twice, 1 dc in next 5 sts, sl st to first dc, turn (14 sts).

Row 6: 1 dc in each st, turn.

Row 7: 1 ch, 1 dc in each st, sl st to first dc, turn.

Row 8: 1 dc in each st, turn.

Row 9 (inc): 1 ch, 1 dc in next 6 sts, (dc2inc) twice, 1 dc in next 6 sts, sl st to first dc, turn (16 sts).

Row 10: 1 dc in each st, turn.

Row 11: 1 ch, 1 dc in each st, sl st to first dc, turn.

Row 12: 1 dc in each st, turn.

Row 13 (inc): 1 ch, 1 dc in next 7 sts, (dc2inc) twice, 1 dc in next 7 sts, sl st to first dc, turn (18 sts).

Row 14: 1 dc in each st, turn.

Row 15 (inc): 1 ch, 1 dc in next 8 sts, (dc2inc) twice, 1 dc in next 8 sts, sl st to first dc, turn (20 sts).
Row 16: 1 dc in each st, turn.
Row 17 (inc): 1 ch, 1 dc in next 9 sts, (dc2inc) twice, 1 dc in next 9 sts, sl st to first dc, turn (22 sts).
Row 18: 1 dc in each st, turn.
Row 19 (inc): 1 ch, 1 dc in next 10 sts, (dc2inc) twice, 1 dc in next 10 sts, sl st to first dc, turn (24 sts).
Row 20: 1 dc in each st, turn.
Row 21 (inc): 1 ch, 1 dc in next 11 sts, (dc2inc) twice, 1 dc in next 11 sts, sl st to first dc, turn (26 sts).
Row 22: 1 dc in each st, turn.
Row 23 (inc): 1 ch, 1 dc in next 12 sts, (dc2inc) twice, 1 dc in next 12 sts, sl st to first dc, turn (28 sts).
Row 24: 1 dc in each st, turn.
Row 25 (inc): 1 ch, 1 dc in next 13 sts, (dc2inc) twice, 1 dc in next 13 sts, sl st to first dc, turn (30 sts).
Row 26: 1 dc in each st, turn.
Row 27 (inc): 1 ch, (2 dc, dc2inc, 2 dc) 6 times, sl st to first dc, turn (36 sts).
Row 28: 1 dc in each st, turn.
Stuff the tail to within the last three rows before continuing, using the end of the hook to push the stuffing right into the tip.

SHAPE END OF BODY

The following is worked in short rows.
Row 1 (RS) (inc): 1 ch, 1 dc in next 17 dc, (dc2inc) twice, 1 dc in next 7 dc, sl st in next dc, turn, finishing 9 sts before the end of the row (38 sts).
Row 2 (WS): 1 dc in same dc as sl st, 1 dc in next 19 dc, sl st in next dc, turn.
Row 3 (inc): 1 dc in same dc as sl st, 1 dc in next 9 dc, (dc2inc) twice, 1 dc in next 10 dc, sl st in next dc, turn (40 sts).
Row 4: 1 dc in same dc as sl st, 1 dc in next 25 dc, sl st in next dc, turn.
Row 5 (inc): 1 dc in same dc as sl st, 1 dc in next 12 dc, (dc2inc) twice, 1 dc in next 13 dc, sl st in next dc, turn (42 sts).
Row 6: 1 dc in same dc as sl st, 1 dc in next 31 dc, sl st in next dc, turn.
Row 7 (inc): 1 dc in same dc as sl st, 1 dc in next 15 dc, (dc2inc) twice, 1 dc in next 16 dc, sl st in next dc, turn (44 sts).
Row 8: 1 dc in same dc as sl st, 1 dc in next 37 dc, sl st in next dc, turn.
Row 9 (inc): 1 dc in same dc as sl st, 1 dc in next 18 dc, (dc2inc) twice, 1 dc in next 19 dc, sl st in next dc, turn (46 sts).
Row 10: 1 dc in same dc as sl st, 1 dc in next 43 dc, sl st in next dc, turn.
Row 11 (inc): 1 dc in same dc as sl st, 1 dc in next 21 dc, (dc2inc) twice, 1 dc in next 22 dc, sl st to first dc, turn (48 sts).
Row 12: 1 dc in each st, turn.

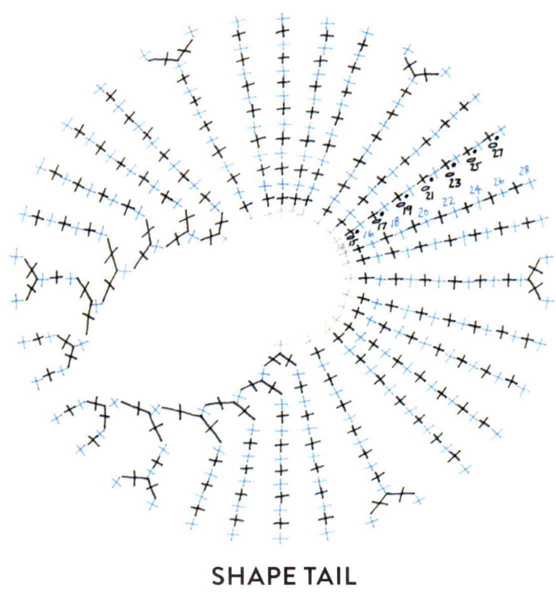

SHAPE TAIL
ROWS 15–28

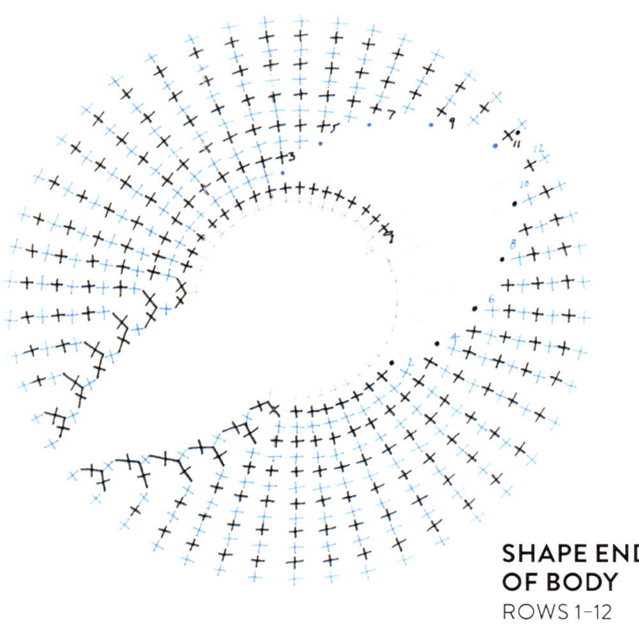

SHAPE END OF BODY
ROWS 1–12

SHAPE MIDDLE OF BODY

The puff stitches are crocheted on the wrong side of the work, as they will appear on the reverse side.

See page 159 for instructions to make a 3-htr puff.

Row 13 (inc): 1 ch, (6 dc, dc2inc) 6 times, 1 dc in next 6 dc, sl st to first dc, turn (54 sts).

Row 14: 1 dc in each st, turn.

Row 15: 1 ch, 1 dc in each st, sl st to first dc, turn.

Row 16: 1 dc in each st, turn.

Row 17 (inc): 1 ch, (7 dc, dc2inc) 3 times, 1 dc in next 6 dc, (dc2inc, 7 dc) 3 times, sl st to first dc, turn (60 sts).

Row 18: 1 dc in each st, turn.

Row 19: 1 ch, 1 dc in each st, sl st to first dc, turn.

Rows 20–21: As rows 18–19.

Row 22: 1 dc in next 27 dc, 3-htr puff in next dc, 1 dc in next 4 dc, 3-htr puff in next dc, 1 dc in next 27 dc, turn.

Row 23: 1 ch, 1 dc in each st, sl st to first dc, turn.

Row 24: 1 dc in next 22 dc, 3-htr puff in next dc, 1 dc in next 14 dc, 3-htr puff in next dc, 1 dc in next 22 dc, turn.

Row 25: 1 ch, 1 dc in each st, sl st to first dc, turn.

Row 26: 1 dc in next 17 dc, 3-htr puff in next dc, 1 dc in next 9 dc, 3-htr puff in next dc, 1 dc in next 4 dc, 3-htr puff in next dc, 1 dc in next 9 dc, 3-htr puff in next dc, 1 dc in next 17 dc, turn.

Row 27 (dec): 1 ch, 1 dc in next 16 sts, dc2tog, 1 dc in next 7 sts, dc2tog, 1 dc in next 6 sts, dc2tog, 1 dc in next 7 sts, dc2tog, 1 dc in next 16 sts, sl st to first dc, turn (56 sts).

Row 28: 1 dc in next 21 dc, 3-htr puff in next dc, 1 dc in next 12 dc, 3-htr puff in next dc, 1 dc in next 21 dc, turn.

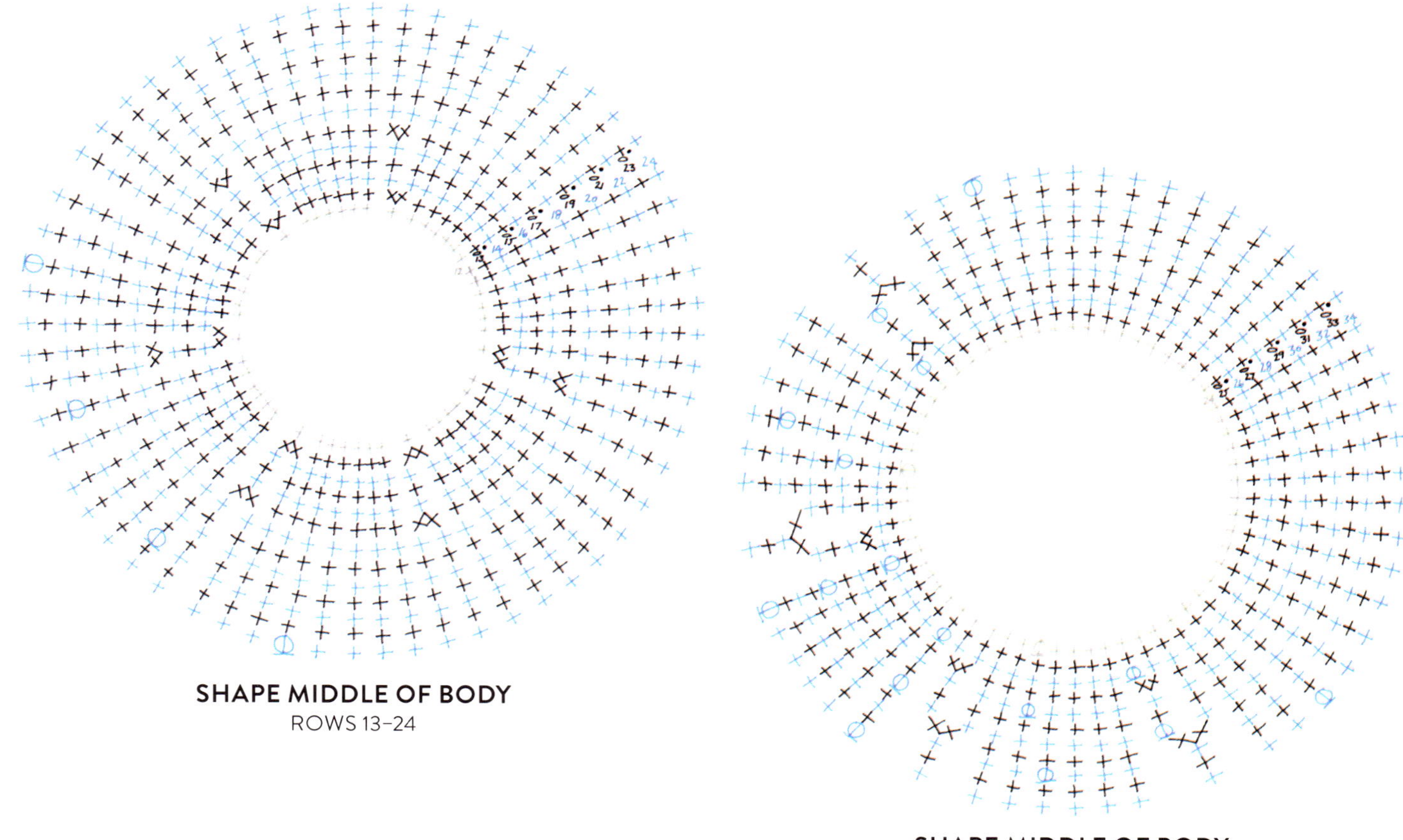

SHAPE MIDDLE OF BODY
ROWS 13–24

SHAPE MIDDLE OF BODY
ROWS 25–34

Row 29: 1 ch, 1 dc in each st, sl st to first dc, turn.

Row 30: 1 dc in next 16 dc, 3-htr puff in next dc, 1 dc in next 8 dc, 3-htr puff in next dc, 1 dc in next 4 dc, 3-htr puff in next dc, 1 dc in next 8 dc, 3-htr puff in next dc, 1 dc in next 16 dc, turn.

Row 31 (dec): 1 ch, 1 dc in next 15 sts, dc2tog, (6 dc, dc2tog) 3 times, 1 dc in next 15 sts, sl st to first dc, turn (52 sts).

Row 32: 1 dc in next 19 dc, 3-htr puff in next dc, 1 dc in next 12 dc, 3-htr puff in next dc, 1 dc in next 19 dc, turn.

Row 33: 1 ch, 1 dc in each st, sl st to first dc, turn.

Row 34: 1 dc in next 12 dc, 3-htr puff in next dc, 1 dc in next 10 dc, 3-htr puff in next dc, 1 dc in next 4 dc, 3-htr puff in next dc, 1 dc in next 10 dc, 3-htr puff in next dc, 1 dc in next 12 dc, turn.

Stuff the body to within the last three rows before continuing.

SHAPE FRONT OF BODY

Row 35 (dec): 1 ch, 1 dc in next 14 sts dc2tog, 1 dc in next 5 sts, dc2tog, 1 dc in next 6 sts, dc2tog, 1 dc in next 5 sts, dc2tog, 1 dc in next 14 sts, sl st to first dc, turn (48 sts).

Row 36: 1 dc in next 16 dc, 3-htr puff in next dc, 1 dc in next 14 dc, 3-htr puff in next dc, 1 dc in next 16 dc, turn.

Row 37: 1 ch, 1 dc in each st, sl st to first dc, turn.

Row 38: 1 dc in next 21 dc, 3-htr puff in next dc, 1 dc in next 4 dc, 3-htr puff in next dc, 1 dc in next 21 dc, turn.

Row 39 (dec): 1 ch, (5 dc, dc2tog) 3 times, 1 dc in next 6 dc, (dc2tog, 5 dc) 3 times, sl st to first dc, turn (42 sts).

Row 40: 1 dc in each st, turn.

Row 41: 1 ch, 1 dc in each st, sl st to first dc, turn.

Row 42: 1 dc in each st, turn.

Row 43 (dec): 1 ch, (4 dc, dc2tog) 3 times, 1 dc in next 6 dc, (dc2tog, 4 dc) 3 times, sl st to first dc, turn (36 sts).

Row 44: 1 dc in each st, turn.

Insert more stuffing before continuing.

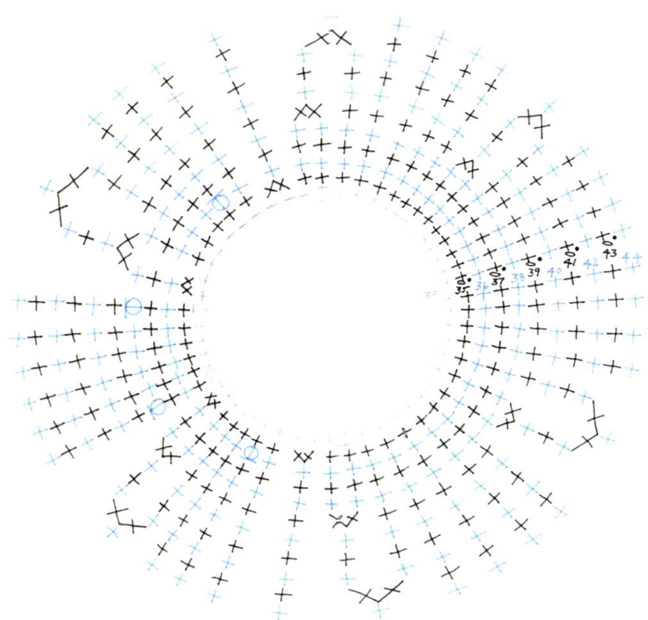

SHAPE FRONT OF BODY
ROWS 35–44

NECK

Row 45: 1 ch, 1 dc in each st, sl st to first dc, turn.
Row 46: 1 dc in each st, turn.
Rows 47–48: As rows 45–46.
Do not fasten off.

JOIN FRILL TO NECK

Row 49: 1 ch, 1 dc in next 6 dc, place the back of the frill against the RS of the body, aligning the 24 stitches of the lower edge of the frill with the next 24 sts of the neck. Holding the pieces together, work 1 dc into each of the next 24 sts of both pieces at the same time to join, 1 dc in the next 6 dc of the neck, sl st to first dc, turn.
Row 50: 1 dc in each st, turn.
Do not fasten off.

HEAD

The next 6 rows are not joined with a slip stitch at the end to leave an opening for stuffing.
Row 51 (RS) (dec): 1 ch, 1 dc in next 15 dc, dc2tog, 1 dc in next 2 dc, dc2tog, 1 dc in next 15 dc, turn (34 sts).
Row 52 (WS) (dec): 1 ch, 1 dc in next 14 dc, dc2tog, 1 dc in next 2 dc, dc2tog, 1 dc in next 14 dc, turn (32 sts).
Row 53 (dec): 1 ch, 1 dc in next 13 dc, dc2tog, 1 dc in next 2 dc, dc2tog, 1 dc in next 13 dc, turn (30 sts).
Row 54 (dec): 1 ch, 1 dc in next 12 dc, dc2tog, 1 dc in next 2 dc, dc2tog, 1 dc in next 12 dc, turn (28 sts).
Row 55 (dec): 1 ch, 1 dc in next 11 dc, dc2tog, 1 dc in next 2 dc, dc2tog, 1 dc in next 11 dc, turn (26 sts).
Row 56 (dec): 1 ch, 1 dc in next 10 dc, dc2tog, 1 dc in next 2 dc, dc2tog, 1 dc in next 10 dc, turn (24 sts).
Row 57: 1 ch, 1 dc in each st, sl st to first dc to join, turn.
Row 58: 1 dc in each st, turn.
Do not fasten off.

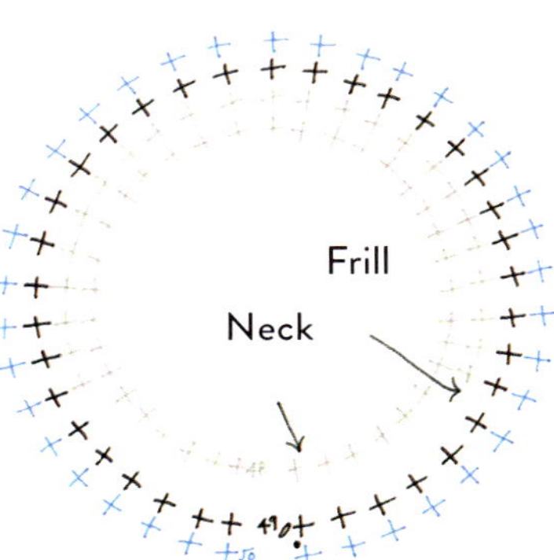

JOIN FRILL TO NECK
ROWS 49–50

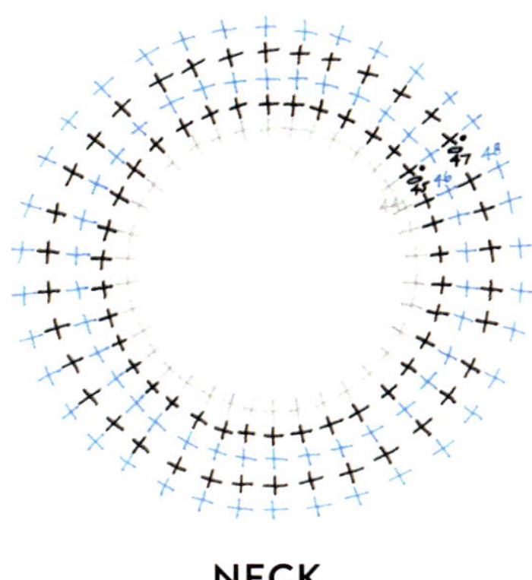

NECK
ROWS 45–48

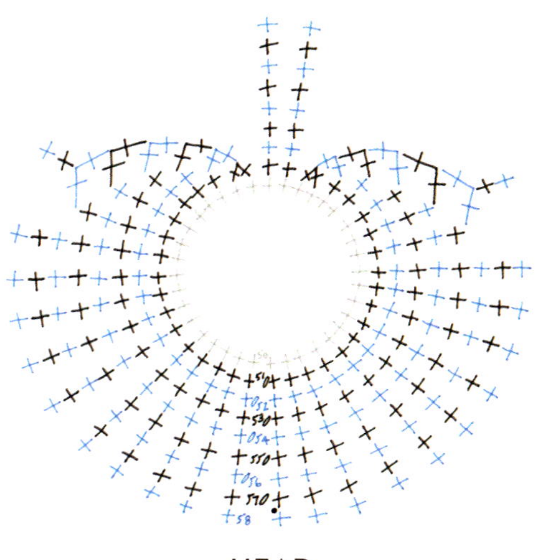

HEAD
ROWS 51–58

SHAPE SNOUT

The following is worked in short rows.

Row 1 (RS): 1 ch, 1 dc in next 14 sts, sl st in next st, turn, leaving the remaining 9 sts unworked.

Row 2 (WS): 1 dc in same dc as sl st, 1 dc in next 5 dc, sl st in next dc, turn.

Row 3: 1 dc in same dc as sl st, 1 dc in next 7 dc, sl st in next dc, turn.

Row 4: 1 dc in same dc as sl st, 1 dc in next 9 dc, sl st in next dc, turn.

Row 5: 1 dc in same dc as sl st, 1 dc in next 5 dc, place marker in last dc, 1 dc in next 12 dc, sl st in next dc.

Fasten off, leaving the next 5 sts of row 1 unworked.

Stuff the neck and head before continuing.

MOUTH

With 2.5mm hook and C, make 11 ch.

Row 1 (RS): 3 dc in second ch from hook, 1 dc in next ch, 1 htr in next 4 ch, place a marker on the second htr st, 1 dc in next 3 ch, 3 dc in end ch; working in opposite side of each ch, 1 dc in next 3 ch, 1 htr in next 4 ch, 1 dc in next ch (22 sts).

Fasten off.

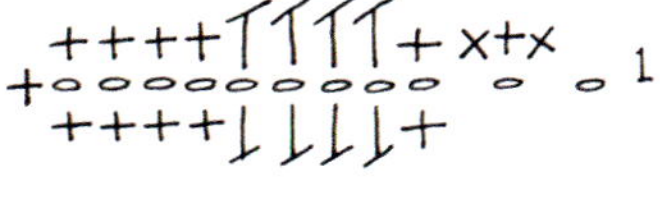

MOUTH
ROW 1

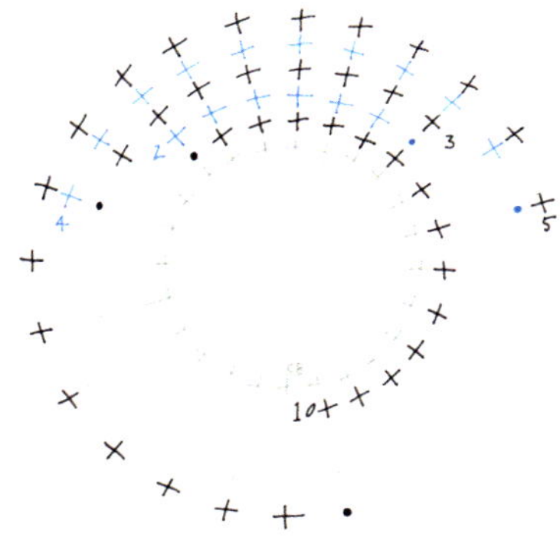

SHAPE SNOUT
ROWS 1–5

BEAK
ROUND 1

BEAK

With 2.5mm hook and RS of work facing, join B with a sl st to the back loop only of the marked st on row 5 of the snout.

Round 1 (RS): 1 dc in same st as sl st, 1 dc in the back loop only of the next 23 sts (24 sts).

Do not fasten off.

TOP BEAK

Row 1 (RS): Dc2tog, sl st in next dc, turn (1 st).

Row 2 (WS): 1 dc in same st as sl st, 1 dc in next 2 dc, sl st in next dc, turn (3 sts).

Row 3: 1 dc in same dc as sl st, 1 dc in next 4 dc, sl st in next dc, turn (5 sts).

Row 4: 1 dc in same dc as sl st, 1 dc in next 6 dc, sl st in next dc, turn (7 sts).

Row 5: 1 dc in same dc as sl st, 1 dc in next 8 dc, sl st in next dc, turn (9 sts).

Row 6: 1 dc in same dc as sl st, 1 dc in next 10 dc (11 sts).

Fasten off.

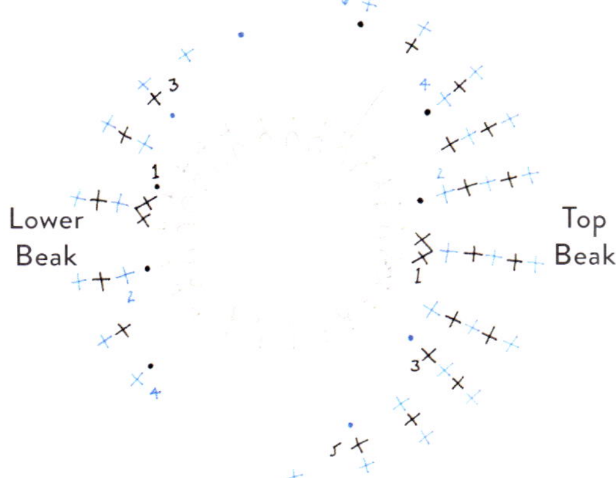

TOP BEAK
ROWS 1–6

LOWER BEAK
ROWS 1–4

LOWER BEAK

With 2.5mm hook and RS of work facing, skip the next 5 sts from the top beak and join B with a sl st to the next st.

Row 1 (RS): Starting in same st as sl st, dc2tog, sl st in next dc, turn (1 st).

Rows 2–3: As rows 2–3 of top beak.

Row 4: 1 dc in same dc as sl st, 1 dc in next 6 dc, sl st in next dc, turn (7 sts).

Do not fasten off.

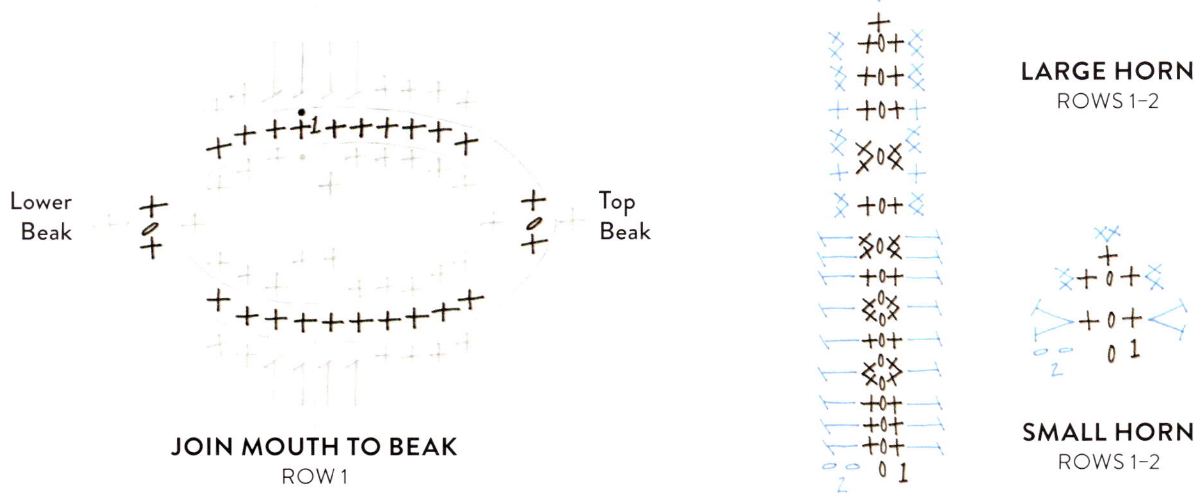

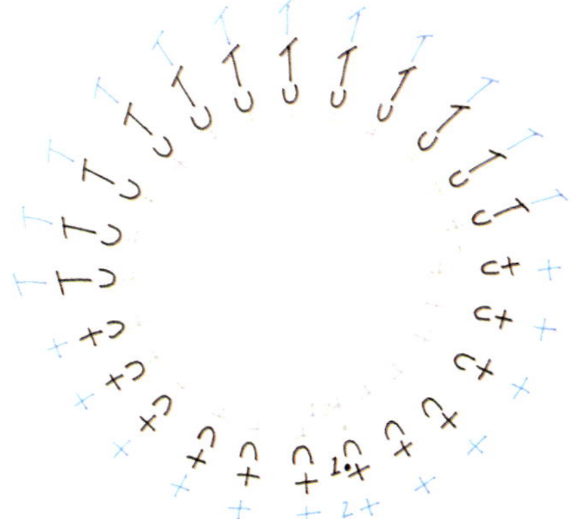

JOIN MOUTH TO BEAK

Row 1 (RS): Insert the mouth into the beak, with WS together, aligning the marker on the mouth with the same st as the sl st at the end of the last row of the lower beak. With yarn B and the lower beak facing, 1 dc in the same st as the sl st and the marked htr of the mouth at the same time to join; working into each stitch of the beak and mouth at the same time, 1 dc in the next 4 sts, 1 ch, 1 dc in the same st as last dc at the tip of the lower beak, 1 dc in the next 11 sts, 1 ch, 1 dc in the same st as last dc at the tip of the top beak, 1 dc in next 6 sts, sl st to next st and fasten off (24 sts).

SNOUT EDGING

With 2.5mm hook and RS of the lower beak facing, join C with a sl st to the first of the 24 unworked front loops of the snout, under the lower beak.

Round 1 (RS): Starting in the same st as sl st, *1 dc in the next 6 sts, 1 htr in the next 12 sts, 1 dc in the next 6 sts*.

Round 2: Rep from * to * of Round 1, working in both loops of each st, sl st to first st and fasten off.

HORNS

LARGE HORNS (MAKE 2)

With 2.25mm hook and B, make 16 ch.

Row 1 (WS): 1 dc in second ch from hook, 1 dc in next 2 ch, (dc2tog, 1 dc) twice, (dc2inc, 1 dc) twice, 1 dc in next ch, 3 dc in end ch; working in opposite side of each ch, 1 dc in next ch, (1 dc, dc2inc) twice, (1 dc, dc2tog) twice, 1 dc in next 3 ch, turn (31 sts).

Row 2 (RS): 2 ch, 1 htr in next 9 sts, (dc2inc, 1 dc) twice, (dc2inc) 5 times, (1 dc, dc2inc) twice, 1 htr in next 9 sts (40 sts).

Fasten off, leaving a long tail of yarn.

SMALL HORN

With 2.25mm hook and B, make 3 ch.

Row 1 (WS): 1 dc in second ch from hook, 3 dc in end ch, 1 dc in opposite side of next ch, turn (5 sts).

Row 2 (RS): 2 ch, htr2inc, (dc2inc) 3 times, htr2inc (10 sts).

Fasten off, leaving a long tail of yarn.

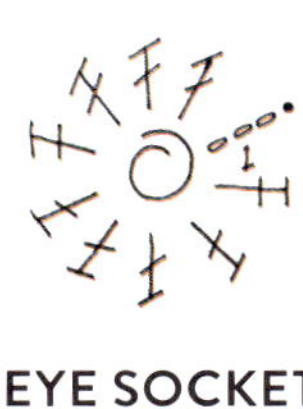

EYE SOCKET
ROUND 1

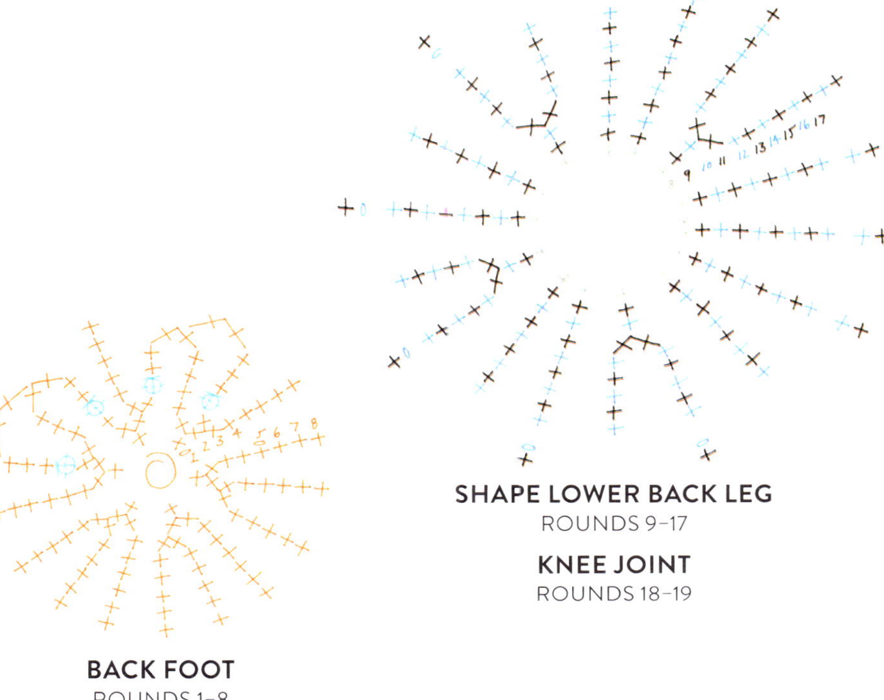

BACK FOOT
ROUNDS 1–8

SHAPE LOWER BACK LEG
ROUNDS 9–17

KNEE JOINT
ROUNDS 18–19

EYE SOCKET
(make 2)

With 2.25mm hook and A, make a magic loop.
Round 1 (RS): 3 ch, 9 tr into loop, sl st to third of 3 ch.
Fasten off, leaving a long tail of yarn.

BACK LEGS
(make 2)

FOOT
The bobbles that form the toes appear on the reverse side of the work. This will be the right side. See page 158 for instructions to make bobble (mb).
Starting at the base of the foot, with 2.5mm hook and A, make a magic loop.
Round 1 (WS): 1 ch, 6 dc into loop (6 sts).
Round 2 (inc): (Dc2inc) 6 times (12 sts). Pull tightly on short end of yarn to close loop.
Round 3 (inc): (Dc2inc, 1 dc) 6 times (18 sts).
Round 4: 1 dc in next dc, join B and carry unused yarn on the WS of the work; (mb with B, 1 dc in next dc with A) 4 times, 1 dc in next 9 dc with A, turn to RS.
Continue with A.
Round 5 (RS): 1 ch, 1 dc in each st.
Round 6: 1 dc in each st.
Round 7 (dec): 1 dc in next 11 dc, (dc2tog, 1 dc) twice, 1 dc in next dc (16 sts).
Round 8 (dec): 1 dc in next 10 dc, (dc2tog, 1 dc) twice (14 sts).

SHAPE LOWER BACK LEG
Rounds 9–10: 1 dc in each dc.
Round 11 (inc): (Dc2inc, 2 dc) 4 times, 1 dc in next 2 dc (18 sts).
Rounds 12–16: 1 dc in each dc.
Round 17: 1 dc in next 3 dc, finishing in line with the first toe, 15 sts before the end of the round.

KNEE JOINT
Round 18: 6 ch, skip next 12 dc, 1 dc in next 6 dc.
Round 19: 1 dc in next 6 ch, 1 dc in next 6 dc (12 sts).
Fasten off and thread tail of yarn through last round of stitches. Pull tightly on end of yarn to close and fasten off.

SHAPE THIGH

With RS facing, join A with a sl st to the first of the 12 skipped sts of the lower back leg.

Round 1: 1 dc in same dc as sl st, 1 dc in next 11 dc, 1 dc in opposite side of next 6 ch of the knee joint (18 sts).

Round 2 (inc): (1 dc, dc2inc) 3 times, (dc2inc, 1 dc) 3 times, 1 dc in next 6 dc (24 sts).

Round 3: 1 dc in each dc.

Round 4 (inc): (2 dc, dc2inc) 6 times, 1 dc in next 6 dc (30 sts).

Rounds 5–6: 1 dc in each dc.

Round 7 (inc): (2 dc, dc2inc, 2 dc) 6 times (36 sts).

Rounds 8–12: 1 dc in each dc.

Round 13 (dec): (Dc2tog, 4 dc) 6 times (30 sts).

Round 14 (dec): (Dc2tog, 3 dc) 6 times (24 sts).

Stuff the leg before continuing.

Round 15 (dec): (Dc2tog, 2 dc) 6 times (18 sts).

Round 16 (dec): (Dc2tog, 1 dc) 6 times (12 sts).

Round 17 (dec): (Dc2tog) 6 times (6 sts).

Fasten off and thread the tail of yarn through the last round of stitches. Pull tightly on the end of yarn to close and fasten off.

FRONT LEGS
(make 2)

FOOT

Starting at the base of the foot, with 2.5mm hook and A, make a magic loop.

Round 1 (WS): 1 ch, 6 dc into loop (6 sts).

Round 2 (inc): (Dc2inc) 6 times (12 sts). Pull tightly on short end of yarn to close loop.

Round 3 (inc): (Dc2inc, 1 dc) 6 times (18 sts).

Join B and carry unused yarn on the WS of the work.

Round 4: (Mb with B, 1 dc in next dc with A) 4 times, mb with B, 1 dc in next 9 dc with A, turn.

Continue with A.

Round 5 (RS): 1 ch, 1 dc in each st.

Round 6: 1 dc in each st.

Round 7 (dec): 1 dc in next 11 dc, (dc2tog, 1 dc) twice, 1 dc in next dc (16 sts).

Round 8 (dec): 1 dc in next 10 dc, (dc2tog, 1 dc) twice (14 sts).

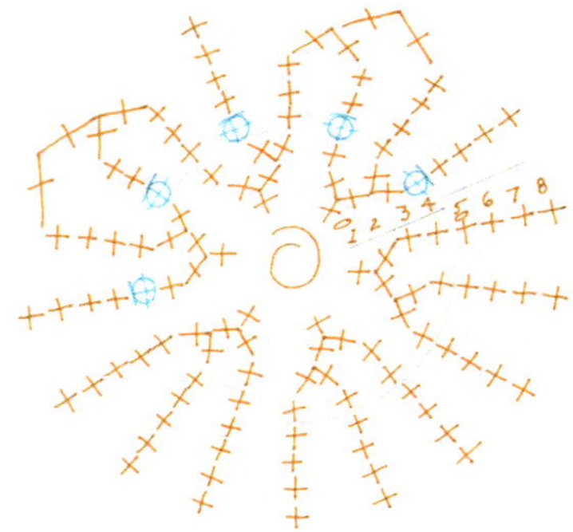

FRONT FOOT
ROUNDS 1–8

SHAPE THIGH
ROUNDS 1–17

SHAPE LOWER FRONT LEG

Rounds 9–11: 1 dc in each dc.
Round 12: 1 dc in next 9 dc, finishing at the side of the leg, 5 sts before the end of the round.

ELBOW JOINT

Round 13: 6 ch, skip next 8 dc, 1 dc in next 6 dc.
Round 14: 1 dc in next 6 ch, 1 dc in next 6 dc (12 sts).
Fasten off and thread tail of yarn through last round of stitches. Pull tightly on end of yarn to close and fasten off.

SHAPE SHOULDER

With RS facing, join A with a sl st to the first of the 8 skipped sts of the lower front leg.
Round 1: 1 dc in same dc as sl st, 1 dc in next 7 dc, 1 dc in opposite side of next 6 ch of the elbow joint (14 sts).
Round 2 (inc): 1 dc in next dc, dc2inc, 1 dc in next 4 dc, (dc2inc, 2 dc) twice, dc2inc, 1 dc in next dc (18 sts).
Rounds 3–10: 1 dc in each dc.
Stuff the leg before continuing.
Round 11 (dec): (Dc2tog, 1 dc) 6 times (12 sts).
Round 12 (dec): (Dc2tog) 6 times (6 sts).
Fasten off and thread the tail of yarn through the last round of stitches. Pull tightly on the end of yarn to close and fasten off.

MAKING UP

HEAD

If using safety eyes, attach them before stuffing the head. Poke the post of the safety eye through the centre of the eye socket. Pull tightly on the short end of yarn to close the loop around the post of the safety eye, before attaching it to the head (see page 163).

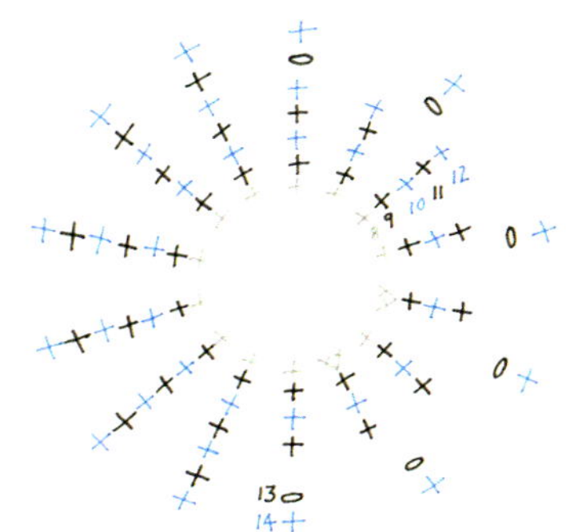

SHAPE LOWER FRONT LEG
ROUNDS 9–12

ELBOW JOINT
ROUNDS 13–14

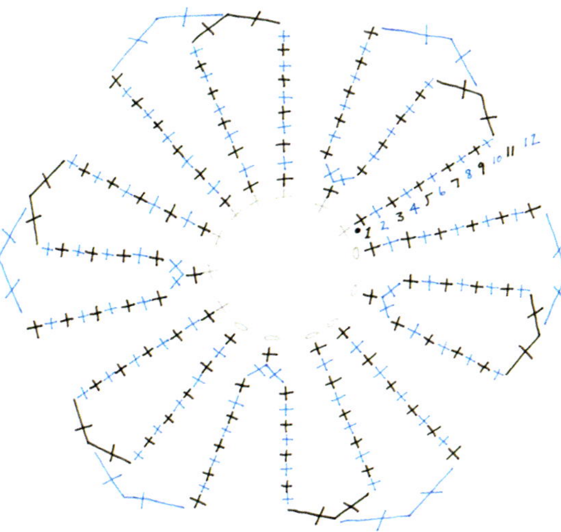

SHAPE SHOULDER
ROUNDS 1–12

Stuff the head, pushing the stuffing into the beak with the end of the hook and keeping the inside of the mouth flat. Sew together the open edges of the head with yarn A.

Use the long tails of yarn left after fastening off the frill to sew the open edges together on each side.

If using looped glass eyes, poke the loop of an eye through the centre of each eye socket before attaching each one to the head using $23\frac{5}{8}$in (60cm) length of clear invisible or strong sewing thread (see page 163). Use the tail of yarn left after fastening off the sockets to neatly sew the edges to the head. Embroider the nostrils in satin stitch (see page 164), using two strands of embroidery thread.

HORNS

Fold the horn, WS together and matching the stitches on each side. Use the tail of yarn left after fastening off to sew the stitches together. Stuff the horns, using the end of a crochet hook to push the stuffing right into the tips. Position the large horns with the seams facing the front of the head and the seams of the small horn facing the frill. Sew the horns in place, stitching all around the lower edges to attach them securely.

Weave in all the yarn ends.

LEGS

Follow the instructions on page 164 to attach the legs, using 63in (160cm) length of yarn A or strong thread for each pair of legs.

PACHYCEPHALOSAURUS

THE PACHYCEPHALOSAURUS IS A SMALL PROJECT THAT FEATURES A GEOMETRIC PATTERN RUNNING DOWN ITS BACK. THIS DINOSAUR CAN SIMPLIFIED BY OMITTING THE PATTERN AND WORKING WITH FEWER COLOURS.

MATERIALS

- Drops Alpaca, 100% alpaca (183yd/167m per 50g ball):
  1 × 50g ball in 9024 Dark Blush (A)
  1 × 50g ball in 4010 Light Lavender (B)
  1 × 50g ball in 9033 Strawberry Cream (C)
  1 × 50g ball in 5565 Light Maroon Mix (D)
- 1 pair of 5/32–3/16in (4–5mm) looped glass teddy bear eyes or safety eyes
- Clear invisible or strong thread to attach the looped glass eyes
- Stranded embroidery thread in black, such as Anchor Stranded Cotton, shade 0403, for the nostrils
- 2.5mm (UK12:US-) crochet hook
- Blunt-ended yarn needle
- Toy stuffing

SIZE

Approximately 9½in (24cm) long and 5½in (14cm) tall

TENSION

27 sts and 30 rows to 4in (10cm) over double crochet using 2.5mm hook and yarn A. Use larger or smaller hook if necessary to obtain correct tension.

METHOD

The head is worked in rounds of double crochet. The dome is produced by making a number of chain stitches, skipping the stitches under the snout and crocheting into the remaining stitches at the top of the head. Bobble stitches form the spikes around the edge of the dome.

The head is finished by crocheting into the skipped stitches of the snout and the opposite side of the chain stitches of the dome. The neck, body and tail are continued from the head and crocheted in rows, using colourwork to produce a geometric pattern that runs down the back of the dinosaur. Short rows shape the front of the body, and the curl in the tip of the tail is formed by increasing and decreasing the stitches.

KEY

- Magic loop
- Chain (ch)
- Slip stitch (sl st)
- Double crochet (dc)
- Dc2inc
- Dc2tog
- Make bobble (mb)
- Work into back loop only
- Work into front loop only

COLOUR

- A
- C
- D

The arms and legs are crocheted in rounds. The arms are started at the elbow joint. The forearm and upper arm are worked separately from the last round of the elbow. The bends in the legs are created by making a length of chain stitches and skipping a number of stitches of the previous row. The stitches of the following row are gathered together to form the joints. The skipped stitches and the opposite side of the chain stitches are then crocheted into to begin the upper parts of the legs. The limbs are attached to the body so they are movable.

Looped glass or safety eyes are attached to a crocheted disc before sewing them to the head. The Pachycephalosaurus is finished with nostrils embroidered in satin stitch and a scattering of French knots over the snout.

1 ch at beg of the row/round does not count as a st throughout.

HEAD

BEAK

Starting at the front of the beak, with 2.5mm hook and B, make a magic loop.

Round 1: 1 ch, 6 dc into loop (6 sts).

Round 2 (inc): (Dc2inc, 1 dc) 3 times (9 sts). Pull tightly on short end of yarn to close loop.

Round 3: 1 dc in each st. Join A in last dc. Carry B on WS of work.

SNOUT

Round 4 (inc): (Dc2inc, 2 dc) 3 times (12 sts).

Rounds 5–6: 1 dc in each st.

Round 7 (inc): (Dc2inc, 3 dc) 3 times (15 sts).

BEAK
ROUNDS 1–3

SNOUT
ROUNDS 4–7

DOME

Round 1: 11 ch, skip next 6 dc, 1 dc in next 9 dc.

Round 2: 1 dc in next 11 ch, 1 dc in next 9 dc, join B in last dc (20 sts). Fasten off A and continue with B.

DOME SPIKES

See page 158 for instructions to make bobble (mb).

Round 3: 1 dc in each st.

Round 4: Sl st in front loop only of next dc, *(sl st, mb, sl st) in front loop only of next dc, sl st in front loop only of next dc; rep from * 4 more times, 1 dc in both loops of next 9 dc.

SHAPE TOP OF DOME

Round 5: 1 dc in unworked back loops of next 11 sts of round 3, 1 dc in both loops of next 9 sts of previous round.

Round 6: 1 dc in next 11 dc, finishing 9 sts before the end of the round.

Round 7 (dec): (Dc2tog, 2 dc) 5 times (15 sts).

Round 8 (dec): (Dc2tog, 1 dc) 5 times (10 sts).

Round 9 (dec): (Dc2tog) 5 times (5 sts).

Fasten off and thread the tail of yarn through the last row of stitches. Pull tightly on the end of yarn to close and fasten off.

FINISH HEAD

The following is worked in rows. With 2.5mm hook and RS of head facing, join A with a sl st to first of unworked 6 dc of snout.

Row 1 (RS) (dec): 1 dc in same dc as sl st, (dc2tog) twice, 1 dc in next dc, 1 dc in the opposite side of the 11 ch sts of the dome, sl st to first dc, turn (15 sts).

Row 2 (WS): 1 dc in each st to end, join C in last dc, turn. Do not fasten off.

If using safety eyes, attach them at this stage. Poke the post of the safety eye through the centre of the eye socket. Pull tightly on the short end of yarn to close the loop around the post of the safety eye, before attaching it to the head (see page 163).

EYE SOCKET

(make 2)

With 2.5mm hook and A, make a magic loop.

Round 1 (RS): 1 ch, 6 dc into loop, sl st to first dc.

Fasten off.

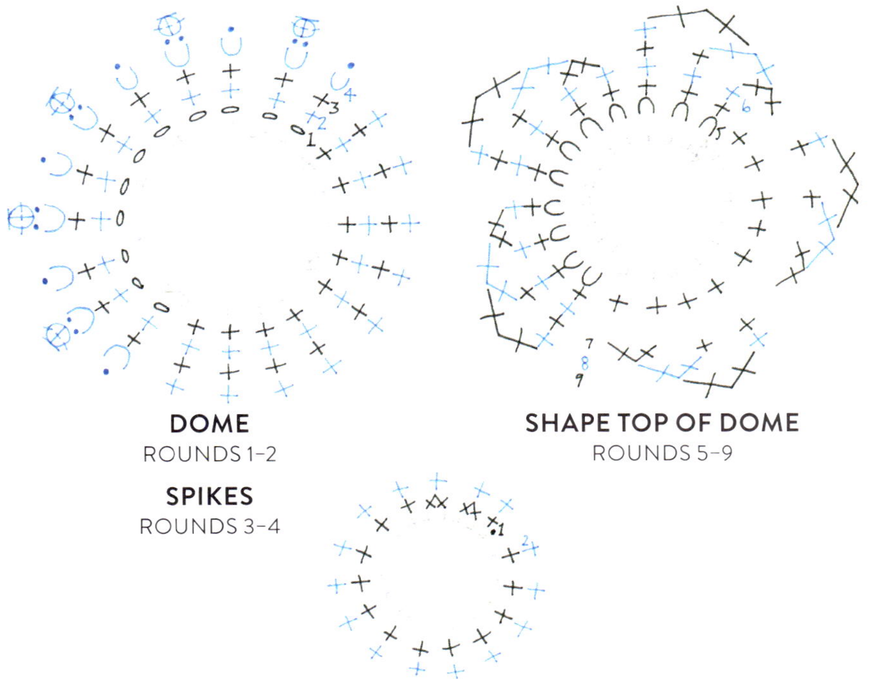

DOME
ROUNDS 1–2

SPIKES
ROUNDS 3–4

SHAPE TOP OF DOME
ROUNDS 5–9

FINISH HEAD
ROWS 1–2

EYE SOCKET
ROW 1

BODY

NECK

Carry unused yarn on WS of work.

Row 1: 1 ch, 1 dc in next 4 dc with C, 1 dc in next 11 dc with A, sl st to first dc, turn.

Row 2: 1 dc in next 11 dc with A, 1 dc in next 4 dc with C, turn.

Row 3: As row 1.

Row 4: 1 dc in next 11 dc with A, 1 dc in next 3 dc with C, sl st in next dc, turn.

SHAPE BASE OF NECK

The following is worked in short rows.

Row 5 (RS) (inc): 1 dc in same dc as sl st, (dc2inc) twice, 1 dc in next dc with C, 1 dc in next 2 dc with A, sl st in next dc, turn (17 sts).

Row 6 (WS): 1 dc in same dc as sl st, 1 dc in next 2 dc with A, 1 dc in next 6 dc with C, 1 dc in next 4 dc with A, turn.

Row 7 (inc): 1 ch, 1 dc in next 4 dc with A, 1 dc in next 2 dc with C, (dc2inc) twice, 1 in next 2 dc; with A, 1 dc in next 4 dc, join D in last dc, 1 dc in next 3 dc with D, sl st to first dc, turn (19 sts).

Row 8: 1 dc in next 3 dc with D, 1 dc in next 4 dc with A, 1 dc in next 8 dc with C, turn, finishing 4 sts before the end of the row.

Stuff the head and neck to within the last three rows before continuing.

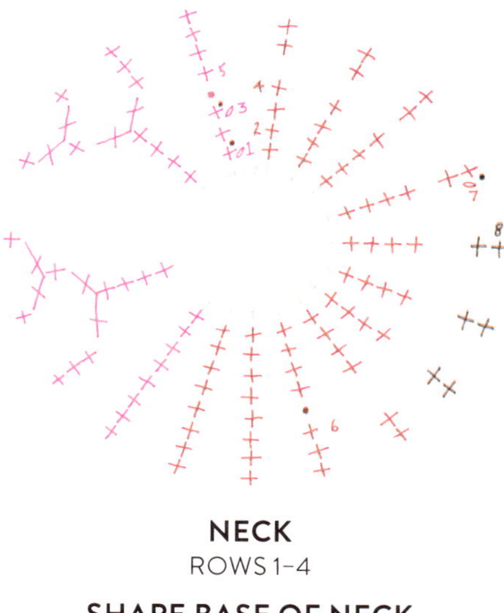

NECK
ROWS 1–4

SHAPE BASE OF NECK
ROWS 5–8

SHAPE FRONT OF BODY

Row 9 (inc): 1 ch, 1 dc in next 8 dc with C, 1 dc in next 4 dc with A, dc2inc with D, 1 dc in next dc, dc2inc; with A, 1 dc in next 4 dc, sl st to first dc, turn (21 sts).

Row 10: 1 dc in next 4 dc with A, 1 dc in next 5 dc with D, 1 dc in next 4 dc with A, 1 dc in next 8 dc with C, turn.

Row 11 (inc): 1 ch, 1 dc in next 8 dc with C, 1 dc in next 3 dc with A, dc2inc; with D, 1 dc in next dc, (dc2inc, 1 dc) twice; with A, dc2inc, 1 dc in next 3 dc, sl st to first dc, turn (25 sts).

Row 12: 1 dc in next 5 dc with A, 1 dc in next 7 dc with D, 1 dc in next 5 dc with A, 1 dc in next 8 dc with C, turn.

Row 13 (inc): 1 ch, 1 dc in next 8 dc with C, 1 dc in next 4 dc with A, dc2inc; with D, 1 dc in next 2 dc, (dc2inc, 1 dc) twice, 1 dc in next dc; with A, dc2inc, 1 dc in next 4 dc, sl st to first dc, turn (29 sts).

Row 14: 1 dc in next 6 dc with A, 1 dc in next 9 dc with D, 1 dc in next 6 dc with A, 1 dc in next 8 dc with C, turn.

Row 15 (inc): 1 ch, 1 dc in next 8 dc with C, 1 dc in next 8 dc with A, dc2inc; 1 dc in next 3 dc with D, dc2inc with A, 1 dc in next 8 dc, sl st to first dc, turn (31 sts).

Row 16: 1 dc in next 10 dc with A, 1 dc in next 3 dc with D, 1 dc in next 10 dc with A, 1 dc in next 8 dc with C, turn.

Row 17 (inc): 1 ch, 1 dc in next 8 dc with C, 1 dc in next 10 dc with A, dc2inc with D, 1 dc in next dc, dc2inc; with A, 1 dc in next 10 dc, sl st to first dc, turn (33 sts).

Row 18: 1 dc in next 10 dc with A, 1 dc in next 5 dc with D, 1 dc in next 10 dc with A, 1 dc in next 8 dc with C, turn.

Row 19 (inc): 1 ch, 1 dc in next 8 dc with C, 1 dc in next 10 dc with A, 1 dc in next dc with D, (dc2inc, 1 dc) twice; with A, 1 dc in next 10 dc, sl st to first dc, turn (35 sts).

Row 20: 1 dc in next 10 dc with A, 1 dc in next 7 dc with D, 1 dc in next 10 dc with A, 1 dc in next 8 dc with C, turn.

SHAPE MIDDLE OF BODY

Row 21: 1 ch, 1 dc in next 8 dc with C, 1 dc in next 9 dc with A, 1 dc in next 9 dc with D, 1 dc in next 9 dc with A, sl st to first dc, turn.

Row 22: 1 dc in next 9 dc with A, 1 dc in next 9 dc with D, 1 dc in next 9 dc with A, 1 dc in next 8 dc with C, turn.

Row 23: 1 ch, 1 dc in next 8 dc with C, 1 dc in next 12 dc with A, 1 dc in next 3 dc with D, 1 dc in next 12 dc with A, sl st to first dc, turn.

Row 24: 1 dc in next 12 dc with A, 1 dc in next 3 dc with D, 1 dc in next 12 dc with A, 1 dc in next 8 dc with C, turn.

Row 25: 1 ch, 1 dc in next 8 dc with C, 1 dc in next 11 dc with A, 1 dc in next 5 dc with D, 1 dc in next 11 dc with A, sl st to first dc, turn.

Row 26: 1 dc in next 11 dc with A, 1 dc in next 5 dc with D, 1 dc in next 11 dc with A, 1 dc in next 8 dc with C, turn.

Row 27: 1 ch, 1 dc in next 8 dc with C, 1 dc in next 10 dc with A, 1 dc in next 7 dc with D, 1 dc in next 10 dc, sl st to first dc, turn.

Row 28: 1 dc in next 10 dc with A, 1 dc in next 7 dc with D, 1 dc in next 10 dc with A, 1 dc in next 8 dc with C, turn.

Stuff the body to within the last three rows before continuing.

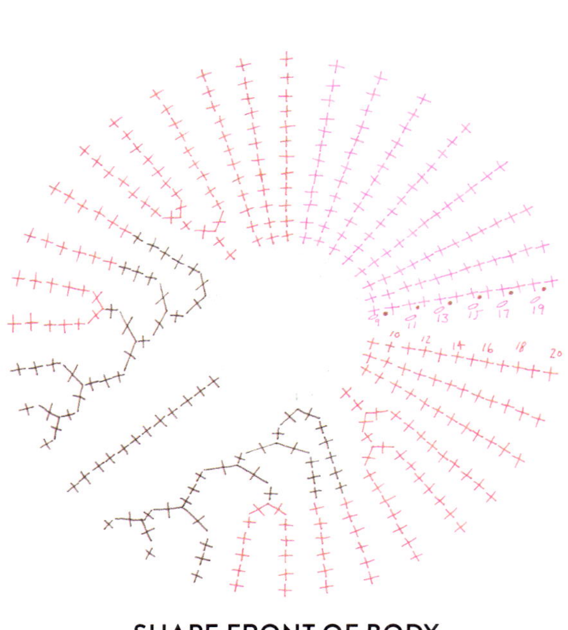

SHAPE FRONT OF BODY
ROWS 9–20

SHAPE MIDDLE OF BODY
ROWS 21–28

SHAPE END OF BODY

Row 29 (dec): 1 ch, 1 dc in next 8 dc with C, dc2tog with A, 1 dc in next 7 dc; with D, 1 dc in next 9 dc; with A, 1 dc in next 7 dc, dc2tog, sl st to first dc, turn (33 sts).

Row 30: 1 dc in next 8 dc with A, 1 dc in next 9 dc with D, 1 dc in next 8 dc with A, 1 dc in next 8 dc with C, turn.

Row 31 (dec): 1 ch, 1 dc in next 8 dc with C, dc2tog with A, 1 dc in next 9 dc; with D, 1 dc in next 3 dc, 1 dc in next 9 dc with A, dc2tog, sl st to first dc, turn (31 sts).

Row 32: 1 dc in next 10 dc with A, 1 dc in next 3 dc with D, 1 dc in next 10 dc with A, 1 dc in next 8 dc with C, turn.

Row 33 (dec): 1 ch, dc2tog, 1 dc in next 4 dc, dc2tog with C, 1 dc in next 9 dc with A, 1 dc in next 5 dc with D, 1 dc in next 9 dc with A, sl st to first dc, turn (29 sts).

Row 34: 1 dc in next 9 dc with A, 1 dc in next 5 dc with D, 1 dc in next 9 dc with A, 1 dc in next 6 dc with C, turn.

Row 35 (dec): 1 ch, 1 dc in next 6 dc, with C, dc2tog with A, 1 dc in next 6 dc; 1 dc in next 7 dc with D, 1 dc in next 6 dc with A, dc2tog, sl st to first dc, turn (27 sts).

Row 36: 1 dc in next 7 dc with A, 1 dc in next 7 dc with D, 1 dc in next 7 dc with A, 1 dc in next 6 dc with C, turn.

Row 37 (dec): 1 ch, 1 dc in next 6 dc with C, dc2tog with A, 1 dc in next 4 dc; 1 dc in next 9 dc with D, 1 dc in next 4 dc with A, dc2tog, sl st to first dc, turn (25 sts).

Row 38: 1 dc in next 5 dc with A, 1 dc in next 9 dc with D, 1 dc in next 5 dc with A, 1 dc in next 6 dc with C, turn.

Row 39 (dec): 1 ch, dc2tog, 1 dc in next 2 dc, dc2tog with C, dc2tog with A, 1 dc in next 6 dc; with D, 1 dc in next 3 dc, 1 dc in next 6 dc with A, dc2tog, sl st to first dc, turn (21 sts).

Row 40: 1 dc in next 7 dc with A, 1 dc in next 3 dc with D, 1 dc in next 7 dc with A, 1 dc in next 4 dc with C, turn. Insert more stuffing before continuing.

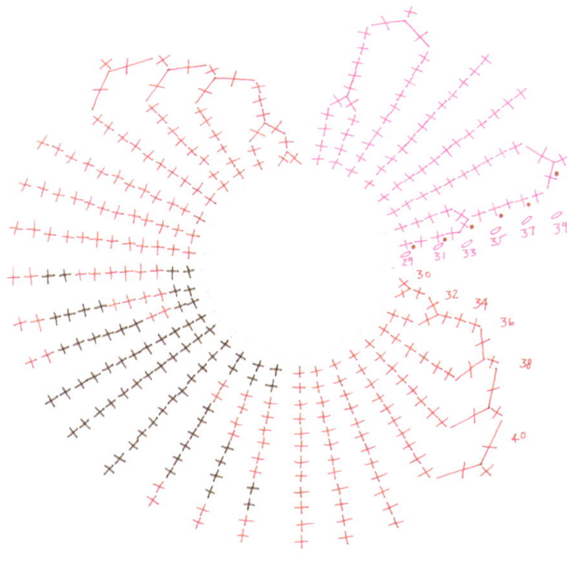

SHAPE END OF BODY
ROWS 29–40

SHAPE TAIL

Row 41 (dec): 1 ch, 1 dc in next 4 dc with C, dc2tog with A, 1 dc in next 3 dc, dc2tog; with D, 1 dc in next 3 dc, dc2tog with A, 1 dc in next 3 dc, dc2tog, sl st to first dc, turn (17 sts).

Row 42: 1 dc in next 5 dc with A, 1 dc in next 3 dc with D, 1 dc in next 5 dc with A, 1 dc in next 4 dc with C, turn.

Row 43 (dec): 1 ch, 1 dc in next 4 dc with C, dc2tog with D, 1 dc in next 9 dc, dc2tog, sl st to first dc, turn (15 sts).

Row 44: 1 dc in next 11 dc with D, 1 dc in next 4 dc with C, turn.

Row 45 (dec): 1 ch, 1 dc in next 4 dc with C, dc2tog with A, 1 dc in next 7 dc, dc2tog, sl st to first dc, turn (13 sts).

Row 46: 1 dc in next 9 dc with A, 1 dc in next 4 dc with C, turn.

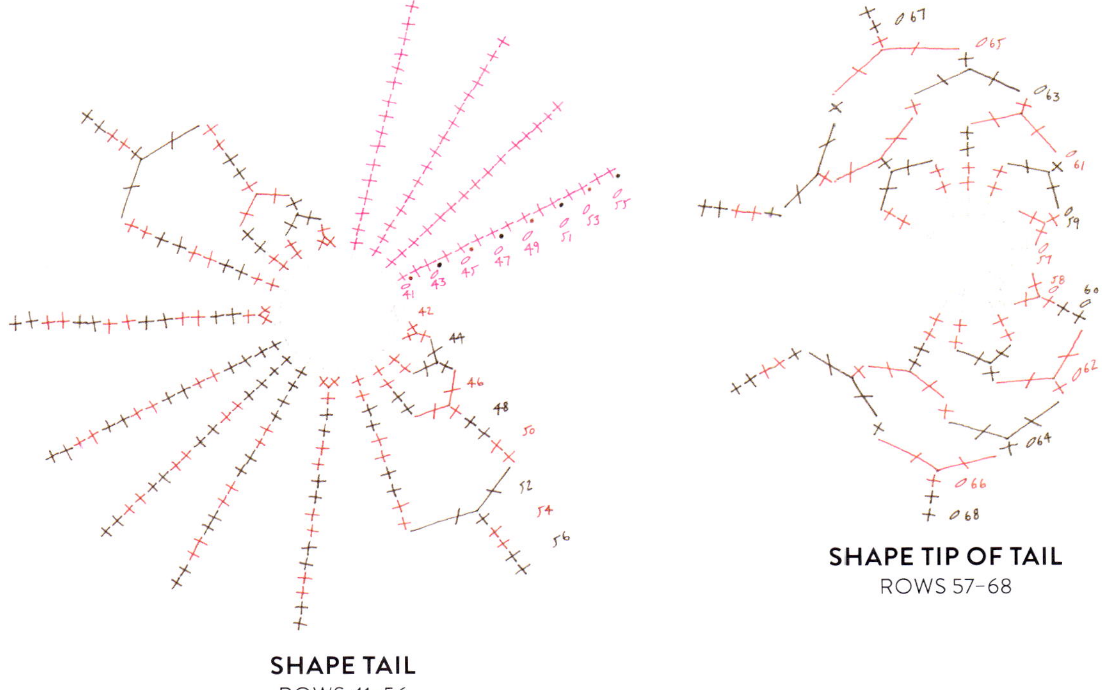

SHAPE TIP OF TAIL
ROWS 57–68

SHAPE TAIL
ROWS 41–56

Row 47: 1 ch, 1 dc in next 4 dc with C, 1 dc in next 9 dc with D, sl st to first dc, turn.
Row 48: 1 dc in next 9 dc with D, 1 dc in next 4 dc with C, turn.
Row 49: 1 ch, 1 dc in next 4 dc with C, 1 dc in next 9 dc with A, sl st to first dc, turn.
Row 50: 1 dc in next 9 dc with A, 1 dc in next 4 dc with C, turn.
Row 51 (dec): 1 ch, 1 dc in next 4 dc with C, dc2tog with D, 1 dc in next 5 dc, dc2tog, sl st to first dc, turn (11 sts).
Row 52: 1 dc in next 7 dc with D, 1 dc in next 4 dc with C, turn.
Row 53: 1 ch, 1 dc in next 4 dc with C, 1 dc in next 7 dc with A, sl st to first dc, turn.
Row 54: 1 dc in next 7 dc with A, 1 dc in next 4 dc with C, turn.
Row 55: 1 ch, 1 dc in next 4 dc with C, 1 dc in next 7 dc with D, sl st to first dc, turn.
Row 56: 1 dc in next 7 dc with D, 1 dc in next 2 dc with C, turn, finishing 2 sts before the end of the row.
Use the end of the crochet hook to push more stuffing into the tail before continuing.

SHAPE TIP OF TAIL

The following rows are not joined with a slip stitch at the end.
Row 57 (dec): 1 ch, dc2tog with A, 1 dc in next 7 dc, dc2tog in the unworked sts of the previous row, turn (9 sts).
Row 58: 1 ch, 1 dc in each st to end with A, turn.
Row 59 (dec): 1 ch, (dc2tog, 1 dc) 3 times with D, turn (6 sts).
Row 60: 1 dc in each st to end with D, turn.
Row 61: 1 ch, dc2tog, (dc2inc) twice, dc2tog with A, turn.
Row 62: 1 dc in each st to end with A, turn.
Rows 63–64: Rep rows 61–62 with D.
Row 65 (dec): 1 ch, dc2tog, 1 dc in next 2 dc, dc2tog with A, turn (4 sts).
Row 66: 1 dc in each st to end with A, turn.
Rows 67–68: 1 dc in each st to end with D, turn.
Fasten off, leaving a long tail of D at the end. Thread the tail of yarn through the last row of stitches and pull tightly to gather the end. Sew the open edges together, matching the rows and inserting stuffing into the tip of the tail before closing the seam.

LEGS
(make 2)

FOOT

With 2.5mm hook and A, make a magic loop.

Round 1: 1 ch, 5 dc into loop (5 sts).

Round 2 (inc): (Dc2inc) 5 times (10 sts).

Pull tightly on short end of yarn to close loop.

Round 3 (inc): (Dc2inc, 1 dc) 5 times (15 sts).

DIVIDE FOR TOES

Round 4: 9 ch, skip next 6 dc, 1 dc in next 9 dc.

Round 5: 1 dc in next 9 ch, 1 dc in next 9 dc.

Continue on these 18 sts.

SHAPE FIRST TOE

Round 1: 1 dc in next 3 dc, skip next 12 dc, 1 dc in next 3 dc.

Continue on these 6 sts.

Rounds 2–4: 1 dc in each st.

Fasten off and thread the tail of yarn through the last round of stitches. Pull tightly to close the end and fasten off.

SHAPE MIDDLE TOE

With RS facing, join A with a sl st to the first of the 12 skipped sts.

Round 1: 1 dc in the same dc as the sl st, 1 dc in next 3 dc, skip next 6 dc, 1 dc in next 3 dc.

Continue on these 6 sts.

Rounds 2–4: 1 dc in each st.

Fasten off and finish as for first toe.

SHAPE THIRD TOE

With RS facing, join A with a sl st to the first of the 6 skipped sts.

Round 1: 1 dc in the same dc as the sl st, 1 dc in next 5 dc (6 sts).

Rounds 2–4: 1 dc in each st.

Fasten off and finish as for first toe.

FOOT
ROUNDS 1–3
DIVIDE FOR TOES
ROUNDS 4–5

SHAPE FIRST TOE
ROUNDS 1–4

SHAPE MIDDLE TOE
ROUNDS 1–4

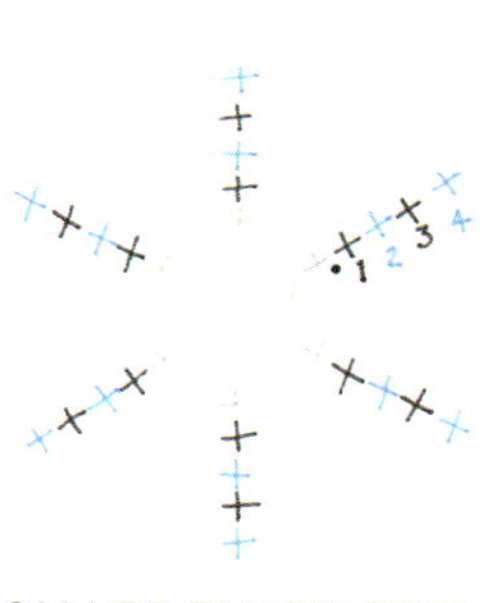

SHAPE THIRD TOE
ROUNDS 1–4

SHAPE FOOT

With RS facing, join A with a sl st to the first of the 6 skipped sts of the foot.

Round 1: 1 dc in same dc as sl st, 1 dc in next 5 dc, 1 dc in opposite side of next 9 ch (15 sts).

Round 2: 1 dc in each st.

Round 3 (dec): (Dc2tog, 1 dc) 5 times (10 sts).

Round 4: 1 dc in each st.

Round 5: 1 dc in next 5 dc, finishing at the side of the leg, 5 sts before the end of the round.

ANKLE JOINT

Round 6: 5 ch, skip next 5 dc, 1 dc in next 5 dc.

Round 7: 1 dc in next 5 ch, 1 dc in next 5 dc (10 sts).

Fasten off and thread tail of yarn through last round of stitches. Pull tightly on end of yarn to close and fasten off.

Stuff the toes and foot before continuing.

SHAPE LOWER LEG

With RS facing, join A with a sl st to the first of the 5 skipped sts of the foot.

Round 1: 1 dc in same dc as sl st, 1 dc in next 4 dc, 1 dc in opposite side of next 5 ch of ankle joint (10 sts).

Round 2: 1 dc in each st.

Round 3 (inc): (Dc2inc, 1 dc) 5 times (15 sts).

Rounds 4–6: 1 dc in each st.

Round 7: 1 dc in next 8 dc, finishing at the side of the leg, 7 sts before the end of the round.

KNEE JOINT

Round 8: 5 ch, skip next 10 dc, 1 dc in next 5 dc at the front of the leg.

Round 9: 1 dc in next 5 ch, 1 dc in next 5 dc (10 sts).

Fasten off and thread tail of yarn through last round of stitches. Pull tightly on end of yarn to close and fasten off.

SHAPE THIGH

With RS facing, join A with a sl st to the first of the 10 skipped sts of the lower leg.

Round 1: 1 dc in same dc as sl st, 1 dc in next 9 dc, 1 dc in opposite side of next 5 ch of the knee joint (15 sts).

Round 2 (inc): (Dc2inc, 1 dc) 5 times, 1 dc in next 5 dc (20 sts).

Round 3 (inc): (Dc2inc, 3 dc) 5 times (25 sts).

Rounds 4–8: 1 dc in each st.

Round 9 (dec): (Dc2tog, 3 dc) 5 times (20 sts).

Stuff the leg before continuing.

Round 10 (dec): (Dc2tog, 2 dc) 5 times (15 sts).

Round 11 (dec): (Dc2tog, 1 dc) 5 times (10 sts).

Round 12 (dec): (Dc2tog) 5 times (5 sts).

Fasten off and thread the tail of yarn through the last round of stitches. Pull tightly on the end of yarn to close and fasten off.

SHAPE FOOT
ROUNDS 1–5
ANKLE JOINT
ROUNDS 6–7

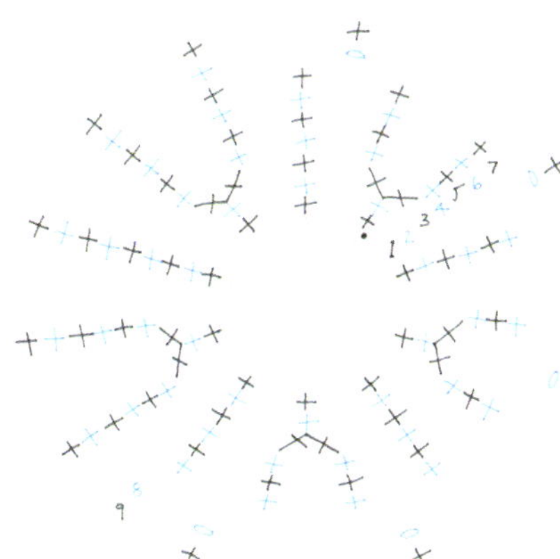

SHAPE LOWER LEG
ROUNDS 1–7
KNEE JOINT
ROUNDS 8–9

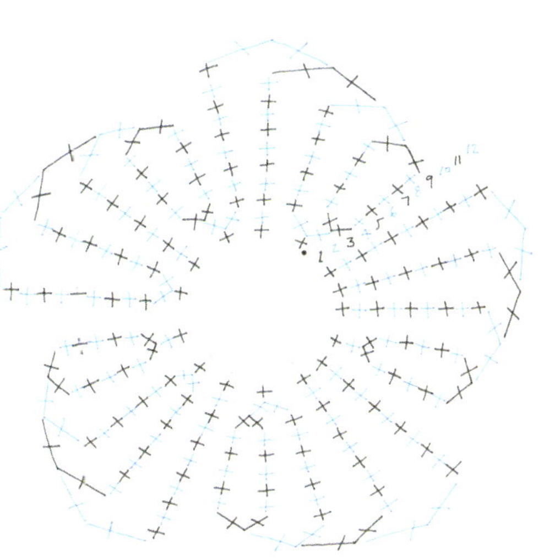

SHAPE THIGH
ROUNDS 1–12

ARMS
(make 2)

ELBOW JOINT

With 2.5mm hook and A, make a magic loop.

Round 1: 1 ch, 6 dc into loop (6 sts).

Round 2 (inc): (Dc2inc, 1 dc) 3 times (9 sts).

Pull tightly on short end of yarn to close loop.

Round 3 (inc): (Dc2inc, 2 dc) 3 times (12 sts).

Round 4 (inc): (Dc2inc, 1 dc) 6 times (18 sts).

FOREARM

Round 5: 1 dc in next 4 dc, skip next 10 dc, 1 dc in next 4 dc.

Continue on these 8 sts.

Rounds 6–7: 1 dc in each st.

HAND

Round 8 (dec): (Dc2tog, 2 dc) twice (6 sts).

Round 9 (inc): (Dc2inc, 2 dc) twice (8 sts).

Round 10 (inc): (Dc2inc, 3 dc) twice (10 sts).

Round 11: 1 dc in each st.

Round 12 (dec): (Dc2tog) 5 times (5 sts).

Fasten off and thread tail of yarn through last round of stitches. Pull tightly on end of yarn to close and fasten off.

Stuff the arm before continuing; stuff the hand lightly.

UPPER ARM

With RS facing, join A with a sl st to the first of the 10 skipped sts of the elbow joint.

Round 1: 1 dc in same dc as sl st, 1 dc in next 9 dc (10 sts).

Rounds 2–4: 1 dc in each st.

Stuff the upper arm before continuing.

Round 5 (dec): (Dc2tog) 5 times (5 sts).

Fasten off and thread tail of yarn through last round of stitches. Pull tightly on end of yarn to close and fasten off.

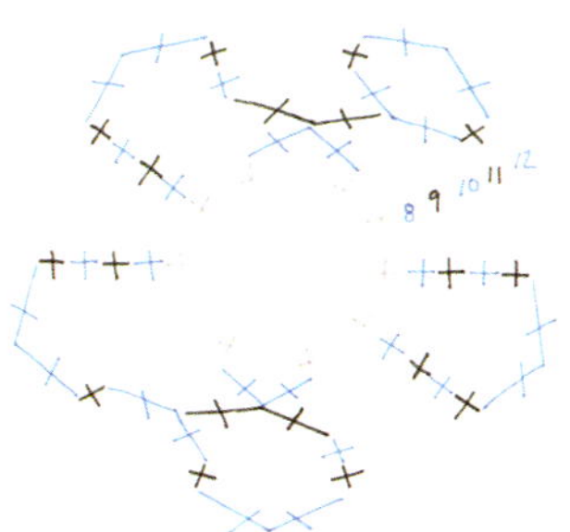

HAND
ROUNDS 8–12

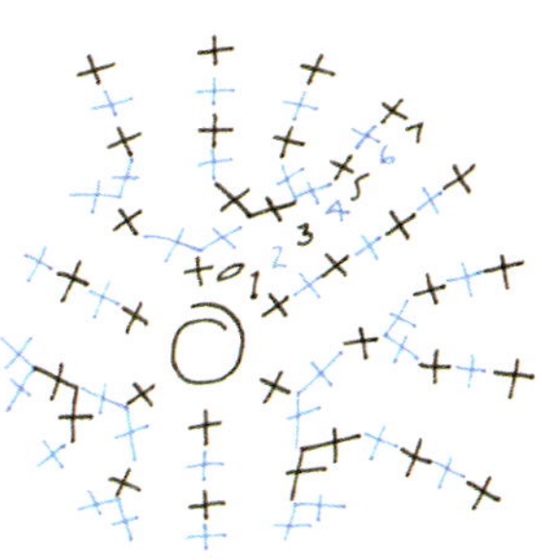

ELBOW JOINT
ROUNDS 1–4

FOREARM
ROUNDS 5–7

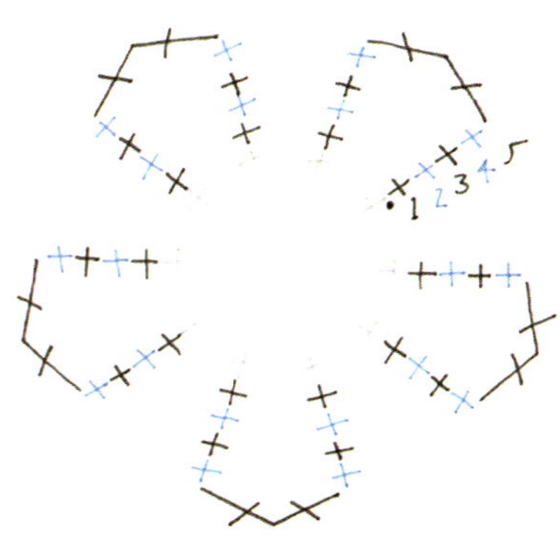

UPPER ARM
ROUNDS 1–5

MAKING UP

HEAD

If using looped glass eyes, poke the loop of an eye through the centre of each eye socket before attaching each one to the head using 23⅝in (60cm) length of clear invisible or strong sewing thread (see page 163).

Using yarn B, embroider a cluster of French knots (see page 165) for the bumps that run down the centre of the snout.

Embroider the nostrils in satin stitch (see page 164), using two strands of embroidery thread.

Finish the mouth with an embroidered horizontal straight stitch (see page 164) across the beak in yarn A.

ARMS AND LEGS

Sew together the gaps between the toes and at the bend in the arms. Flatten the hands. Embroider four straight stitches on each hand with yarn D to define the line between each finger.

Follow the instructions on page 164 to attach the limbs, using a 51in (130cm) length of yarn A or strong thread for the arms and 59in (150cm) length for the legs.

Weave in all the yarn ends.

SPINOSAURUS

THE SPINOSAURUS IS CROCHETED USING VARIOUS STITCH TECHNIQUES, AND FEATURES A RIBBED SAIL AND A PICOT EDGING.

MATERIALS

- Jamieson & Smith 2ply jumper weight (4ply equivalent), 100% Shetland wool (114yd/105m per 25g ball):
  3 × 25g balls in FC39 Mix (A)
  1 × 25g ball in 1284 Mix (B)
- 2¼yd (2m) length of 4ply white yarn, such as 1 Optic White (C)
- 1 pair of 5/32–3/16in (4–5mm) looped glass teddy bear eyes or safety eyes
- Clear invisible or strong thread to attach the looped glass eyes
- Stranded embroidery thread in black, such as Anchor Stranded Cotton, shade 0403, for the nostrils
- 2.25mm (UK13:USB/1) and 2.5mm (UK12:US-) crochet hooks
- Stitch markers
- Blunt-ended yarn needle
- Toy stuffing
- 4 pipe cleaners, each measuring 9¾in (25cm) long to strengthen the legs (optional: not suitable for young children)

SIZE

Approximately 19¼in (49cm) long

TENSION

26 sts and 28 rows to 4in (10cm) over double crochet using 2.5mm hook and yarn A. Use larger or smaller hook if necessary to obtain correct tension.

METHOD

The upper and lower jaws are worked in rows of double crochet. The pieces are joined and the back of the head is completed in rows. The roof and floor of the mouth are worked in one piece. Various stitches are used to form the teeth and buccal flaps, crocheted into the back loops of the mouth, leaving the unworked loops to attach the mouth to the jaw.

The first row of the neck is crocheted into the unworked stitches of the lower jaw and around the edges of the rows at the back of the head. The neck, body and tail are crocheted in one piece. The front of the body is shaped by working in short rows.

The sail and tail fin are each made in two pieces, that are joined together with a picot edging.

KEY

- Magic loop
- Chain (ch)
- Slip stitch (sl st)
- Double crochet (dc)
- Dc2inc
- Dc3inc
- Dc2tog
- Half treble (htr)
- Treble (tr)
- Htr2inc
- Work into back loop only
- Work into front loop only

The arms and legs are crocheted in rounds. The bends in the limbs are formed by making a length of chain stitches and skipping a number of stitches of the previous row. The stitches of the following row are gathered together to form the joints. The skipped stitches and the opposite side of the chain stitches are then crocheted into to begin the upper parts of the arms and legs. The limbs are attached to the body so they are movable.

Glass or safety eyes, attached to a crocheted disc, and simple embroidered nostrils complete the finishing touches.

1 ch and 2 ch at beg of the row/round do not count as a st throughout.

HEAD

UPPER JAW

With 2.5mm hook and A, make 3 ch.

Row 1 (RS): 2 dc in second ch from hook, 2 dc in next ch, turn (4 sts).

Row 2 (WS) (inc): 1 ch, 1 dc in next dc, (dc2inc) twice, 1 dc in next dc, turn (6 sts).

Rows 3–4: 1 ch, 1 dc in each st, turn.

Row 5 (dec): 1 ch, 1 dc in next dc, (dc2tog) twice, 1 dc in next dc, turn (4 sts).

Row 6: 1 ch, 1 dc in each st, turn.

Row 7 (inc): 1 ch, 1 dc in next dc, (dc2inc) twice, 1 dc in next dc, turn (6 sts).

Row 8: 1 ch, 1 dc in each st, turn.

Row 9 (inc): 1 ch, (1 dc, dc2inc, 1 dc) twice, turn (8 sts).

Rows 10–12: 1 ch, 1 dc in each st, turn.
Row 13 (inc): 1 ch, (dc2inc, 1 dc) twice, (1 dc, dc2inc) twice, turn (12 sts).
Rows 14–18: 1 ch, 1 dc in each st.
Place a marker at each end of the last row.
Fasten off.

LOWER JAW

With 2.5mm hook and A, make 3 ch.
Rows 1–16: As for rows 1–16 of upper jaw.
Place a marker at each end of the last row.
Fasten off.

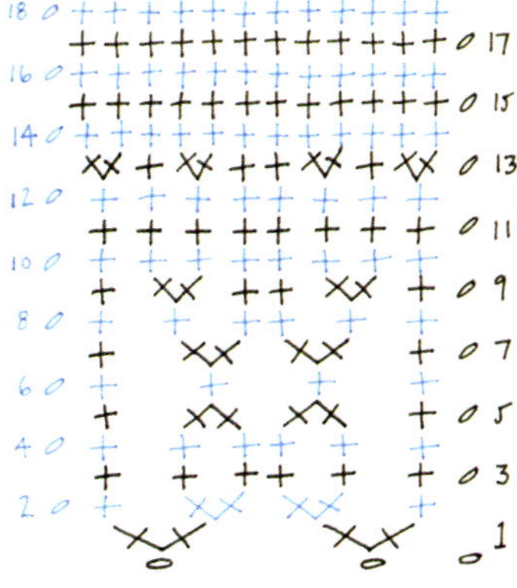

UPPER JAW
ROWS 1–18
LOWER JAW
FOLLOW ROWS 1–16 ONLY

SHAPE BACK OF HEAD

With RS of lower jaw facing, skip the first 9 sts and join A with a sl st to the next dc.
Row 1 (RS): 1 dc in same st as sl st, 1 dc in next 2 dc; with RS facing, work 1 dc in each st of the upper jaw; with RS facing, work 1 dc in first 3 dc of lower jaw to join, turn, leaving the centre 6 sts of the lower jaw unworked.
Continue on these 18 sts.
Row 2 (WS): 1 ch, 1 dc in each st, turn.
Rows 3–8 (dec): 1 ch, dc2tog, 1 dc in each dc to last 2 sts, dc2tog, turn (6 sts).
Fasten off and thread the tail of yarn through the last round of stitches. Pull tightly on the end of yarn and fasten off.

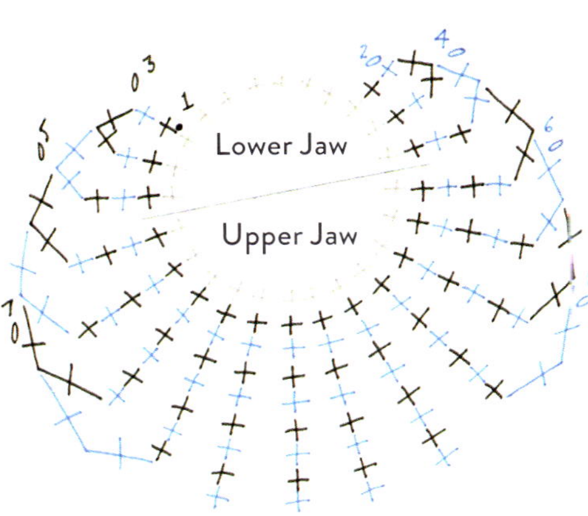

SHAPE BACK OF HEAD
ROWS 1–8

MOUTH

With 2.5mm hook and B, make 39 ch.
Row 1 (RS): 1 dc in second ch from hook, 1 dc in next 9 ch, 1 htr in next 5 ch, 1 tr in next 10 ch, place a marker on the sixth tr st, 1 htr in next 5 ch, 1 dc in each ch to end; working in opposite side of each ch, 1 dc in next 8 ch, 1 htr in next 5 ch, 1 tr in next 10 ch, place a marker on the fifth tr st, 1 htr in next 5 ch, 1 dc in each ch to end (76 sts).
Fasten off.

TEETH

With 2.25mm hook and WS of the mouth facing, skip the marked stitch of the shorter end of the mouth and the next 5 sts.
Next: *With C, (sl st in back loop only of next st, 2 ch, sl st in second ch from hook, sl st in back loop only of next st)* 12 times to finish the lower set of teeth. Fasten off.
Next: With WS of mouth facing, skip the next 12 sts from the last tooth made; rep from * to * 14 times to finish the top set of teeth.

BUCCAL FLAPS

*With 2.25mm hook and WS of the mouth facing, skip the first 6 stitches from the last tooth and join B with a sl st to the back loop only of the next st.

Next: *Working in back loops only, 1 dc in same st as sl st, 1 dc in next st, 1 htr in next 4 sts. Fasten off, leaving a long tail of yarn* (6 sts).

Rotate the mouth and rep from * to * to make a second flap to match the first on the other side of the mouth.

Sew the tops of the buccal flaps to the back loops only of the corresponding 6 sts on the opposite side of the mouth to connect the roof and floor of the mouth, leaving the front loops of the stitches unworked to join the mouth to the jaw.

JAW EDGING

With 2.5mm hook and RS facing, join A with a sl st to the st at the edge of row 16 of the lower jaw, indicated by the marker.

Round 1 (RS): Starting in the same st as the sl st, work 1 dc into each stitch at the edge of the next 16 rows, 2 dc in the opposite side of each of the next 2 ch, 1 dc into each stitch at the edge of the next 16 rows, finishing at the corner of the other side of the jaw, indicated by the marker; work 1 dc into each stitch at the edge of the next 18 rows of the upper jaw, 2 dc in the opposite side of each of the next 2 ch, 1 dc into each stitch at the edge of the next 18 rows, finishing at the marked stitch of the corner of the other side of the jaw (76 sts).

Do not fasten off.

JOIN MOUTH TO JAW

Round 2 (RS): Insert the mouth into the head, with WS together, matching the stitches and aligning the markers of the mouth with the markers of the lower jaw. With the lower jaw facing and working into the back loops only of each stitch of the jaws and the unworked loops of the mouth at the same time to join, 1 dc in the next 76 sts, sl st to next st and fasten off.

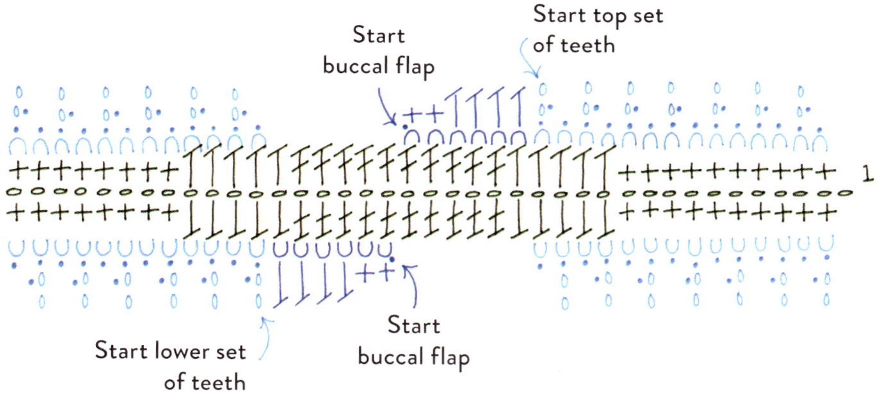

MOUTH
ROW 1
TEETH & BUCCAL FLAPS

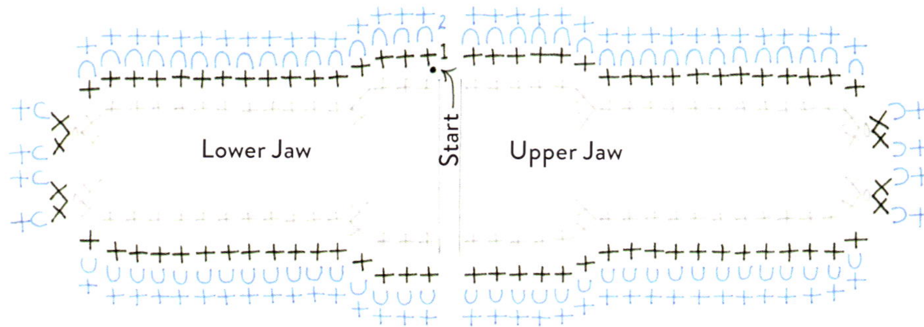

JAW EDGING
ROUND 1
JOIN MOUTH TO JAW
ROUND 2
Insert hook into each stitch of both pieces at the same time to join

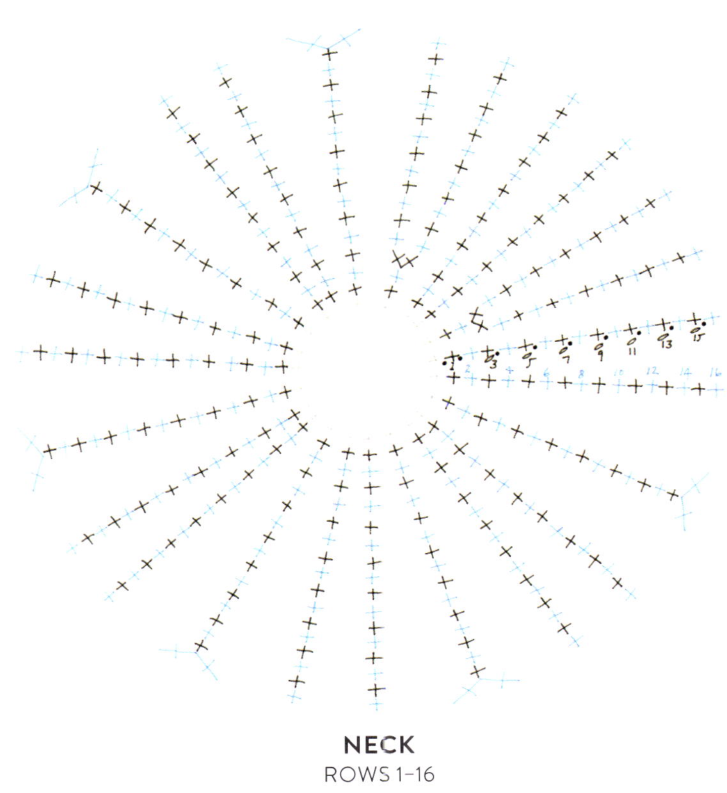

NECK
ROWS 1–16

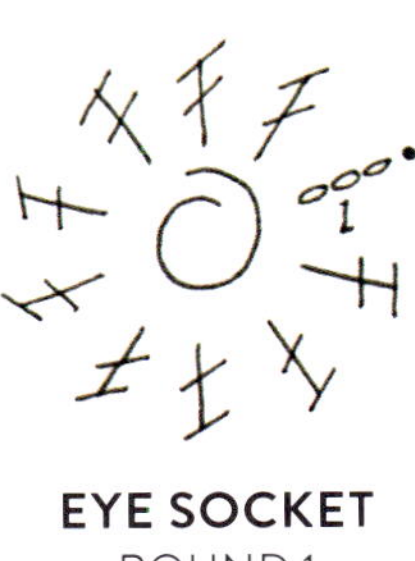

EYE SOCKET
ROUND 1

EYE SOCKET
(make 2)

With 2.25mm hook and A, make a magic loop.
Round 1 (RS): 3 ch, 9 tr into loop, sl st to third of 3 ch.
Fasten off, leaving a long tail of yarn.
If using safety eyes, attach them at this stage. Poke the post of the safety eye through the centre of the eye socket. Pull tightly on the short end of yarn to close the loop around the post of the safety eye, before attaching it to the head (see page 163).

BODY

NECK
With 2.5mm hook and RS of head facing, join A with a sl st to first of unworked 6 dc of lower jaw.
Row 1 (RS): 1 dc in same dc as sl st, 1 dc in next 5 dc, work 8 dc evenly along the edge of rows of the first side of the head, work 8 dc evenly along the edge of rows down the other side of the head, sl st to first dc, turn (22 sts).
Row 2 (WS): 1 dc in each st, turn.
Row 3 (inc): 1 ch, (1 dc, dc2inc, 1 dc) twice, 1 dc in next 16 dc, sl st to first dc, turn (24 sts).
Row 4: 1 dc in each st, turn.
Row 5: 1 ch, 1 dc in each st, sl st to first dc, turn.
Rows 6–15: Rep rows 4–5 5 times.
Row 16 (inc): (1 dc, dc2inc, 1 dc) 6 times, 1 dc in next 6 dc, sl st in first dc, turn (30 sts).
Before continuing, stuff the head to the beginning of the neck, keeping the inside of the mouth flat.

SHAPE FRONT OF BODY

The following is worked in short rows.

Row 1 (RS) (inc): 1 dc in same dc as sl st, 1 dc in next 3 dc, (dc2inc) twice, 1 dc in next 4 dc, sl st in next dc, turn (32 sts).

Row 2 (WS): 1 dc in same dc as sl st, 1 dc in next 13 dc, sl st in next dc, turn.

Row 3 (inc): 1 dc in same dc as sl st, 1 dc in next 6 dc, (dc2inc) twice, 1 dc in next 7 dc, sl st in next dc, turn (34 sts).

Row 4: 1 dc in same dc as sl st, 1 dc in next 19 dc, sl st in next dc, turn.

Row 5 (inc): 1 dc in same dc as sl st, 1 dc in next 9 dc, (dc2inc) twice, 1 dc in next 10 dc, sl st in next dc, turn (36 sts).

Row 6: 1 dc in same dc as sl st, 1 dc in next 25 dc, sl st in next dc, turn.

Row 7 (inc): 1 dc in same dc as sl st, 1 dc in next 12 dc, (dc2inc) twice, 1 dc in next 13 dc, sl st in next dc, turn (38 sts).

Row 8: 1 dc in same dc as sl st, 1 dc in next 31 dc, sl st in next dc, turn.

Row 9 (inc): 1 dc in same dc as sl st, 1 dc in next 15 dc, (dc2inc) twice, 1 dc in next 16 dc, sl st in next dc, turn (40 sts).

Row 10: 1 dc in same dc as sl st, 1 dc in next 37 dc, sl st in next dc, turn.

Row 11 (inc): 1 dc in same dc as sl st, 1 dc in next 18 dc, (dc2inc) twice, 1 dc in next 19 dc, sl st in first dc, turn (42 sts).

Row 12: 1 dc in each st, turn.

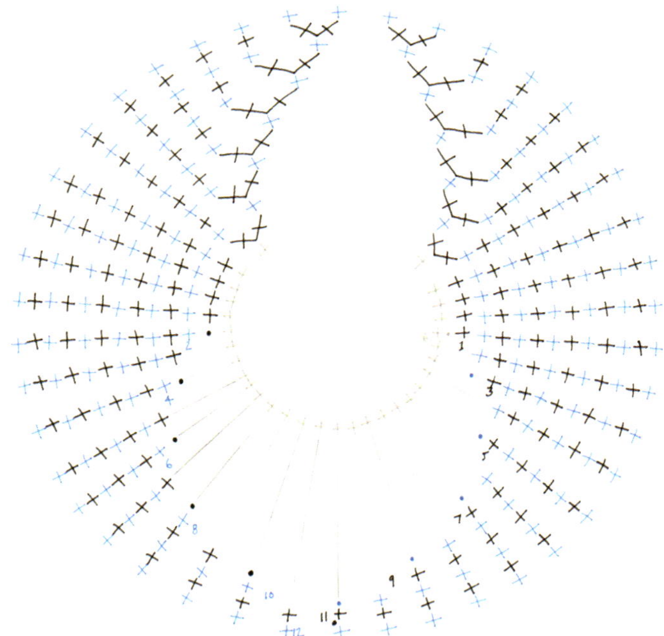

SHAPE FRONT OF BODY
ROWS 1–12

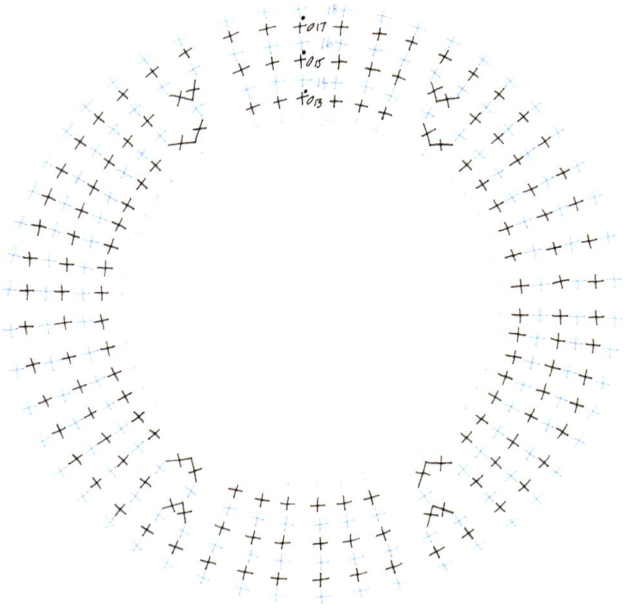

SHAPE MIDDLE OF BODY
ROWS 13–18

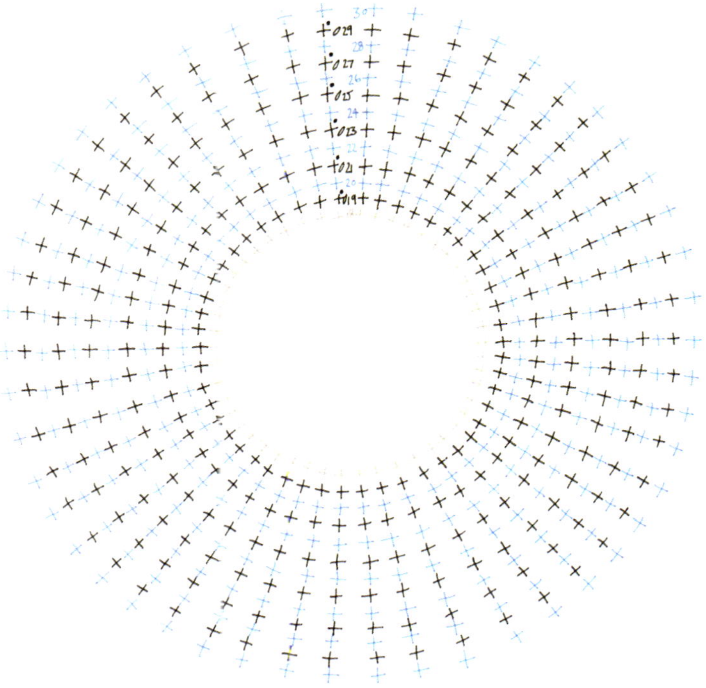

SHAPE MIDDLE OF BODY
ROWS 19–30

SHAPE MIDDLE OF BODY

Row 13 (inc): 1 ch, (3 dc, dc2inc, 13 dc, dc2inc, 3 dc) twice, sl st to first dc, turn (46 sts).

Row 14: 1 dc in each st, turn.

Row 15 (inc): 1 ch, (3 dc, dc2inc, 15 dc, dc2inc, 3 dc) twice, sl st to first dc, turn (50 sts).

Row 16: 1 dc in each st, turn.

Row 17: 1 ch, 1 dc in each st, sl st to first dc, turn.

Row 18: 1 dc in each st, turn.

Rows 19–30: Rep rows 17–18 6 times.

Stuff the neck before continuing.

SHAPE END OF BODY

Row 31 (dec): 1 ch, (3 dc, dc2tog, 15 dc, dc2tog, 3 dc) twice, sl st to first dc, turn (46 sts).

Row 32: 1 dc in each st, turn.

Row 33 (dec): 1 ch, (3 dc, dc2tog, 13 dc, dc2tog, 3 dc) twice, sl st to first dc, turn (42 sts).

Row 34: 1 dc in each st, turn.

Before continuing, stuff the body to within the last three rows.

Row 35 (dec): 1 ch, (3 dc, dc2tog, 11 dc, dc2tog, 3 dc) twice, sl st to first dc, turn (38 sts).

Row 36: 1 dc in each st, turn.

Row 37 (dec): 1 ch, (3 dc, dc2tog, 9 dc, dc2tog, 3 dc) twice, sl st to first dc, turn (34 sts).

Row 38: 1 dc in each st, turn.
Row 39 (dec): 1 ch, (3 dc, dc2tog, 7 dc, dc2tog, 3 dc) twice, sl st to first dc, turn (30 sts).
Row 40: 1 dc in each st, turn.
Row 41 (dec): 1 ch, (3 dc, dc2tog, 5 dc, dc2tog, 3 dc) twice, sl st to first dc, turn (26 sts).
Row 42: 1 dc in each st, turn.
Insert more stuffing before continuing.

SHAPE TAIL

Row 43 (dec): 1 ch, 1 dc in next 3 dc, dc2tog, 1 dc in next 16 dc, dc2tog, 1 dc in next 3 dc, sl st to first dc, turn (24 sts).
Row 44: 1 dc in each st, turn.
Row 45: 1 ch, 1 dc in each st, sl st to first dc, turn.
Row 46: 1 dc in each st, turn.
Row 47 (dec): 1 ch, 1 dc in next 3 dc, dc2tog, 1 dc in next 14 dc, dc2tog, 1 dc in next 3 dc, sl st to first dc, turn (22 sts).
Row 48: 1 dc in each st, turn.
Row 49: 1 ch, 1 dc in each st, sl st to first dc, turn.
Row 50: 1 dc in each st, turn.
Row 51 (dec): 1 ch, 1 dc in next 3 dc, dc2tog, 1 dc in next 12 dc, dc2tog, 1 dc in next 3 dc, sl st to first dc, turn (20 sts).
Row 52: 1 dc in each st, turn.
Row 53: 1 ch, 1 dc in each st, sl st to first dc, turn.
Row 54: 1 dc in each st, turn.
Row 55 (dec): 1 ch, 1 dc in next 3 dc, dc2tog, 1 dc in next 10 dc, dc2tog, 1 dc in next 3 dc, sl st to first dc, turn (18 sts).
Row 56: 1 dc in each st, turn.

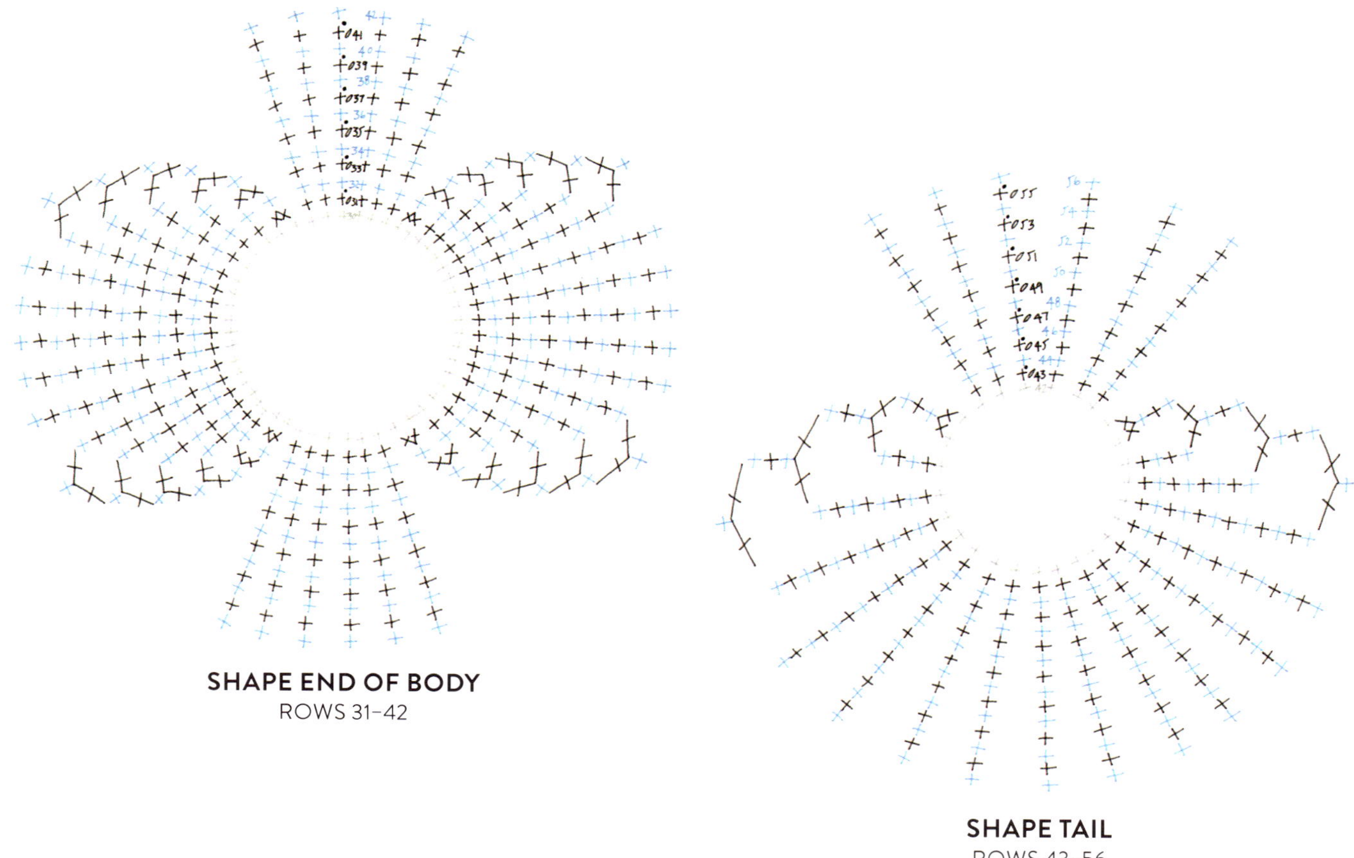

SHAPE END OF BODY
ROWS 31–42

SHAPE TAIL
ROWS 43–56

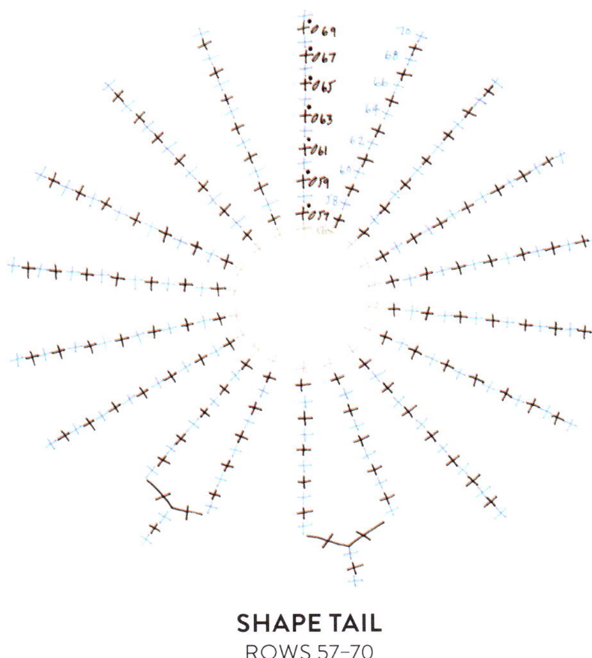

SHAPE TAIL
ROWS 57–70

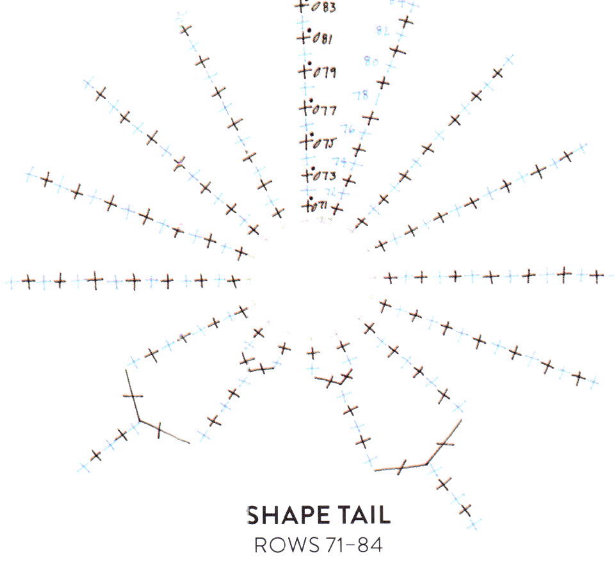

SHAPE TAIL
ROWS 71–84

Row 57: 1 ch, 1 dc in each st, sl st to first dc, turn.
Row 58: 1 dc in each st, turn.
Stuff the tail to within the last three rows before continuing.
Rows 59–66: Rep rows 57–58 4 times.
Row 67 (dec): 1 ch, 1 dc in next 7 dc, (dc2tog) twice, 1 dc in next 7 dc, sl st to first dc, turn (16 sts).
Row 68: 1 dc in each st, turn.
Row 69: 1 ch, 1 dc in each st, sl st to first dc, turn.
Row 70: 1 dc in each st, turn.
Rows 71–72: Rep rows 69–70.
Insert more stuffing before continuing.
Row 73 (dec): 1 ch, 1 dc in next 6 dc, (dc2tog) twice, 1 dc in next 6 dc, sl st to first dc, turn (14 sts).
Row 74: 1 dc in each st, turn.
Row 75: 1 ch, 1 dc in each st, sl st to first dc, turn.
Row 76: 1 dc in each st, turn.
Rows 77–78: Rep rows 75–76.
Row 79 (dec): 1 ch, 1 dc in next 5 dc, (dc2tog) twice, 1 dc in next 5 dc, sl st to first dc, turn (12 sts).
Row 80: 1 dc in each st, turn.
Row 81: 1 ch, 1 dc in each st, sl st to first dc, turn.
Row 82: 1 dc in each st, turn.
Rows 83–84: Rep rows 81–82.
Use the end of the crochet hook to push more stuffing into the tail before continuing.

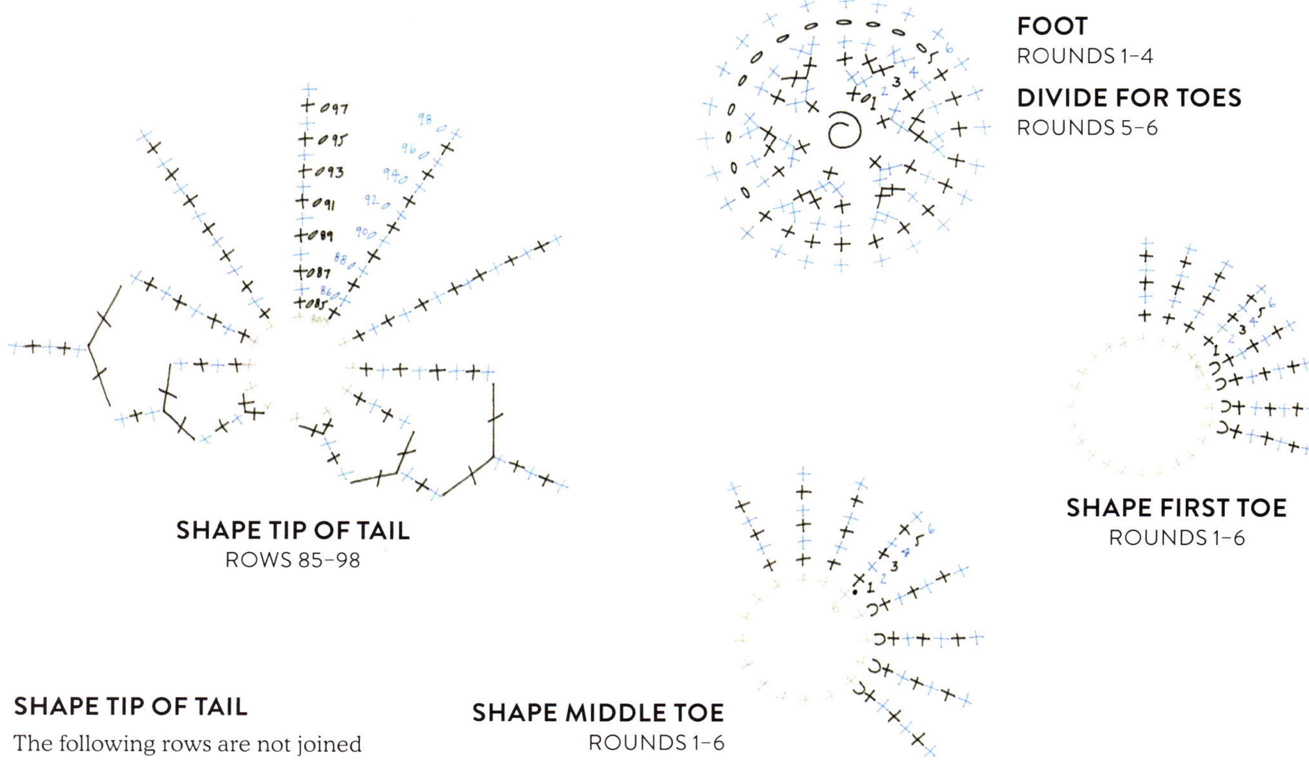

SHAPE TIP OF TAIL

The following rows are not joined with a slip stitch at the end.

Row 85 (dec): 1 ch, 1 dc in next 4 dc, (dc2tog) twice, 1 dc in next 4 dc, turn (10 sts).

Rows 86–88: 1 ch, dc in each st, turn.

Row 89 (dec): 1 ch, 1 dc in next 3 dc, (dc2tog) twice, 1 dc in next 3 dc, turn (8 sts).

Rows 90–92: 1 ch, dc in each st, turn.

Row 93 (dec): 1 ch, 1 dc in next 2 dc, (dc2tog) twice, 1 dc in next 2 dc, turn (6 sts).

Rows 94–98: 1 ch, dc in each st, turn.

Fasten off, leaving a long tail of yarn at the end. Thread the tail of yarn through the last round of stitches and pull tightly to gather the end. Sew the open edges together, inserting stuffing into the tip of the tail before closing the seam.

LEGS
(make 2)

FOOT

With 2.5mm hook and A, make a magic loop.

Round 1: 1 ch, 6 dc into loop (6 sts).

Round 2 (inc): (Dc2inc) 6 times (12 sts).

Pull tightly on short end of yarn to close loop.

Round 3 (inc): (Dc2inc, 1 dc) 6 times (18 sts).

Round 4 (inc): (Dc2inc, 2 dc) 6 times (24 sts).

DIVIDE FOR TOES

Round 5: 12 ch, skip next 12 dc, 1 dc in next 12 dc.

Round 6: 1 dc in next 12 ch, 1 dc in next 12 dc.

Continue on these 24 sts.

SHAPE FIRST TOE

Round 1: 1 dc in next 4 dc, skip next 16 dc, 1 dc in back loop only of next 4 dc.

Continue on these 8 sts.

Rounds 2–6: 1 dc in each st.

Fasten off and thread the tail of yarn through the last round of stitches. Pull tightly to close the end and fasten off.

SHAPE MIDDLE TOE

With RS facing, join A with a sl st to the first of the 16 skipped sts.

Round 1: 1 dc in the same dc as the sl st, 1 dc in next 3 dc, skip next 8 dc, 1 dc in back loop only of next 4 dc. Continue on these 8 sts.

Rounds 2–6: 1 dc in each st.

Fasten off and finish as for first toe.

SHAPE THIRD TOE

With RS facing, join A with a sl st to the first of the 8 skipped sts.

Round 1: 1 dc in the same dc as the sl st, 1 dc in next 3 dc, 1 dc in back loop only of next 4 dc (8 sts).

Rounds 2–6: 1 dc in each st.

Fasten off and finish as for first toe.

WEBBED BASE

With RS of the base of the foot facing, join A with a sl st to the first of the 12 unworked front loops below the toes.

Row 1: 1 dc in the same dc as the sl st, 1 dc in next 11 loops, turn (12 sts).

Row 2 (inc): 1 ch, dc2inc, 1 dc in next 10 dc, dc2inc, turn (14 sts).

Row 3: 1 ch, 1 dc in each st, turn.

Row 4 (inc): 1 ch, dc2inc, 1 dc in next 12 dc, dc2inc, turn (16 sts).

Row 5: 1 ch, 1 dc in each st, turn.

Fasten off, leaving a long tail of yarn.

SHAPE FOOT

With RS facing, join A with a sl st to the first of the 12 skipped sts of the foot.

Round 1: 1 dc in same dc as sl st, 1 dc in next 11 dc, 1 dc in opposite side of next 12 ch (24 sts).

Round 2: 1 dc in each st.

Round 3 (dec): (Dc2tog, 2 dc) 6 times (18 sts).

Round 4 (dec): (Dc2tog, 1 dc) 6 times (12 sts).

Rounds 5–7: 1 dc in each st.

Round 8: 1 dc in next 8 dc, finishing at the side of the leg, 4 sts before the end of the round.

Stuff the toes before continuing.

ANKLE JOINT

Round 9: 6 ch, skip next 6 dc, 1 dc in next 6 dc.

Round 10: 1 dc in next 6 ch, 1 dc in next 6 dc (12 sts).

Fasten off and thread tail of yarn through last round of stitches. Pull tightly on end of yarn to close and fasten off.

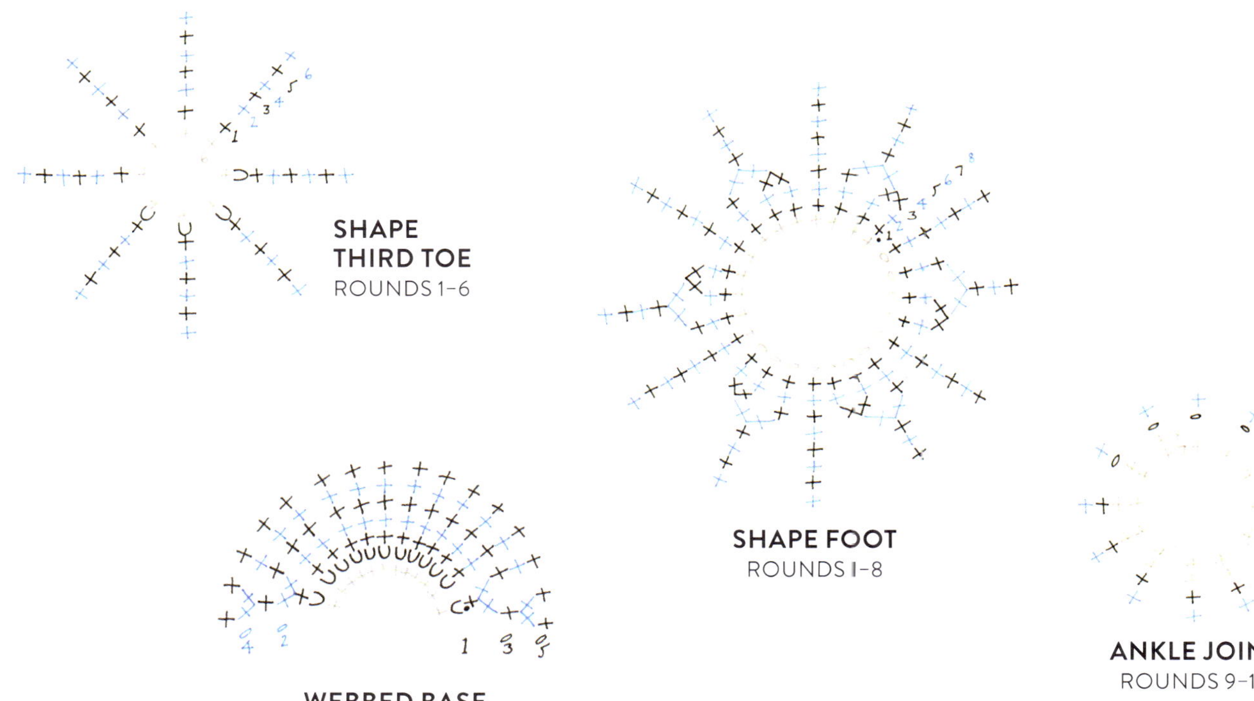

SHAPE THIRD TOE
ROUNDS 1–6

WEBBED BASE
ROWS 1–5

SHAPE FOOT
ROUNDS 1–8

ANKLE JOINT
ROUNDS 9–10

SHAPE LOWER LEG

With RS facing, join A with a sl st to the first of the 6 skipped sts of the foot.

Round 1: 1 dc in same dc as sl st, 1 dc in next 5 dc, 1 dc in opposite side of next 6 ch of ankle joint (12 sts).

Rounds 2–3: 1 dc in each st.

Round 4 (inc): (Dc2inc, 1 dc) 6 times (18 sts).

Rounds 5–6: 1 dc in each st.

Round 7: 1 dc in next 9 dc, finishing at the side of the leg, 9 sts before the end of the round.

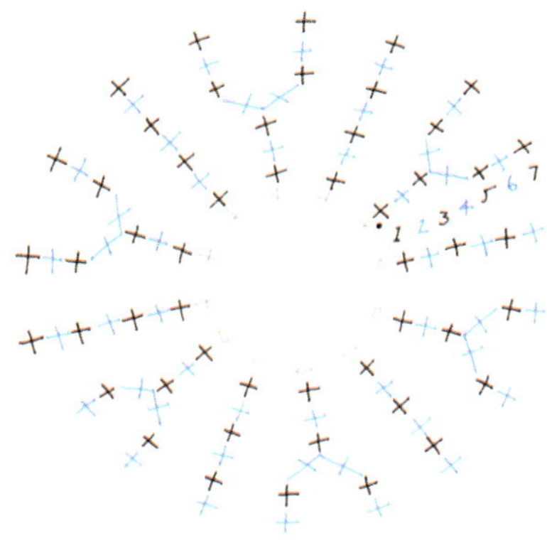

SHAPE LOWER LEG
ROUNDS 1–7

KNEE JOINT
ROUNDS 8–9

KNEE JOINT

Round 8: 6 ch, skip next 12 dc, 1 dc in next 6 dc at the front of the leg.

Round 9: 1 dc in next 6 ch, 1 dc in next 6 dc (12 sts).

Fasten off and thread tail of yarn through last round of stitches. Pull tightly on end of yarn to close and fasten off.

Hold two pipe cleaners together and make a bend in the middle. Twist the four lengths together, keeping a small loop at the bend. Bend back the sharp ends. Insert the twisted pipe cleaners into the leg, pushing the looped end into the foot. Push stuffing into the lower leg and foot, around the pipe cleaner.

SHAPE THIGH

With RS facing, join A with a sl st to the first of the 12 skipped sts of the lower leg.

Round 1: 1 dc in same dc as sl st, 1 dc in next 11 dc, 1 dc in opposite side of next 6 ch of the knee joint (18 sts).

Round 2 (inc): (Dc2inc, 1 dc) 6 times, 1 dc in next 6 dc (24 sts).

Round 3: 1 dc in each st.

Round 4 (inc): (Dc2inc, 3 dc) 6 times (30 sts).

Round 5: 1 dc in each st.

Round 6 (inc): (Dc2inc, 4 dc) 6 times (36 sts).

Rounds 7–9: 1 dc in each st.

Round 10 (dec): (Dc2tog, 4 dc) 6 times (30 sts).

Round 11 (dec): (Dc2tog, 3 dc) 6 times (24 sts).

Stuff the thigh before continuing, keeping the twisted pipe cleaners in the middle of the leg. Bend back any excess pipe cleaner and cover the top with stuffing.

Round 12 (dec): (Dc2tog, 2 dc) 6 times (18 sts).

Round 13 (dec): (Dc2tog, 1 dc) 6 times (12 sts).

Round 14 (dec): (Dc2tog) 6 times (6 sts).

Fasten off and thread the tail of yarn through the last round of stitches. Pull tightly on the end of yarn to close and fasten off.

ARMS
(make 2)

WRIST JOINT

With 2.5mm hook and A, make a magic loop.

Round 1: 1 ch, 6 dc into loop (6 sts).

Round 2 (inc): (Dc2inc) 6 times (12 sts).

Pull tightly on short end of yarn to close loop.

DIVIDE FOR FINGERS

Round 3: 6 ch, skip next 6 dc, 1 dc in next 6 dc.

Round 4: 1 dc in next 6 ch, 1 dc in next 6 dc (12 sts).

Continue on these 12 sts.

Round 5 (inc): (dc2inc, 1 dc) 6 times (18 sts).

SHAPE FIRST FINGER

Round 1: 1 dc in next 3 dc, skip next 12 dc, 1 dc in next 3 dc.

Continue on these 6 sts.

Rounds 2–6: 1 dc in each st.

Fasten off and thread the tail of yarn through the last round of stitches. Pull tightly to close the end and fasten off.

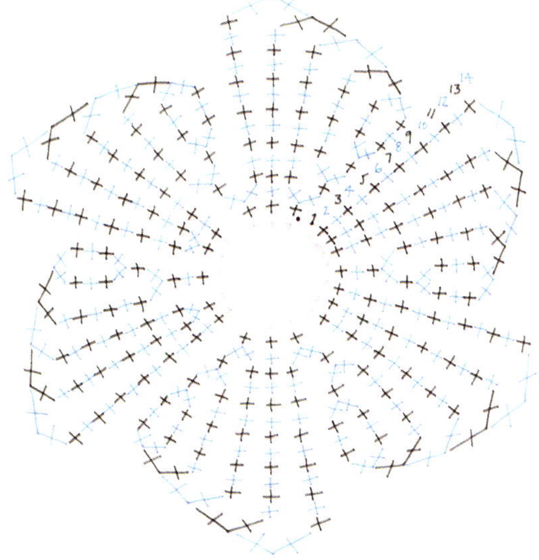

SHAPE THIGH
ROUNDS 1–14

WRIST JOINT
ROUNDS 1–2

DIVIDE FOR FINGERS
ROUNDS 3–5

SHAPE FIRST FINGER
ROUNDS 1–6

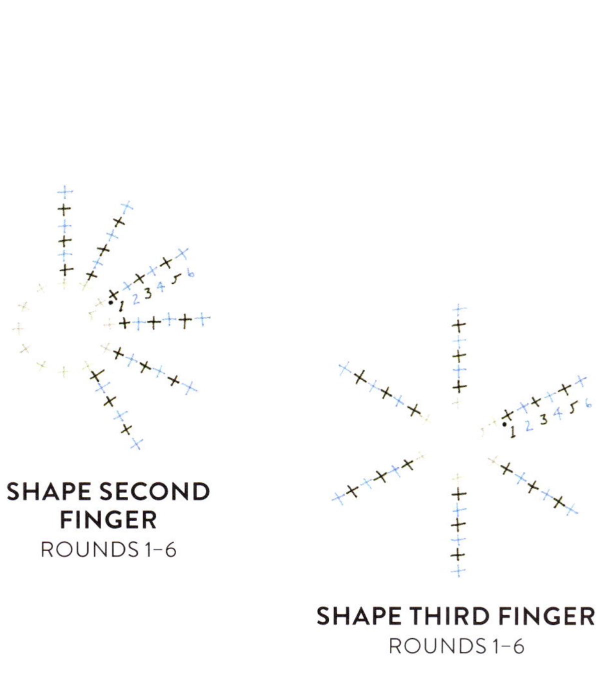

SHAPE SECOND FINGER
ROUNDS 1–6

SHAPE THIRD FINGER
ROUNDS 1–6

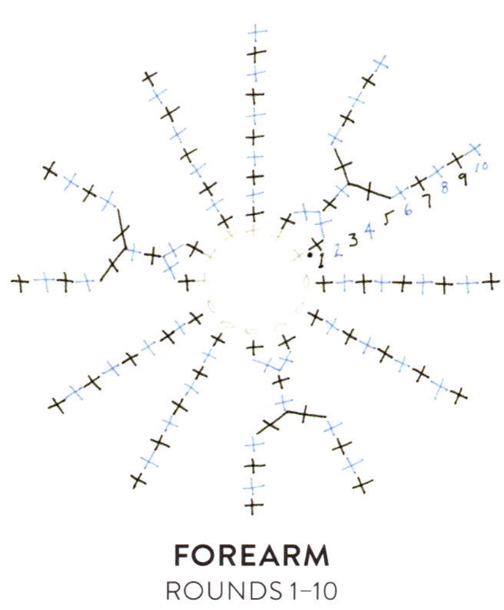

FOREARM
ROUNDS 1–10

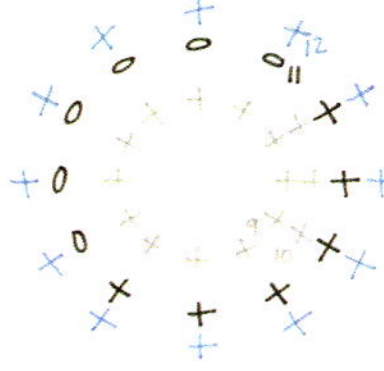

ELBOW JOINT
ROUNDS 11–12

SHAPE SECOND FINGER

With RS facing, join A with a sl st to the first of the 12 skipped sts.

Round 1: 1 dc in the same dc as the sl st, 1 dc in next 2 dc, skip next 6 dc, 1 dc in next 3 dc.

Continue on these 6 sts.

Rounds 2–6: 1 dc in each st.

Fasten off and thread the tail of yarn through the last round of stitches. Pull tightly to close the end and fasten off.

SHAPE THIRD FINGER

With RS facing, join A with a sl st to the first of the 6 skipped sts.

Round 1: 1 dc in the same dc as the sl st, 1 dc in next 5 dc (6 sts).

Rounds 2–6: 1 dc in each st.

Fasten off and finish as for first finger.

FOREARM

With RS facing, join A with a sl st to the first of the 6 skipped sts of the wrist joint.

Round 1: 1 dc in same dc as sl st, 1 dc in next 5 dc, 1 dc in opposite side of next 6 ch (12 sts).

Round 2 (dec): (Dc2tog, 2 dc) 3 times (9 sts).

Rounds 3–4: 1 dc in each st.

Round 5 (inc): (Dc2inc, 2 dc) 3 times (12 sts).

Rounds 6–9: 1 dc in each st.

Round 10: 1 dc in next 3 dc, finishing at the side of the hand, 9 sts before the end of the round.

Stuff the fingers before continuing.

ELBOW JOINT

Round 11: 6 ch, skip next 6 dc, 1 dc in next 6 dc.

Round 12: 1 dc in next 6 ch, 1 dc in next 6 dc (12 sts).

Fasten off and thread tail of yarn through last round of stitches. Pull tightly on end of yarn to close and fasten off.

UPPER ARM

With RS facing, join A with a sl st to the first of the 6 skipped sts of the forearm.

Round 1: 1 dc in same dc as sl st, 1 dc in next 5 dc, 1 dc in opposite side of next 6 ch of the elbow joint (12 sts).

Rounds 2–9: 1 dc in each st.

Stuff the arm before continuing.

Round 10 (dec): (Dc2tog) 6 times (6 sts).

Fasten off and thread tail of yarn through last round of stitches. Pull tightly on end of yarn to close and fasten off.

SAIL

With 2.5mm hook and A, make 11 ch.

Row 1: 2 dc in second ch from hook, 1 dc in next 9 ch, turn (11 sts).

Work the stitches of rows 2–23 into the back loops only to produce a rib effect.

Row 2 (inc): 1 ch, 1 dc in each dc to last st, dc2inc, turn (12 sts).

Row 3: 1 ch, dc2inc, 1 dc in each st to last 2 sts, dc2tog, turn.

Row 4 (dec): 1 ch, 1 dc in each st, turn.

Row 5 (inc): 1 ch, dc2inc, 1 dc in each st, turn (13 sts).

Row 6: 1 ch, 1 dc in each st, turn.

Row 7 (inc): 1 ch, dc2inc, 1 dc in each st, turn (14 sts).

Rows 8–18: 1 ch, 1 dc in each st, turn.

Row 19 (inc): 1 ch, 1 dc in each dc to last st, dc2inc, turn (15 sts).

Rows 20–21: 1 ch, 1 dc in each st, turn.

Row 22 (dec): 2 ch, 1 htr in next 3 dc, 1 dc in each dc to last 2 sts, dc2tog, turn (14 sts).

Row 23 (inc): 1 ch, 1 dc in next 10 dc, 1 htr in next 3 sts, htr2inc, turn (15 sts).

Do not fasten off.

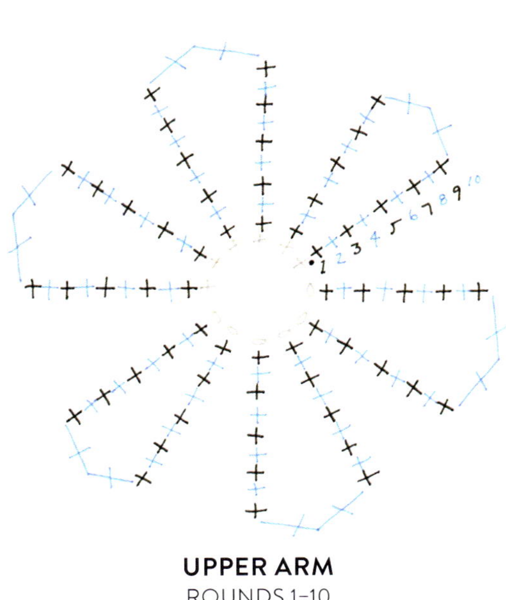

UPPER ARM
ROUNDS 1–10

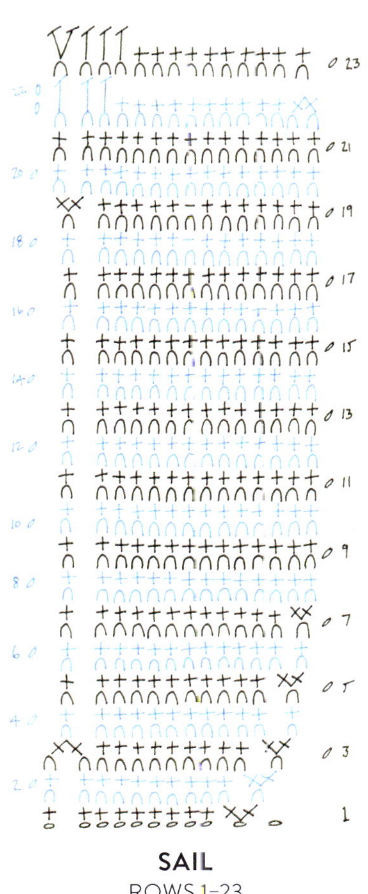

SAIL
ROWS 1–23

SAIL EDGING

Row 1: 1 ch, dc2inc, 1 dc in next 13 sts, dc2inc, work 22 dc evenly along the edges of the rows; working in the opposite side of each ch, dc2inc, 1 dc in next 8 ch, dc2inc. Join B in last dc, turn (51 sts).
Fasten off A, leaving a long tail of yarn. Continue with B.
Row 2 (inc): 1 ch, dc2inc, 1 dc in next 12 sts, dc2inc, 1 dc in next 3 sts, dc2inc, 1 dc in next 15 sts, (dc2inc) 3 times, 1 dc in next 14 sts, dc2inc (58 sts).
Fasten off.
Make a second piece to match the first. Turn work at the end of the last row. Do not fasten off.

JOIN SAIL PIECES

Hold the two sail pieces together, matching the shaping and aligning the stitches.
Row 3 (inc): Working into each stitch of both pieces at the same time to join, 1 ch, 1 dc in next 5 sts, *2 ch, sl st in second ch from hook, 3 dc*; rep from * to * 3 more times, 2 ch, sl st in second ch from hook, 1 dc in next st, dc2inc, rep from * to * 7 times, 2 ch, sl st in second ch from hook, dc2inc, 1 dc in next st; rep from * to * 5 times; 1 dc in next st (60 sts, 18 picots).
Fasten off.

TAIL FIN

With 2.5mm hook and A, make 55 ch.
Row 1: 1 dc in second ch from hook, 1 dc in next ch, 1 htr in next ch, 1 tr in next 40 ch, 1 htr in next 3 ch, 1 dc in next 7 ch, 3 dc in end ch. Join B in last dc, turn (56 sts).
Fasten off A, leaving a long tail of yarn. Continue with B.
Row 2 (inc): 1 ch, 1 dc in next dc, dc3inc, 1 dc in next 51 sts, (dc2inc) 3 times (61 sts).
Fasten off.
Make a second piece to match the first. Turn work at the end of the last row. Do not fasten off.

JOIN TAIL FIN PIECES

Hold the two pieces together, matching the shaping and aligning the stitches.
Row 3 (inc): Working into each stitch of both pieces at the same time to join, 1 ch, dc2inc, 1 dc in next 2 sts, (2 ch, sl st in second ch from hook, 3 dc) 18 times, 2 ch, sl st in second ch from hook,1 dc in next st, dc3inc, 1 dc in next 2 sts (64 sts, 19 picots).
Fasten off, leaving a long tail of B.

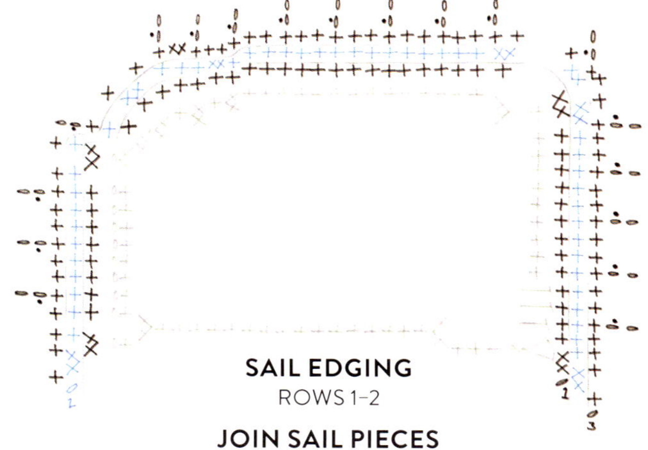

SAIL EDGING
ROWS 1–2

JOIN SAIL PIECES
ROW 3
Insert hook into each stitch of both pieces at the same time to join

TAIL FIN
ROWS 1–2

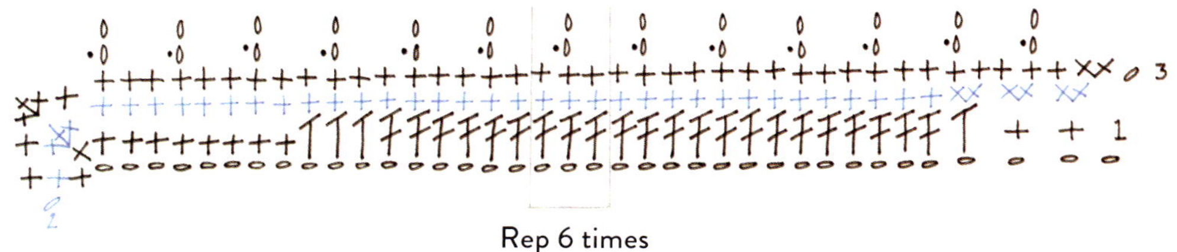

JOIN TAIL-FIN PIECES
ROW 3
Insert hook into each stitch of both pieces at the same time to join

MAKING UP

HEAD

If using looped glass eyes, poke the loop of an eye through the centre of each eye socket before attaching each one to the head using 23⅝in (60cm) length of clear invisible or strong sewing thread (see page 163). Use the tail of yarn left after fastening off the sockets to neatly sew the edges to the head.

Embroider the nostrils in satin stitch (see page 164), using two strands of embroidery thread.

SAIL AND TAIL FIN

Lightly stuff the sail, keeping it flat. Position the curved edge of the sail towards the front of the body, behind the neck, and align the open edges with the joined edges of the body that run down the centre of the dinosaur's back. Use the tails of yarn left after fastening off to sew each side of the sail in place.

Use the tails of yarn to sew the tail fin in place, directly behind the sail, with the curved end at the tip of the tail. Sew each side of the fin to the joined edges of the rows running down the centre of the tail. Sew the four stitches of the tail fin and sail together, where the edges meet.

ARMS AND LEGS

Sew together the gaps between the fingers and toes. Use the tail of yarn left after fastening off to sew the webbed base in place, stitching all around the edges of the toes to attach them securely to the base.

Follow the instructions on page 164 to attach the limbs, using a 59in (150cm) length of yarn A or strong thread for the arms and 63in (160cm) length for the legs.

Weave in all the yarn ends.

ANKYLOSAURUS

PUFF AND BOBBLE STITCHES ARE USED TO CREATE THE ROWS OF VARIOUS SIZED PLATES OF ARMOUR OVER THE BODY OF THIS ANKYLOSAURUS, WHICH IS WORKED IN THREE COLOURS.

MATERIALS

- Scheepjes Metropolis, 75% extra fine merino wool, 25% nylon (219yd/200m per 50g ball):
  1 × 50g ball in 006 Taipei (A)
  1 × 50g ball in 053 Santiago (B)
  1 × 50g ball in 054 Johannesburg (C)
- 52in (132cm) length of 4ply yarn in pink, such as Scheepjes Metropolis 052 Bangalore, for the mouth (D)
- 1 pair of 5/32–3/16in (4–5mm) looped glass teddy bear eyes or safety eyes
- Clear invisible or strong thread to attach the looped glass eyes
- Stranded metallic embroidery thread in black, such as DMC Light Effects, shade E310, for the nostrils
- 2.25mm (UK13:USB/1) and 2.5mm (UK12:US-) crochet hooks
- Stitch marker
- Blunt-ended yarn needle
- Toy stuffing

SIZE

Approximately 13¾in (35cm) long

TENSION

27 sts and 27 rows to 4in (10cm) over double crochet using 2.5mm hook and yarn A. Use larger or smaller hook if necessary to obtain correct tension.

METHOD

The Ankylosaurus is crocheted from the tail up and worked in three colours. The tail club is started with a number of chain stitches and worked in increasing rounds of double crochet, ending with the shaping at the top and long stitches to accentuate the club shape. The opposite side of the chain, at the base of the club, is crocheted into to begin the tail and continued in rows. Puff stitches and large bobble stitches form the bony plates of armour running over the back of the dinosaur, and the textured section down the centre of the head. The body is stuffed as it is crocheted.

The lower beak is crocheted in rounds and the top beak is worked in short rows. An edging of double crochet, half treble and treble stitches is crocheted at the front of the snout, overlapping the beak. The horns are worked in two pieces and joined by crocheting into each stitch of both pieces at the same time. They are stuffed and sewn to the head at an angle.

The legs are worked in rounds of double crochet with bobble stitches forming the claws. The bends in the legs are made by working a length of chain stitches and skipping a number of stitches of the previous row. The stitches of the following row are gathered together to form the elbow and knee joints. The first round of the tops of the legs are crocheted into the skipped stitches and the opposite side of the chain stitches. The movable legs are attached using matching yarn or strong thread.

The Ankylosaurus is finished with looped glass or safety eyes attached to a crocheted eye socket and simple embroidered nostrils.

1 ch and 2 ch at beg of the row/round do not count as a st throughout.

KEY

- Magic loop
- Chain (ch)
- Slip stitch (sl st)
- Double crochet (dc)
- Dc2inc
- Dc3inc
- Dc2tog
- Half treble (htr)
- Treble (tr)
- 2-htr puff
- Make bobble (mb)
- 6-tr bobble
- Work into back loop only
- Work into front loop only

COLOUR

 A

 B

 C

TAIL CLUB

With 2.5mm hook and A, make 12 ch, join with a sl st to the first ch to form a ring.

Round 1: 1 dc in each ch (12 sts).

Round 2 (inc): (Dc2inc, 1 dc) 6 times (18 sts).

Round 3 (inc): (Dc2inc, 2 dc) 6 times (24 sts).

Round 4 (inc): (Dc2inc, 3 dc) 6 times (30 sts).

Round 5 (inc): (Dc2inc, 4 dc) 6 times (36 sts).

Rounds 6–9: 1 dc in each st.

Do not fasten off.

SHAPE TOP OF CLUB

Round 1: 1 dc in next 6 dc, skip next 24 sts, 1 dc in next 6 dc.

Continue on these 12 sts.

Round 2: 1 dc in each st.

Fasten off, leaving a long tail of yarn.

SHAPE MIDDLE OF CLUB

With RS facing, join A with a sl st to the first of the 24 skipped sts.

Round 1: 1 dc in same dc as sl st, 1 dc in next 5 dc, skip next 12 sts, 1 dc in next 6 dc.

Continue on these 12 sts.

Round 2: 1 dc in each st.

Fasten off, leaving a long tail of yarn.

FINISH TOP OF CLUB

With RS facing, join A with a sl st to the first of the 12 skipped sts.

Round 1: 1 dc in same dc as sl st, 1 dc in next 11 dc.

Round 2: 1 dc in each st.

Fasten off, leaving a long tail of yarn.

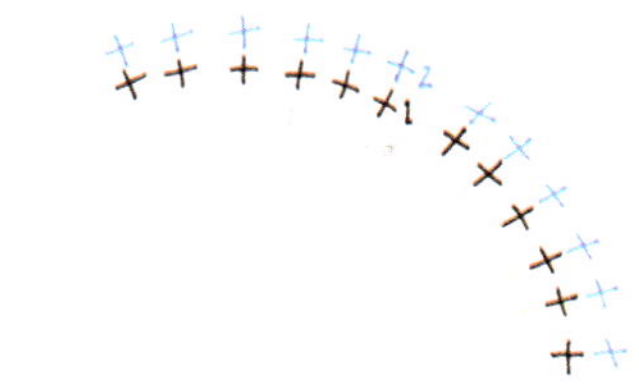

SHAPE TOP OF CLUB
ROUNDS 1–2

SHAPE MIDDLE OF CLUB
ROUNDS 1–2

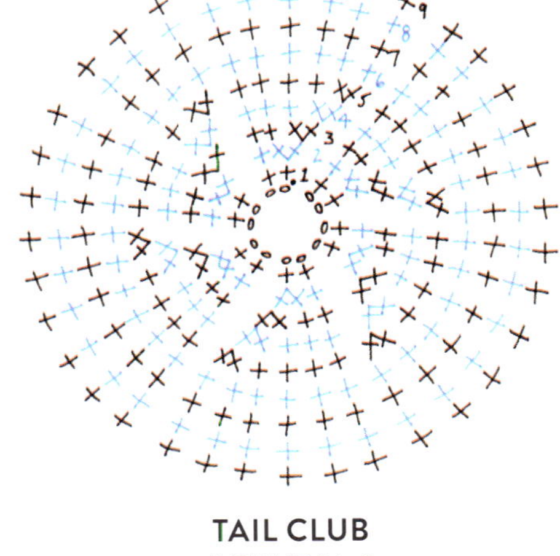

TAIL CLUB
ROUNDS 1–9

FINISH TOP OF CLUB
ROUNDS 1–2

BODY

TAIL

The puff stitches and bobbles are crocheted on the wrong side of the work, as they will appear on the reverse side.

See page 159 for instructions to make a 2-htr puff and a 6-tr bobble.

With RS facing and 2.5mm hook, join B with a sl st to the opposite side of the ch at the side of the tail.

Row 1 (RS): 1 dc in same ch as sl st, 1 dc in next 5 ch, join C in last dc and carry unused yarn on WS of work; 1 dc in next 6 ch with C, sl st to first dc, turn (12 sts).

Row 2 (WS): 1 dc in next 6 sts with C, 1 dc in next 6 sts with B, turn.

Row 3: 1 ch, 1 dc in next 6 sts with B, 1 dc in next 6 sts with C, sl st to first dc, turn.

Row 4: 1 dc in next 6 sts with C, 1 dc in next dc with B, join A and work 2-htr puff, 1 dc in next 2 dc with B, 2-htr puff with A, 1 dc in next dc with B, turn.

Row 5: As row 3.

Row 6: As row 2.

Row 7 (inc): With B, 1 ch, *1 dc in next 2 sts, (dc2inc) twice, 1 dc in next 2 sts; rep from * with C, sl st to first dc, turn (16 sts).

Row 8: 1 dc in next 8 sts with C, (2 dc with B, 2-htr puff with A) twice, 1 dc in next 2 dc with B, turn.

Row 9: 1 ch, 1 dc in next 8 sts with B, 1 dc in next 8 sts with C, sl st to first dc, turn.

Row 10: 1 dc in next 8 sts with C, 1 dc in next 8 sts with B, turn.

Row 11 (inc): With B, 1 ch, *1 dc in next 3 sts, (dc2inc) twice, 1 dc in next 3 sts; rep from * with C, sl st to first dc, turn (20 sts).

Row 12: 1 dc in next 10 sts with C, 1 dc in next 3 dc with B, 2-htr puff with A, 1 dc in next 2 dc with B, 2-htr puff with A, 1 dc in next 3 dc with B, turn.

Row 13: 1 ch, 1 dc in next 10 sts with B, 1 dc in next 10 sts with C, sl st to first dc, turn.

Row 14: 1 dc in next 10 sts with C, 1 dc in next 10 sts with B, turn.

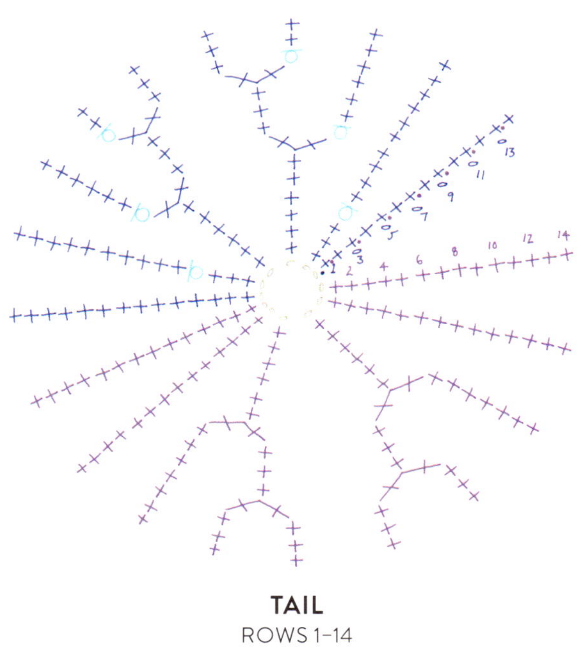

TAIL
ROWS 1–14

Row 15 (inc): With B, 1 ch, *1 dc in next 4 sts, (dc2inc) twice, 1 dc in next 4 sts; rep from * with C, sl st to first dc, turn (24 sts).

Row 16: 1 dc in next 12 sts with C, 1 dc in next dc with B, (2-htr puff with A, 2 dc with B) 3 times, 2-htr puff with A, 1 dc in next dc with B, turn.

Row 17: 1 ch, 1 dc in next 12 sts with B, 1 dc in next 12 sts with C, sl st to first dc, turn.

Row 18: 1 dc in next 12 sts with C, 1 dc in next 12 sts with B, turn.

Row 19 (inc): With B, 1 ch, *1 dc in next 5 sts, (dc2inc) twice, 1 dc in next 5 sts; rep from * with C, sl st to first dc, turn (28 sts).

Row 20: 1 dc in next 14 sts with C, 1 dc in next dc with B, 2-htr puff with A, 1 dc in next 3 dc with B, 2-htr puff with A, 1 dc in next 2 dc with B, 2-htr puff with A, 1 dc in next 3 dc with B, 2-htr puff with A, 1 dc in next dc with B, turn.

Row 21: 1 ch, 1 dc in next 14 sts with B, 1 dc in next 14 sts with C, sl st to first dc, turn.

Row 22: 1 dc in next 14 sts with C, 1 dc in next 14 sts with B, turn.

Row 23 (inc): With B, 1 ch, *1 dc in next 6 sts, (dc2inc) twice, 1 dc in next 6 sts; rep from * with C, sl st to first dc, turn (32 sts).

Row 24: 1 dc in next 16 sts with C, 1 dc in next dc with B, 2-htr puff with A, 1 dc in next 4 dc with B, 2-htr puff with A, 1 dc in next 2 dc with B, 2-htr puff with A, 1 dc in next 4 dc with B, 2-htr puff with A, 1 dc in next dc with B, turn.

Row 25: 1 ch, 1 dc in next 16 sts with B, 1 dc in next 16 sts with C, sl st to first dc, turn.

Row 26: 1 dc in next 16 sts with C, 1 dc in next 16 sts with B, turn.

Row 27 (inc): With B, 1 ch, *1 dc in next 7 sts, (dc2inc) twice, 1 dc in next 7 sts; rep from * with C, sl st to first dc, turn (36 sts).

Row 28: 1 dc in next 18 sts with C, 1 dc in next dc with B, 2-htr puff with A, (4 dc with B, 6-tr bobble with A) twice, 1 dc in next 4 dc with B, 2-htr puff with A, 1 dc in next dc with B, turn.

Stuff the tail to within the last three rows before continuing.

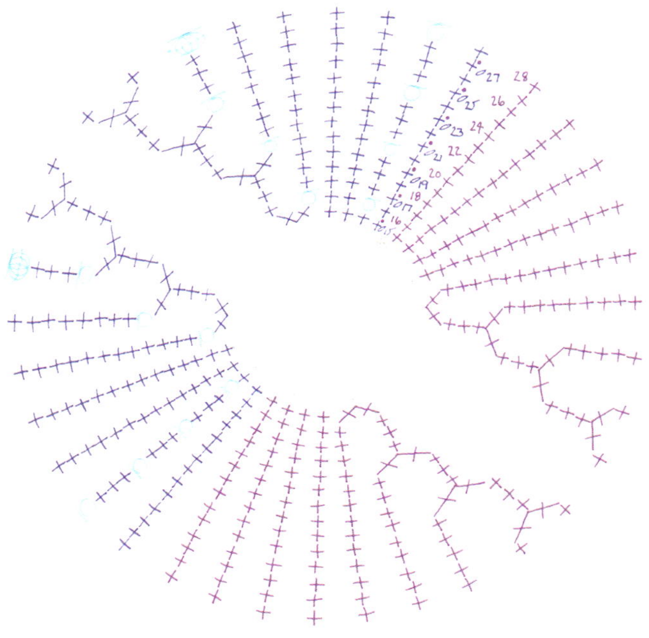

TAIL
ROWS 15–28

SHAPE END OF BODY

Row 29 (inc): With B, 1 ch, *1 dc in next 8 sts, (dc2inc) twice, 1 dc in next 8 sts; rep from * with C, sl st to first dc, turn (40 sts).

Row 30: 1 dc in next 20 sts with C, 1 dc in next 20 sts with B, turn.

Row 31 (inc): With B, 1 ch, *1 dc in next 9 sts, (dc2inc) twice, 1 dc in next 9 sts; rep from * with C, sl st to first dc, turn (44 sts).

Row 32: 1 dc in next 22 sts with C, 1 dc in next dc with B, 2-htr puff with A, 1 dc in next 2 dc with B, 2-htr puff with A, 1 dc in next 3 dc with B, 6-tr bobble with A, 1 dc in next 4 dc with B, 6-tr bobble with A, 1 dc in next 3 dc with B, 2-htr puff with A, 1 dc in next 2 dc with B, 2-htr puff with A, 1 dc in next dc with B, turn.

Row 33 (inc): With B, 1 ch, *1 dc in next 10 sts, (dc2inc) twice, 1 dc in next 10 sts; rep from * with C, sl st to first dc, turn (48 sts).

Row 34: 1 dc in next 24 sts with C, 1 dc in next 24 sts with B, turn.

Row 35 (inc): With B, 1 ch, *1 dc in next 11 sts, (dc2inc) twice, 1 dc in next 11 sts; rep from * with C, sl st to first dc, turn (52 sts).

Row 36: 1 dc in next 26 sts with C, 1 dc in next dc with B, 2-htr puff with A, 1 dc in next 3 dc with B, (6-tr bobble with A, 4 dc with B) 3 times, 6-tr bobble with A, 1 dc in next 3 dc with B, 2-htr puff with A, 1 dc in next dc with B, turn.

Row 37 (inc): With B, 1 ch, *1 dc in next 12 sts, (dc2inc) twice, 1 dc in next 12 sts; rep from * with C, sl st to first dc, turn (56 sts).

Row 38: 1 dc in next 28 sts with C, 1 dc in next 28 sts with B, turn.

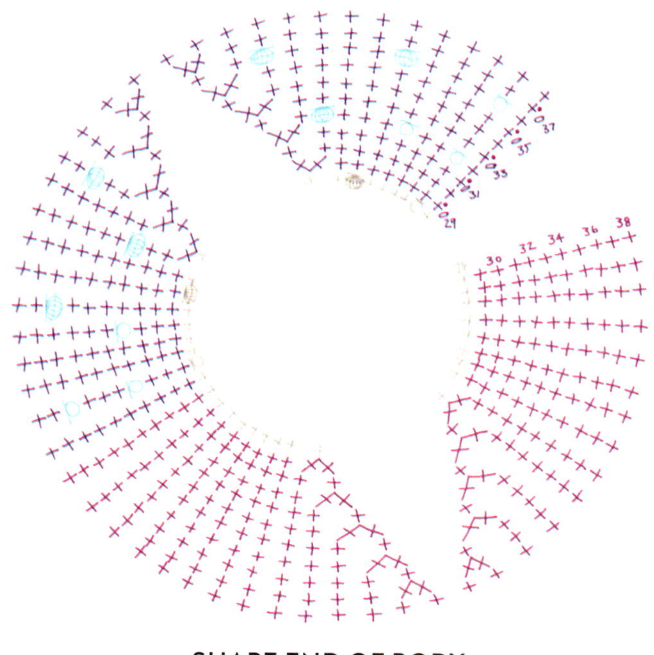

SHAPE END OF BODY
ROWS 29–38

SHAPE MIDDLE OF BODY

Row 39 (inc): With B, 1 ch, *1 dc in next 13 sts, (dc2inc) twice, 1 dc in next 13 sts; rep from * with C, sl st to first dc, turn (60 sts).

Row 40: 1 dc in next 30 sts with C, 1 dc in next 2 dc with B, 2-htr puff with A, (4 dc with B, 6-tr bobble with A) 4 times, 1 dc in next 4 dc with B, 2-htr puff with A, 1 dc in next 2 dc with B, turn.

Row 41: 1 ch, 1 dc in next 30 sts with B, 1 dc in next 30 sts with C, sl st to first dc, turn.

Row 42: 1 dc in next 30 sts with C, 1 dc in next 30 sts with B, turn.

Row 43: As row 41.

Rows 44–51: Rep rows 40–43 twice.

Row 52: As row 40.

Stuff the body to within the last three rows before continuing.

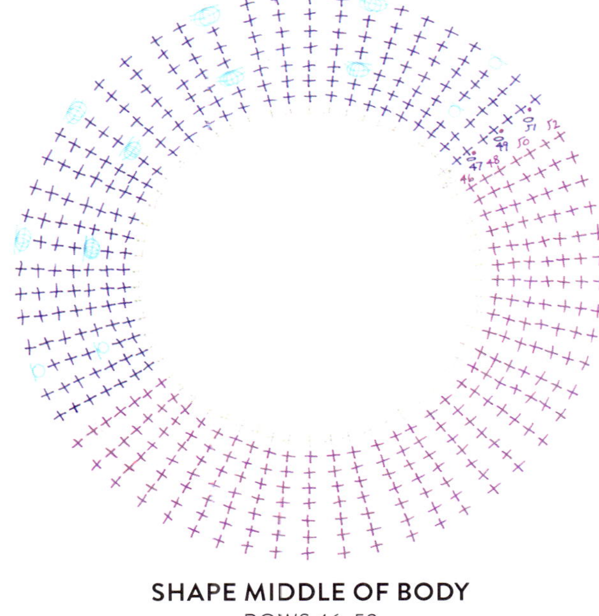

SHAPE MIDDLE OF BODY
ROWS 46–52

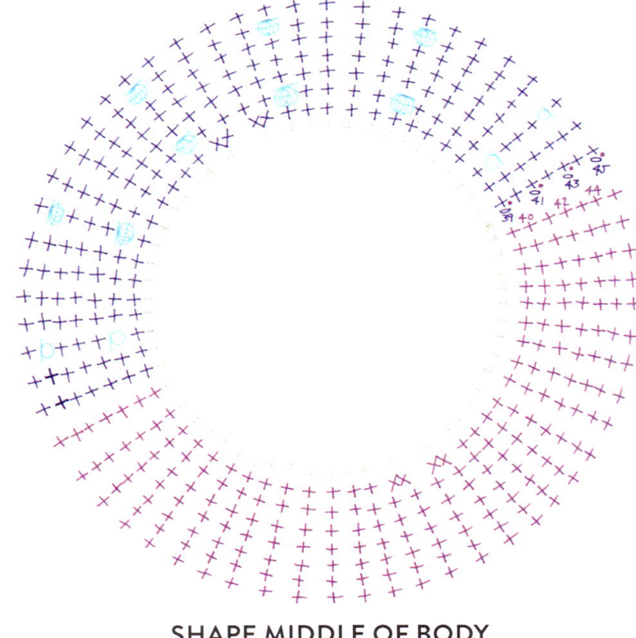

SHAPE MIDDLE OF BODY
ROWS 39–45

SHAPE FRONT OF BODY

Row 53 (dec): With B, 1 ch, *1 dc in next 13 sts, (dc2tog) twice, 1 dc in next 13 sts; rep from * with C, sl st to first dc, turn (56 sts).

Row 54: 1 dc in next 28 sts with C, 1 dc in next 28 sts with B, turn.

Row 55 (dec): With B, 1 ch, *1 dc in next 12 sts, (dc2tog) twice, 1 dc in next 12 sts; rep from * with C, sl st to first dc, turn (52 sts).

Row 56: 1 dc in next 26 sts with C, 1 dc in next dc with B, 2-htr puff with A, 1 dc in next 3 dc with B, (6-tr bobble with A, 4 dc with B) 3 times, 6-tr bobble with A, 1 dc in next 3 dc with B, 2-htr puff with A, 1 dc in next dc with B, turn.

Row 57 (dec): With B, 1 ch, *1 dc in next 11 sts, (dc2tog) twice, 1 dc in next 11 sts; rep from * with C, sl st to first dc, turn (48 sts).

Row 58: 1 dc in next 24 sts with C, 1 dc in next 24 sts with B, turn.

Row 59 (dec): With B, 1 ch, *1 dc in next 10 sts, (dc2tog) twice, 1 dc in next 10 sts; rep from * with C, sl st to first dc, turn (44 sts).

Row 60: 1 dc in next 22 sts with C, 1 dc in next dc with B, 2-htr puff with A, 1 dc in next 2 dc with B, 2-htr puff with A, 1 dc in next 3 dc with B, 6-tr bobble with A, 1 dc in next 4 dc with B, 6-tr bobble with A, 1 dc in next 3 dc with B, 2-htr puff with A, 1 dc in next 2 dc with B, 2-htr puff with A, 1 dc in next dc with B, turn.

Row 61 (dec): With B, 1 ch, *1 dc in next 9 sts, (dc2tog) twice, 1 dc in next 9 sts; rep from * with C, sl st to first dc, turn (40 sts).

Row 62: 1 dc in next 20 sts with C, 1 dc in next 20 sts with B, turn.

Row 63 (dec): With B, 1 ch, *1 dc in next 8 sts, (dc2tog) twice, 1 dc in next 8 sts; rep from * with C, sl st to first dc, turn (36 sts).

Row 64: 1 dc in next 18 sts with C, 1 dc in next dc with B, 2-htr puff with A, (4 dc with B, 6-tr bobble with A) twice, 1 dc in next 4 dc with B, 2-htr puff with A, 1 dc in next dc with B, turn.

Row 65 (dec): With B, 1 ch, *1 dc in next 7 sts, (dc2tog) twice, 1 dc in next 7 sts; rep from * with C, sl st to first dc, turn (32 sts).

Row 66: 1 dc in next 16 sts with C, 1 dc in next 16 sts with B, turn.

Insert more stuffing before continuing.

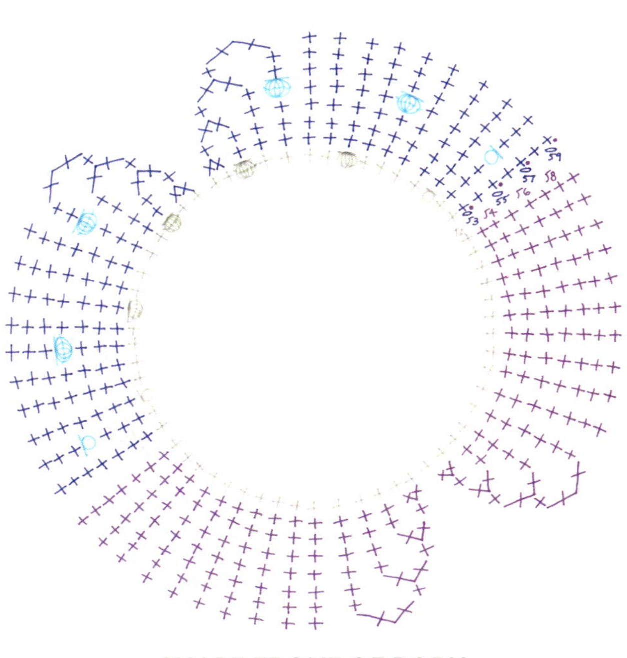

SHAPE FRONT OF BODY
ROWS 53–59

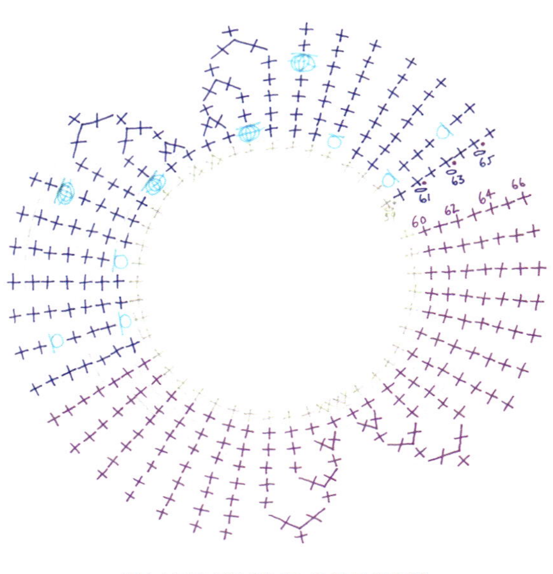

SHAPE FRONT OF BODY
ROWS 60–66

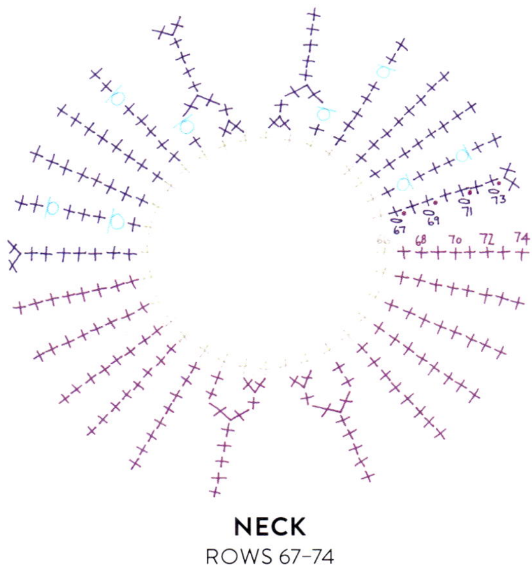

NECK
ROWS 67–74

HEAD
ROWS 75–84

NECK

Row 67 (dec): With B, 1 ch, *1 dc in next 6 sts, (dc2tog) twice, 1 dc in next 6 sts; rep from * with C, sl st to first dc, turn (28 sts).

Row 68: 1 dc in next 14 sts with C, 1 dc in next dc with B, 2-htr puff with A, 1 dc in next 3 dc with B, 2-htr puff with A, 1 dc in next 2 dc with B, 2-htr puff with A, 1 dc in next 3 dc with B, 2-htr puff with A, 1 dc in next dc with B, turn.

Row 69 (dec): With B, 1 ch, *1 dc in next 5 sts, (dc2tog) twice, 1 dc in next 5 sts; rep from * with C, sl st to first dc, turn (24 sts).

Row 70: 1 dc in next 12 sts with C, 1 dc in next 12 sts with B, turn.

Row 71: 1 ch, 1 dc in next 12 sts with B, 1 dc in next 12 sts with C, sl st to first dc, turn.

Row 72: 1 dc in next 12 sts with C, 1 dc in next dc with B, (2-htr puff with A, 2 dc with B) 3 times, 2-htr puff with A, 1 dc in next dc with B, turn.

Row 73: As row 71.

Row 74 (inc): 1 dc in next 12 sts with C, dc2inc with B, 1 dc in next 4 dc, dc2inc, 1 dc in next 5 dc, dc2inc, turn (27 sts).

HEAD

The next 6 rows are not joined with a slip stitch at the end to leave an opening for stuffing.

Row 75 (RS) (inc): With B, 1 ch, (dc2inc, 1 dc) 3 times, 1 dc in next 3 dc, (1 dc, dc2inc) 3 times; with C, 1 dc in next 12 sts, turn (33 sts).

Row 76 (WS): 1 ch, 1 dc in next 12 sts with C, 1 dc in next 7 dc with B, (2-htr puff with A, 1 dc with B) 4 times, 1 dc in next 6 dc, turn.

Row 77: 1 ch, 1 dc in next 21 dc with B, 1 dc in next 12 sts with C, turn.

Rows 78–79: As rows 76–77.

Row 80: As row 76.

Row 81 (dec): With B, 1 ch, 1 dc in next 2 dc, (dc2tog) twice, 1 dc in next 9 dc, (dc2tog) twice, 1 dc in next 2 dc; with C, dc2tog, 1 dc in next 8 sts, dc2tog, sl st to first dc to join, turn (27 sts).

Row 82: 1 dc in next 10 sts with C, 1 dc in next 5 dc with B, (2-htr puff with A, 1 dc with B) 4 times, 1 dc in next 4 dc with B, turn.

Row 83 (dec): With B, 1 ch, 1 dc in next dc, (dc2tog) twice, 1 dc in next 7 dc, (dc2tog) twice, 1 dc in next dc; with C, dc2tog, 1 dc in next 6 sts, dc2tog, sl st to first dc, turn (21 sts).

Row 84: 1 dc in next 8 sts with C, 1 dc in next 3 dc with B, (2-htr puff with A, 1 dc with B) 4 times, 1 dc in next 2 dc with B, join A in last dc, turn.

Do not fasten off.

BEAK

LOWER BEAK

Continue with A, leaving B and C on the RS of the work.
The following is worked in continuous rounds.

Round 1 (RS): 1 ch, 1 dc in back loop only of each st (21 sts).

Round 2 (dec): (1 dc, dc2tog) 4 times in back loops only, 1 dc in back loop only of next dc, (1 dc, dc2tog, 1 dc) twice in both loops (15 sts).

Round 3 (dec): (Dc2tog, 1 dc) 5 times (10 sts).

Round 4 (dec): (Dc2tog) 5 times (5 sts).

Fasten off and thread tail of yarn through last round of stitches. Pull tightly on end of yarn to close and fasten off.

LOWER BEAK
ROUNDS 1–4

TOP BEAK

With 2.5mm hook and RS of work facing, skip the first 4 of the 13 unworked front loops of round 1 of the lower beak and join A with a sl st to the unworked loop of the next st.
The following is worked in short rows.

Row 1 (RS): 1 dc in same st as sl st, 1 dc in next 4 unworked loops, sl st in next loop, turn, leaving the next 3 loops unworked (5 sts).

Row 2 (WS): 1 dc in same st as sl st, 1 dc in next 5 dc, 1 dc in next unworked loop, sl st in next loop, turn (7 sts).

Row 3 (dec): 1 dc in same st as sl st, dc2tog, 1 dc in next 3 dc, dc2tog, 1 dc in next unworked loop, sl st in next loop, turn (7 sts).

Row 4: 1 dc in same st as sl st, 1 dc in next 7 dc, 1 dc in next unworked loop, sl st in next loop, turn (9 sts).

Row 5 (dec): 1 dc in same st as sl st, dc2tog, 1 dc in next 2 dc, 1 htr in next dc, 1 dc in next 2 dc, dc2tog, 1 dc in next unworked loop (9 sts).

Fasten off.

TOP BEAK
ROWS 1–5

SNOUT EDGING

With 2.5mm hook and RS of the top beak facing, work into the unworked front loops of the last row of the head.

Round 1 (RS): With B, sl st into first loop, 2 ch, 1 htr in same st as sl st, 1 tr in next 3 sts, 1 htr in next 5 sts, 1 tr in next 3 sts, 1 htr in next st; with C, 1 dc in next 8 sts, sl st to first htr.

Fasten off.

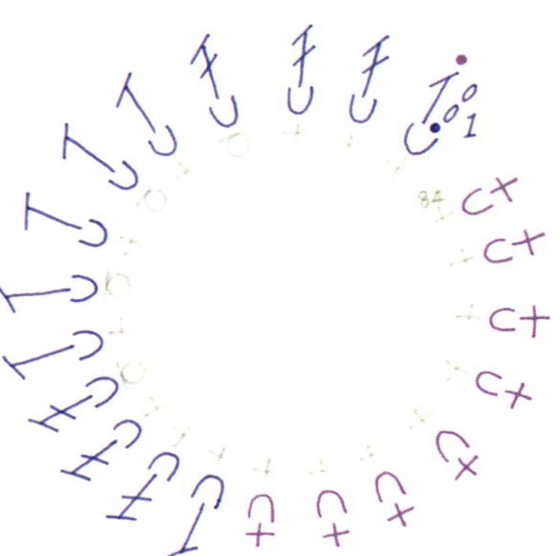

SNOUT EDGING
ROUND 1

HORN
ROWS 1–2

JOIN HORN PIECES
ROW 3
Insert hook into each stitch of both pieces at the same time to join

EYE SOCKET
ROUND 1

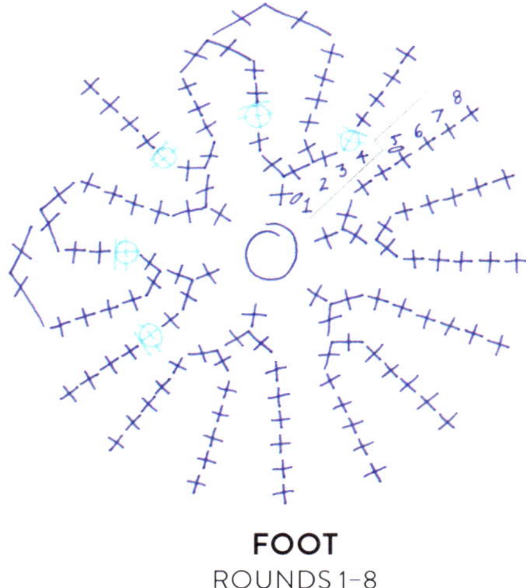

FOOT
ROUNDS 1–8

HORNS
(make 4)

With 2.25mm hook and A, make 4 ch.
Row 1 (WS): 1 dc in second ch from hook, 1 dc in next ch, 3 dc in end ch, 1 dc in opposite side of each ch to end, turn (7 sts).
Row 2 (RS) (inc): 1 ch, 1 dc in next 3 dc, dc3inc, 1 dc in next 3 dc (9 sts).
Fasten off.
Make a second piece to match the first. Do not fasten off.

JOIN HORN PIECES
Place horn pieces with WS together.
Row 3 (inc): Working into back loop only of each st of both pieces at the same time to join, 1 ch, sl st in next 4 sts, dc3inc, sl st in next 4 sts (11 sts).
Fasten off, leaving a long tail of yarn.

EYE SOCKET
(make 2)

With 2.25mm hook and B, make a magic loop.
Round 1 (RS): 2 ch, 9 htr into loop, sl st to second of 2 ch.
Fasten off, leaving a long tail of yarn.

BACK LEGS
(make 2)

FOOT
The bobbles that form the toes appear on the reverse side of the work. This will be the right side. See page 158 for instructions to make bobble (mb).
Starting at the base of the foot, with 2.5mm hook and B, make a magic loop.
Round 1 (WS): 1 ch, 6 dc into loop (6 sts).
Round 2 (inc): (Dc2inc) 6 times (12 sts). Pull tightly on short end of yarn to close loop.
Round 3 (inc): (Dc2inc, 1 dc) 6 times (18 sts).
Join A and carry unused yarn on the WS of the work.
Round 4: (Mb with A, 1 dc in next dc with B) 4 times, mb with A, 1 dc in next 9 dc with B, turn to RS.
Continue with B.
Round 5 (RS): 1 ch, 1 dc in each st.
Round 6: 1 dc in each st.
Round 7 (dec): 1 dc in next 11 dc, (dc2tog, 1 dc) twice, 1 dc in next dc (16 sts).
Round 8 (dec): 1 dc in next 10 dc, (dc2tog, 1 dc) twice (14 sts).

SHAPE LOWER BACK LEG
Rounds 9–10: 1 dc in each dc.
Round 11 (inc): (Dc2inc, 2 dc) 4 times, 1 dc in next 2 dc (18 sts).
Rounds 12–16: 1 dc in each dc.
Round 17: 1 dc in next 3 dc, finishing in line with the first toe, 15 sts before the end of the round.

KNEE JOINT

Round 18: 6 ch, skip next 12 dc, 1 dc in next 6 dc.

Round 19: 1 dc in next 6 ch, 1 dc in next 6 dc (12 sts).

Fasten off and thread tail of yarn through last round of stitches. Pull tightly on end of yarn to close and fasten off.

SHAPE THIGH

With RS facing, join B with a sl st to the first of the 12 skipped sts of the lower back leg.

Round 1: 1 dc in same dc as sl st, 1 dc in next 11 dc, 1 dc in opposite side of next 6 ch of the knee joint (18 sts).

Round 2 (inc): (1 dc, dc2inc) 3 times, (dc2inc, 1 dc) 3 times, 1 dc in next 6 dc (24 sts).

Round 3 (inc): (2 dc, dc2inc) 6 times, 1 dc in next 6 dc (30 sts).

Round 4 (inc): (2 dc, dc2inc, 2 dc) 6 times (36 sts).

Rounds 5–9: 1 dc in each dc.

Round 10 (dec): (Dc2tog, 4 dc) 6 times (30 sts).

Round 11 (dec): (Dc2tog, 3 dc) 6 times (24 sts).

Stuff the leg before continuing.

Round 12 (dec): (Dc2tog, 2 dc) 6 times (18 sts).

Round 13 (dec): (Dc2tog, 1 dc) 6 times (12 sts).

Round 14 (dec): (Dc2tog) 6 times (6 sts).

Fasten off and thread the tail of yarn through the last round of stitches. Pull tightly on the end of yarn to close and fasten off.

FRONT LEGS
(make 2)

FOOT

Work as for back foot (see page 133).

SHAPE LOWER FRONT LEG

Rounds 9–11: 1 dc in each dc.

Round 12: 1 dc in next 9 dc, finishing at the side of the leg, 5 sts before the end of the round.

ELBOW JOINT

Round 13: 6 ch, skip next 8 dc, 1 dc in next 6 dc.

Round 14: 1 dc in next 6 ch, 1 dc in next 6 dc (12 sts).

Fasten off and thread tail of yarn through last round of stitches. Pull tightly on end of yarn to close and fasten off.

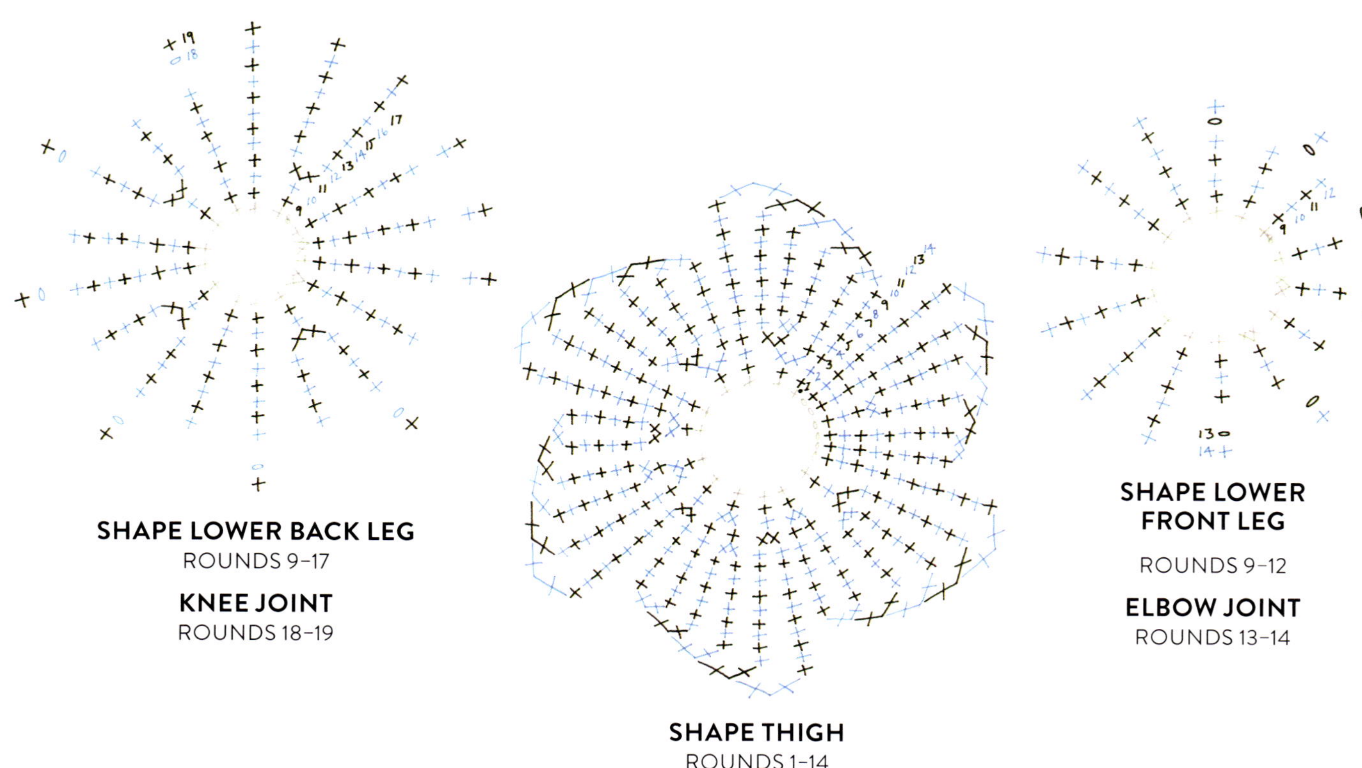

SHAPE LOWER BACK LEG
ROUNDS 9–17
KNEE JOINT
ROUNDS 18–19

SHAPE THIGH
ROUNDS 1–14

SHAPE LOWER FRONT LEG
ROUNDS 9–12
ELBOW JOINT
ROUNDS 13–14

SHAPE SHOULDER

With RS facing, join B with a sl st to the first of the 8 skipped sts of the lower front leg.

Round 1: 1 dc in same dc as sl st, 1 dc in next 7 dc, 1 dc in opposite side of next 6 ch of the elbow joint (14 sts).

Round 2 (inc): 1 dc in next dc, dc2inc, 1 dc in next 4 dc, (dc2inc, 2 dc) twice, dc2inc, 1 dc in next dc (18 sts).

Rounds 3–10: 1 dc in each dc.

Stuff the leg before continuing.

Round 11 (dec): (Dc2tog, 1 dc) 6 times (12 sts).

Round 12 (dec): (Dc2tog) 6 times (6 sts).

Fasten off and thread the tail of yarn through the last round of stitches. Pull tightly on the end of yarn to close and fasten off.

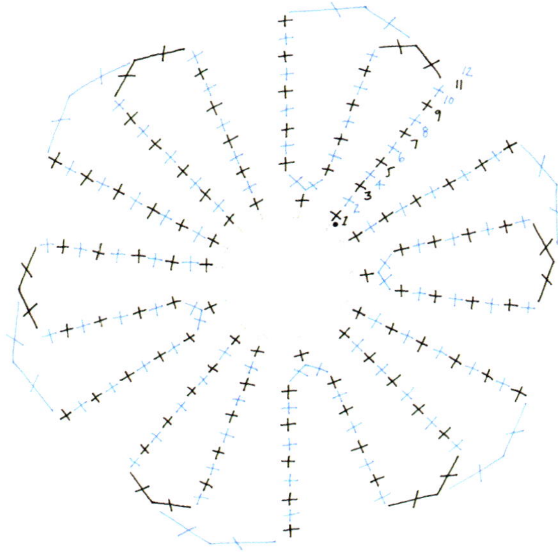

SHAPE SHOULDER
ROUNDS 1–12

MAKING UP

HEAD

If using safety eyes, attach them before stuffing the head. Poke the post of the safety eye through the centre of the eye socket. Pull tightly on the short end of yarn to close the loop around the post of the safety eye, before attaching it to the head (see page 163).

Stuff the head, pushing the stuffing into the beak. Sew together the open edges of the head with yarn B.

If using looped glass eyes, poke the loop of an eye through the centre of each eye socket before attaching each one to the head using 23⅝in (60cm) length of clear invisible or strong sewing thread (see page 163). Use the tail of yarn left after fastening off the sockets to neatly sew the edges to the head.

Using two strands of thread, embroider the nostrils in satin stitch (see page 164) at the top of the snout edging on each side of the head.

HORNS

Stuff the horns using the end of a crochet hook to push the stuffing right into the tips. Position the horns at angles on the head and sew them in place, stitching all around the lower edges to attach them securely, using the tail of yarn left after fastening off.

TAIL CLUB

Stuff the club. Thread the tail of yarn through last round of stitches of the three openings at the top of the tail club. Pull tightly on the ends of yarn to close the openings and fasten off. Sew together any gaps between the domed tops. Thread a yarn needle with a 31½in (80cm) length of yarn A, doubled. Sew two long stitches from the centre of the lower edge of the tail club, over the top of each side of the middle section and back through the centre of the lower edge, to form a V. Pull tightly on the yarn to sink the stitches and define the shaping of the tail club. Fasten off.

LEGS

Follow the instructions on page 164 to attach the legs, using 63in (160cm) length of yarn B or strong thread for each pair of legs.

Weave in all the yarn ends.

VELOCIRAPTOR

THE VELOCIRAPTOR IS CROCHETED USING VARIOUS STITCHES AND TECHNIQUES TO PRODUCE THE DETAILED FEATHERS ON THE TAIL AND WING-LIKE ARMS. THIS PROJECT IS ONE OF THE MORE COMPLEX PATTERNS.

MATERIALS

- King Cole Giza Cotton 4ply, 100% Giza mercerized cotton (175yd/158m per 50g ball), or any 4ply yarn:
  1 × 50g ball in 4844 Platinum (A)
  1 × 50g ball in 2417 Sage (B)
  1 × 50g ball in 2414 Teal (C)
  1 × 50g ball in 4843 Antique (D)
- 1 pair of 5/32–3/16in (4–5mm) looped glass teddy bear eyes or safety eyes
- Clear invisible or strong thread to attach the looped glass eyes
- Stranded embroidery thread in black, such as Anchor Stranded Cotton, shade 0403, for the nostrils
- 1.75mm (UK2:US6), 2.25mm (UK13:USB/1) and 2.5mm (UK12:US-) crochet hooks
- Blunt-ended yarn needle
- Toy stuffing

SIZE

Approximately 10in (25.5cm) long

TENSION

27 sts and 30 rows to 4in (10cm) over double crochet using 2.5mm hook and yarn A. Use larger or smaller hook if necessary to obtain correct tension.

METHOD

The head is worked in rows of double crochet. The first row of the neck is crocheted into unworked stitches underneath the snout and around the edges of the rows at the back of the head. The neck, body and tail are crocheted in one piece, shaping the front of the body by working in short rows. The upward slope of the tail is formed by increasing and decreasing the same number of stitches on the same rows.

The arms and legs are crocheted in rounds. The arms are started at the elbow joint. The forearm and upper arm are worked separately from the last round of the elbow. The fingers are crocheted in rows. The bends in the legs are created by making a length of chain stitches and skipping a number of stitches of the previous row. The stitches of the following row are gathered together to form the joints. The skipped stitches and the opposite side of the chain stitches are then crocheted into to begin the upper parts of the legs. The toes are worked in rounds. A sickle claw is crocheted separately for each foot. Stitches are crocheted together to produce the curve in the claw. The limbs are attached to the body so they are movable.

The arm and tail feathers are crocheted in rows of various stitches.

Slip stitches form the ridge of the eyebrow over the crocheted eye socket. Looped glass or safety eyes are attached to the socket before sewing them to the head. The Velociraptor is finished with nostrils embroidered in satin stitch, and bullion stitches for the claws on the fingers and toes.

1 ch at beg of the row/round does not count as a st throughout.

KEY

- Magic loop
- Chain (ch)
- Slip stitch (sl st)
- Double crochet (dc)
- Dc2inc
- Dc3inc
- Dc2tog
- Half treble (htr)
- Treble (tr)
- Htr2inc
- Tr2inc
- Work into back loop only

COLOUR

- A
- B
- C

HEAD

SNOUT

Starting at the front of the snout, with 2.5mm hook and A, make 4 ch.

Row 1 (RS): 1 dc in second ch from hook, 1 dc in next ch, 3 dc in end ch, 1 dc in opposite side of next 2 ch, turn (7 sts).

Row 2 (WS): 1 ch, 1 dc in each st, turn.

Rows 3–4: As row 2.

Row 5 (inc): 1 ch, 1 dc in next 2 dc, (dc2inc, 1 dc) twice, 1 dc in next dc, turn (9 sts).

Row 6: 1 ch, 1 dc in each st, turn.

SHAPE FACE

Row 7 (inc): 1 ch, dc2inc, 1 dc in next 2 dc, join B in last dc and carry unused yarn on WS of work, 1 dc in next dc with B, dc2inc, 1 dc in next dc; with A, 1 dc in next 2 dc, dc2inc, turn (12 sts).

Row 8: 1 ch, 1 dc in next 4 dc with A, 1 dc in next 4 dc with B, 1 dc in next 4 dc with A, turn.

SNOUT
ROWS 1–6

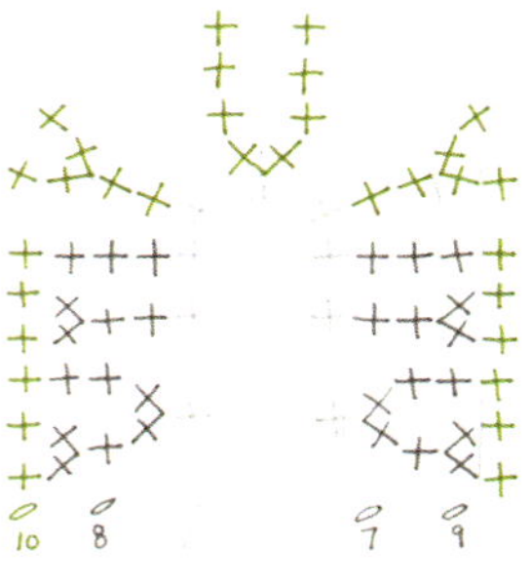

SHAPE FACE
ROWS 7–10

Row 9 (inc): 1 ch, (dc2inc, 1 dc) twice with A, dc2inc with B, 1 dc in next 2 dc, dc2inc, (1 dc, dc2inc) twice with A, turn (18 sts).
Row 10: 1 ch, 1 dc in each st to end with B.
Fasten off, leaving a long tail of A.

SHAPE BACK OF HEAD

With RS of head facing and 2.5mm hook, skip the first 3 sts of the last row and join B with a sl st to the next st.
Row 1 (RS): 1 dc in same dc as sl st, 1 dc in next 11 sts, turn, finishing 3 sts before the end of the row.
Continue on these 12 sts.
Rows 2–4: 1 ch, 1 dc in each st to end, turn.
Row 5 (dec): (Dc2tog) 6 times (6 sts).
Fasten off and thread the tail of yarn through the last row of stitches.
Pull tightly on the end of yarn and fasten off.
Use the tail of yarn A, left after fastening off, to sew together the edges of the snout, matching the rows.

EYE SOCKET
(make 2)

With 2.5mm hook and A, make a magic loop.
Round 1 (RS): 1 ch, 6 dc into loop, join B in last dc (6 sts).
Do not fasten off.

EYEBROW

Row 1 (inc): With B, (dc2inc) twice, sl st in next dc, turn, finishing 3 sts before the end of the row, turn (8 sts).
Row 2 (WS): Sl st in back loop only of next 4 dc, sl st in both loops of next st.
Fasten off, leaving a long tail of B.
If using safety eyes, attach them at this stage. Poke the post of the safety eye through the centre of the eye socket. Pull tightly on the short end of yarn to close the loop around the post of the safety eye, before attaching it to the head (see page 163).

BODY

NECK

With 2.5mm hook and RS of head facing, join B with a sl st to the first of the unworked 3 dc of shape face.
Row 1 (RS): 1 dc in same dc as sl st, 1 dc in next 2 dc, work 5 dc evenly along the edge of rows of the first side of the head, work 5 dc evenly along the edge of rows down the other side of the head, 1 dc in the next 3 unworked stitches of row 10 of shape face, sl st to first dc, turn (16 sts).
Row 2 (WS): 1 dc in each st to end, turn.
Row 3: 1 ch, 1 dc in each st to end, sl st to first dc, turn.
Row 4: 1 dc in each st, sl st in next dc, turn.

EYE SOCKET
ROUND 1

SHAPE BACK OF HEAD
ROWS 1–5

EYEBROW
ROWS 1–2

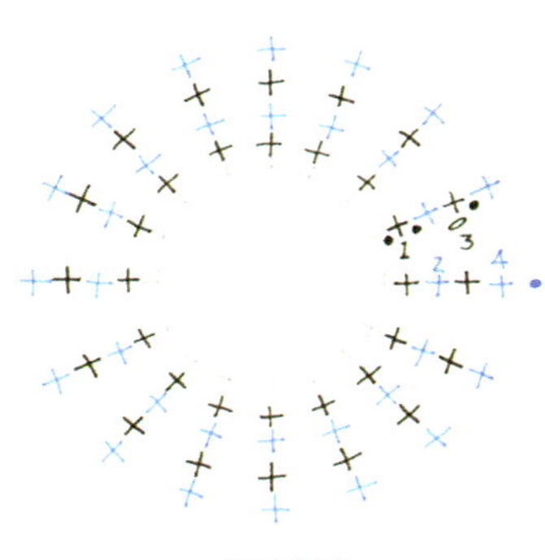

NECK
ROWS 1–4

SHAPE FRONT OF BODY

The following is worked in short rows.

Row 1 (RS) (inc): Starting in same dc as sl st, (dc2inc) twice, sl st in next dc, turn (18 sts).

Row 2 (WS): 1 dc in same dc as sl st, 1 dc in next 5 dc, sl st in next dc, turn.

Row 3 (inc): 1 dc in same dc as sl st, 1 dc in next 2 dc, (dc2inc) twice, 1 dc in next 3 dc, sl st in next dc, turn (20 sts).

Row 4: 1 dc in same dc as sl st, 1 dc in next 11 dc, sl st in next dc, turn.

Row 5 (inc): 1 dc in same dc as sl st, 1 dc in next 5 dc, (dc2inc) twice, 1 dc in next 6 dc, sl st in next dc, turn (22 sts).

Row 6: 1 dc in same dc as sl st, 1 dc in next 17 dc, sl st in next dc, turn.

Row 7 (inc): 1 dc in same dc as sl st, 1 dc in next 8 dc, (dc2inc) twice, 1 dc in next 9 dc, sl st in next dc, turn (24 sts).

Row 8: 1 dc in same dc as sl st, 1 dc in next 23 dc, sl st to first dc, turn.

Stuff the head and neck to within the last three rows before continuing, using the end of the hook to push the stuffing into the end of the snout.

Row 9 (inc): 1 ch, 1 dc in next 11 dc, (dc2inc) twice, 1 dc in next 6 dc, sl st in next dc, turn (26 sts).

Row 10: 1 dc in same dc as sl st, 1 dc in next 17 dc, sl st in next dc, turn.

Row 11 (inc): 1 dc in same dc as sl st, 1 dc in next 8 dc, (dc2inc) twice, 1 dc in next 9 dc, sl st in next dc, turn (28 sts).

Row 12: 1 dc in same dc as sl st, 1 dc in next 23 dc, sl st in next dc, turn.

Row 13 (inc): 1 dc in same dc as sl st, 1 dc in next 11 dc, (dc2inc) twice, 1 dc in next 12 dc, sl st in next dc, turn (30 sts).

Row 14: 1 dc in same dc as sl st, 1 dc in next 29 dc, sl st to first dc, turn.

SHAPE MIDDLE OF BODY

Row 15 (inc): 1 ch, (2 dc, dc2inc, 9 dc, dc2inc, 2 dc) twice, sl st to first dc, turn (34 sts).

Row 16: 1 dc in each st, turn.

Row 17: 1 ch, 1 dc in each st, sl st to first dc, turn.

Rows 18–21: Rep rows 16–17 twice.

Row 22: 1 dc in each st, turn.

Stuff the body to within the last three rows before continuing.

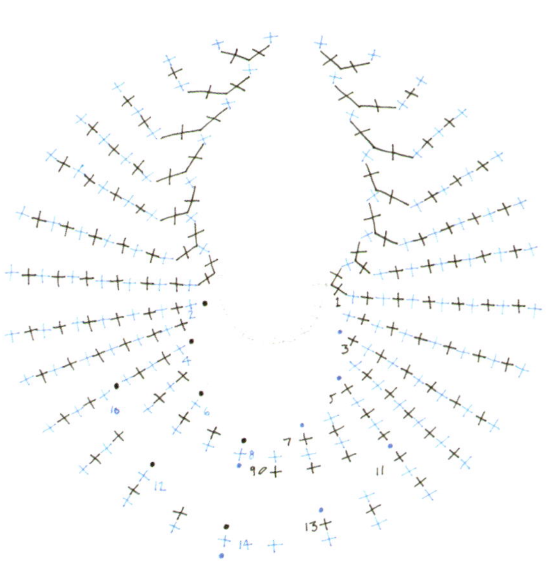

SHAPE FRONT OF BODY
ROWS 1–14

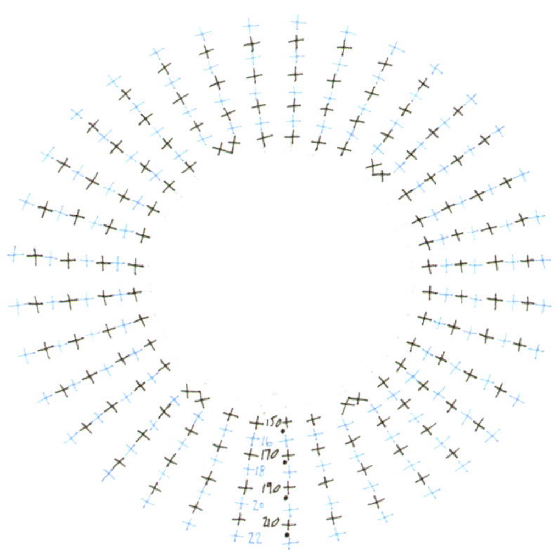

SHAPE MIDDLE OF BODY
ROWS 15–22

SHAPE END OF BODY

Row 23 (dec): 1 ch, 1 dc in next 14 sts, dc2tog, 1 dc in next 2 dc, dc2tog, 1 dc in next 14 sts, sl st to first dc, turn (32 sts).

Row 24 (dec): 1 dc in next 13 sts, dc2tog, 1 dc in next 2 dc, dc2tog, 1 dc in next 13 sts, turn (30 sts).

Row 25 (dec): 1 ch, 1 dc in next 12 sts, dc2tog, 1 dc in next 2 dc, dc2tog, 1 dc in next 12 sts, sl st to first dc, turn (28 sts).

Row 26 (dec): 1 dc in next 11 sts, dc2tog, 1 dc in next 2 dc, dc2tog, 1 dc in next 11 sts, turn (26 sts).

Row 27 (dec): 1 ch, 1 dc in next 10 sts, dc2tog, 1 dc in next 2 dc, dc2tog, 1 dc in next 10 sts, sl st to first dc, turn (24 sts).

Row 28 (dec): 1 dc in next 9 sts, dc2tog, 1 dc in next 2 dc, dc2tog, 1 dc in next 9 sts, turn (22 sts).

Row 29 (dec): 1 ch, 1 dc in next 8 sts, dc2tog, 1 dc in next 2 dc, dc2tog, 1 dc in next 8 sts, sl st to first dc, turn (20 sts).

Row 30 (dec): 1 dc in next 7 sts, dc2tog, 1 dc in next 2 dc, dc2tog, 1 dc in next 7 sts, turn (18 sts).

Insert more stuffing before continuing.

Row 31 (dec): 1 ch, 1 dc in next 6 sts, dc2tog, 1 dc in next 2 dc, dc2tog, 1 dc in next 6 sts, sl st to first dc, turn (16 sts).

Row 32 (dec): 1 dc in next 5 sts, dc2tog, 1 dc in next 2 dc, dc2tog, 1 dc in next 5 sts, turn (14 sts).

Row 33 (dec): 1 ch, 1 dc in next 4 sts, dc2tog, 1 dc in next 2 dc, dc2tog, 1 dc in next 4 sts, sl st to first dc, turn (12 sts).

Row 34: 1 dc in each st, turn.

Row 35 (dec): 1 ch, 1 dc in next 3 sts, dc2tog, 1 dc in next 2 dc, dc2tog, 1 dc in next 3 sts, sl st to first dc, turn (10 sts).

Row 36: 1 dc in each st, turn.

Use the end of the crochet hook to push more stuffing into the body before continuing.

SHAPE UNDERSIDE OF TAIL

The following rows are not joined with a slip stitch at the end.

Row 37 (dec): 1 ch, 1 dc in next 2 sts, (dc2tog, 2 dc) twice, turn (8 sts).

Row 38: 1 ch, 1 dc in each st, turn.

Row 39: 1 ch, dc2inc, dc2tog, 1 dc in next 2 sts, dc2tog, dc2inc, turn.

Rows 40–43: Rep rows 38–39 twice.

Row 44 (dec): 1 ch, (1 dc, dc2tog, 1 dc) twice, turn (6 sts).

Row 45: 1 ch, dc2inc, (dc2tog) twice, dc2inc, turn.

Row 46: 1 ch, 1 dc in each st, turn.

Rows 47–60: Rep rows 45–46 7 times.

Fasten off, leaving a long tail of yarn. Thread the tail of yarn through the last row of stitches and pull tightly to gather the end. Sew the open edges together, matching the rows and inserting stuffing into the tail before closing the seam.

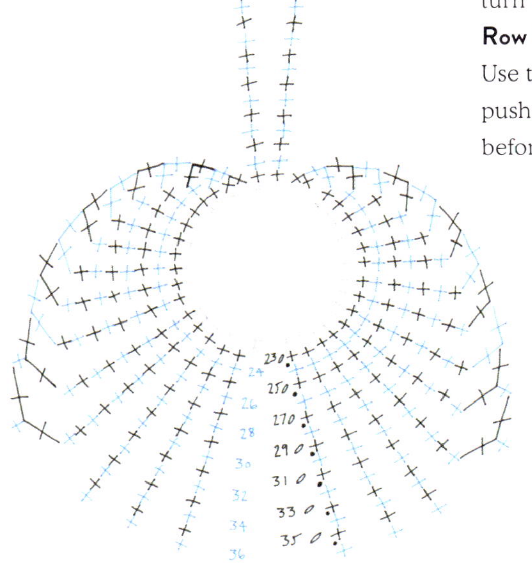

SHAPE END OF BODY
ROWS 23–36

Repeat Repeat

SHAPE UNDERSIDE OF TAIL
ROWS 37–46
FOR ROWS 47–60, REPEAT
ROWS 45–46

UPPERTAIL

With 2.5mm hook and B, make 30 ch.
Row 1: 1 dc in second ch from hook, 1 dc in next 27 ch, 3 dc in end ch, 1 dc in opposite side of next 28 ch. Join C in last dc, turn (59 sts).

TAIL FEATHERS

Row 1 (WS): With C, 3 ch, 3 dc in second ch from hook, 1 dc in next ch, skip first dc of uppertail and sl st in next dc with B, turn (4 sts).
On the following rows, carry the unused yarn along the line of stitches (see page 161).
Row 2 (RS): With B, 1 dc in back loop only of next 2 sts, turn, leaving the last 2 sts unworked (2 sts).
Row 3: With C, 1 ch, dc3inc, 1 dc in next dc, skip next dc of uppertail and sl st in next dc with B, turn (4 sts).
Rows 4–17: Rep rows 2–3 7 times.
Row 18: With B, 1 dc in back loop only of next 3 sts, turn, leaving the last st unworked (3 sts).
Row 19: With C, 1 ch, dc3inc, 1 dc in next 2 dc, skip next dc of uppertail and sl st in next dc with B, turn (5 sts).
Row 20: With B, 1 dc in back loop only of next 3 sts, turn, leaving the last 2 sts unworked (3 sts).
Row 21: As row 19.
Row 22: With B, 1 dc in back loop only of next 4 sts, turn, leaving the last st unworked (4 sts).
Row 23: With C, 1 ch, dc3inc, 1 dc in next 3 dc, skip next dc of uppertail and sl st in next dc with B, turn (6 sts).
Row 24: With B, 1 dc in back loop only of next 4 sts, turn, leaving the last 2 sts unworked (4 sts).
Rows 25–28: Rep rows 23–24 twice.
Row 29: With C, 1 ch, 1 dc and 2 htr in next dc, 1 htr in next dc, 1 dc in next 2 dc, sl st in next dc of uppertail with B, turn (6 sts).
Row 30: With B, 1 dc in back loop only of next 5 sts, turn, leaving the last st unworked (5 sts).
Row 31: With C, 1 ch, 1 dc and 2 htr in next dc, 1 htr in next dc, 1 dc in next 3 dc, sl st in same dc of uppertail as the last sl st with B, turn (7 sts).
Row 32: With B, 1 dc in back loop only of next 6 sts, turn, leaving the last st unworked (6 sts).
Row 33: With C, 1 ch, 1 dc and 2 htr in next dc, 1 htr in next 2 dc, 1 dc in next 3 dc, sl st in next dc of uppertail with B, turn (8 sts).
Row 34: With B, 1 dc in back loop only of next 5 sts, turn, leaving the last 3 sts unworked (5 sts).
Row 35: With C, 1 ch, 1 dc and 2 htr in next dc, 1 htr in next dc, 1 dc in next 3 dc, sl st in next dc of uppertail with B, turn (7 sts).
Row 36: With B, 1 dc in back loop only of next 4 sts, turn, leaving the last 3 sts unworked (4 sts).
Row 37: With C, 1 ch, 1 dc and 2 htr in next dc, 1 htr in next dc, 1 dc in next 2 dc, sl st in same dc of uppertail as the last sl st with B, turn (6 sts).
Row 38: With B, 1 dc in back loop only of next 4 sts, turn, leaving the last 2 sts unworked (4 sts).
Row 39: With C, 1 ch, dc3inc, 1 dc in next 3 dc, sl st in next dc of uppertail with B, turn (6 sts).
Row 40: With B, 1 dc in back loop only of next 4 sts, turn, leaving the last 2 sts unworked (4 sts).
Row 41: With C, 1 ch, dc3inc, 1 dc in next 3 dc, skip next dc of uppertail and sl st in next dc with B, turn (6 sts).

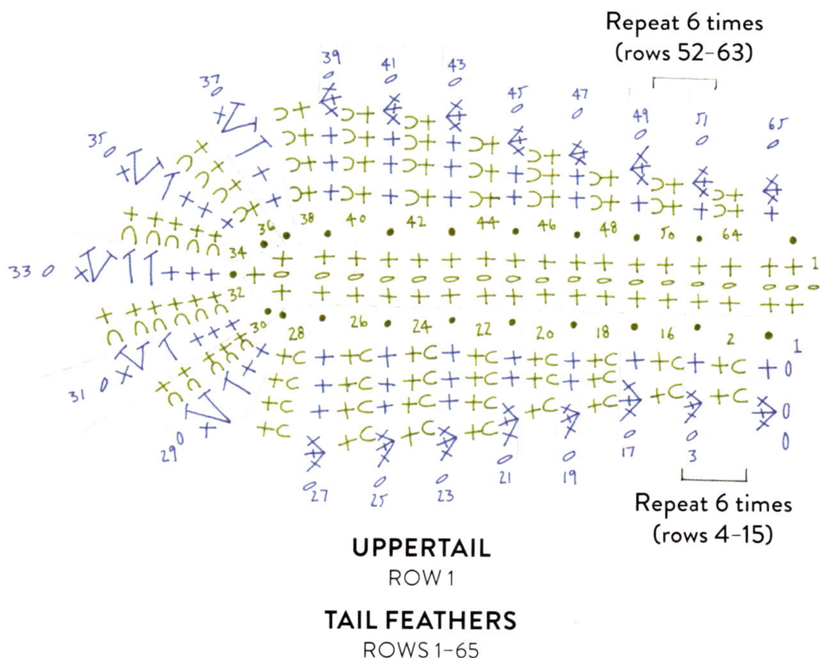

UPPERTAIL
ROW 1
TAIL FEATHERS
ROWS 1–65

Rows 42–43: As rows 40–41.
Row 44: With B, 1 dc in back loop only of next 3 sts, turn, leaving the last 3 sts unworked (3 sts).
Row 45: With C, 1 ch, dc3inc, 1 dc in next 2 dc, skip next dc of uppertail and sl st in next dc with B, turn (5 sts).
Row 46: With B, 1 dc in back loop only of next 3 sts, turn, leaving the last 2 sts unworked (3 sts).
Row 47: As row 45.
Row 48: With B, 1 dc in back loop only of next 2 sts, turn, leaving the last 3 sts unworked (2 sts).
Row 49: With C, 1 ch, dc3inc, 1 dc in next dc, skip next dc of uppertail and sl st in next dc with B, turn (4 sts).
Row 50: With B, 1 dc in back loop only of next 2 sts, turn, leaving the last 2 sts unworked (2 sts).
Row 51: With C, 1 ch, dc3inc, 1 dc in next dc, skip next dc of uppertail and sl st in next dc with B, turn (4 sts).
Rows 52–63: Rep rows 50–51 6 times.
Row 64: As row 50.
Row 65: With C, 1 ch, dc3inc, 1 dc in next dc, skip next 2 dc of uppertail and sl st in last dc with B (4 sts).
Fasten off, leaving a long tail of B.

LEGS
(make 2)

FOOT

With 2.25mm hook and D, make a magic loop.
Round 1: 1 ch, 5 dc into loop (5 sts).
Round 2 (inc): (Dc2inc) 5 times (10 sts).
Pull tightly on short end of yarn to close loop.
Round 3 (inc): (Dc2inc, 1 dc) 5 times (15 sts).

DIVIDE FOR TOES

Round 4: 9 ch, skip next 6 dc, 1 dc in next 9 dc.
Round 5: 1 dc in next 9 ch, 1 dc in next 9 dc.
Continue on these 18 sts.

SHAPE FIRST TOE
ROUNDS 1–4

SHAPE FIRST TOE

Round 1: 1 dc in next 3 dc, skip next 12 dc, 1 dc in next 3 dc.
Continue on these 6 sts.
Rounds 2–4: 1 dc in each st.
Fasten off, leaving a long tail of yarn.

SHAPE MIDDLE TOE

With RS facing and 2.25mm hook, join D with a sl st to the first of the 12 skipped sts.
Round 1: 1 dc in the same dc as the sl st, 1 dc in next 2 dc, skip next 6 dc, 1 dc in next 3 dc.
Continue on these 6 sts.
Rounds 2–4: 1 dc in each st.
Fasten off and thread the tail of yarn through the last round of stitches. Pull tightly to close the end and fasten off.

SHAPE THIRD TOE

With RS facing and 2.25mm hook, join D with a sl st to the first of the 6 skipped sts.
Round 1: 1 dc in the same dc as the sl st, 1 dc in next 5 dc (6 sts).
Rounds 2–4: 1 dc in each st.
Fasten off, leaving a long tail of yarn.

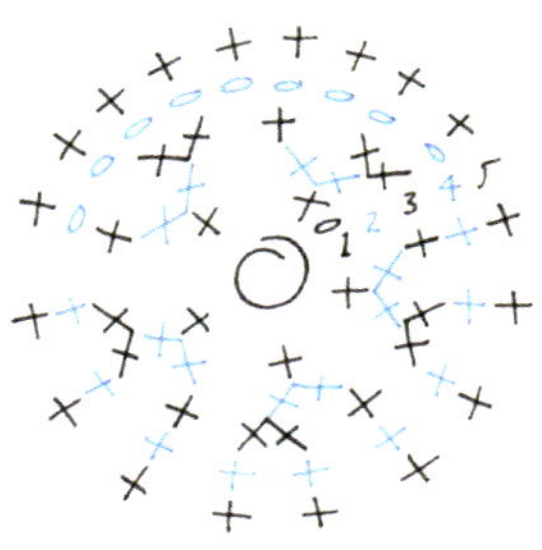

FOOT
ROUNDS 1–3
DIVIDE FOR TOES
ROUNDS 4–5

SHAPE MIDDLE TOE
ROUNDS 1–4

SHAPE THIRD TOE
ROUNDS 1–4

SHAPE FOOT

With RS facing and 2.25mm hook, join D with a sl st to the first of the 6 skipped sts of the foot.

Round 1: 1 dc in same dc as sl st, 1 dc in next 5 dc, 1 dc in opposite side of next 9 ch (15 sts).

Round 2 (dec): 1 dc in next 6 dc, (dc2tog, 1 dc) 3 times (12 sts).

Round 3 (dec): (Dc2tog, 2 dc) 3 times (9 sts).

Rounds 4–6: 1 dc in each st.

Round 7: 1 dc in next 5 dc, finishing at the side of the leg, 4 sts before the end of the round.

ANKLE JOINT

Round 8: 5 ch, skip next 5 dc, 1 dc in next 4 dc.

Round 9: 1 dc in next 5 ch, 1 dc in next 4 dc (9 sts).

Fasten off and thread tail of yarn through last round of stitches. Pull tightly on end of yarn to close and fasten off.

SICKLE CLAW

With 1.75mm hook and A, make 9 ch.

Row 1 (RS) (dec): Starting in second ch from hook, *1 dc in next 2 ch, (dc2tog) twice, 1 dc in next 2 ch*; working in opposite side of each ch, rep from * to * (12 sts).

Fasten off, leaving a long tail of yarn. Fold the claw lengthways, with WS together, matching the stitches on each side. With the tail of yarn left after fastening off, sew together the back loops of stitches on each side of the claw.

SICKLE CLAW
ROW 1

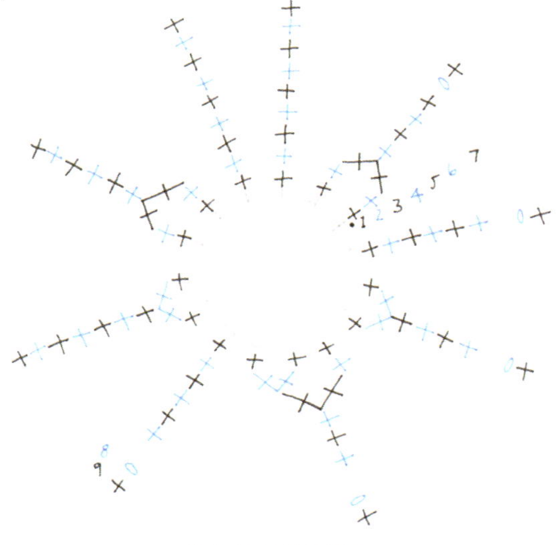

SHAPE FOOT
ROUNDS 1–7

ANKLE JOINT
ROUNDS 8–9

FINISH RIGHT FOOT

Insert the sickle claw just inside the last row of the third toe. Adjust the claw so it faces towards the base of the foot. Thread the length of yarn, left after fastening off the toe, through the last row, pull up tightly around the claw and sew the claw in place. Thread the tails of yarn D, left after fastening off the remaining toes, through the last round of stitches. Pull tightly to close the ends of the toes and fasten off.

Stuff the toes and foot before continuing.

FINISH LEFT FOOT

Finish as for the right foot, attaching the claw to the first toe.

SHAPE LOWER LEG

With RS facing and 2.25mm hook, join D with a sl st to the first of the 5 skipped sts of the foot.

Round 1: 1 dc in same dc as sl st, 1 dc in next 4 dc, 1 dc in opposite side of next 5 ch of ankle joint (10 sts).

Rounds 2–4: 1 dc in each st.

Join B in last dc and change to 2.5mm hook.

Continue with B.

Round 5: 1 dc in each st.

Round 6 (inc): (Dc2inc, 1 dc) 5 times (15 sts).

Round 7 (inc): (Dc2inc, 2 dc) 5 times (20 sts).

Rounds 8–9: 1 dc in each st.

Round 10: 1 dc in next 12 dc, finishing at the side of the leg, 8 sts before the end of the round.

KNEE JOINT

Round 11: 5 ch, skip next 15 dc, 1 dc in next 5 dc at the front of the leg.

Round 12: 1 dc in next 5 ch, 1 dc in next 5 dc (10 sts).

Fasten off and thread tail of yarn B through last round of stitches. Pull tightly on end of yarn to close and fasten off.

SHAPE THIGH

With RS facing and 2.5mm hook, join B with a sl st to the first of the 15 skipped sts of the lower leg.

Round 1: 1 dc in same dc as sl st, 1 dc in next 14 dc, 1 dc in opposite side of next 5 ch of the knee joint (20 sts).

Round 2 (inc): (1 dc, dc2inc, 1 dc) 5 times, 1 dc in next 5 dc (25 sts).

Round 3 (inc): (Dc2inc, 4 dc) 5 times (30 sts).

Rounds 4–5: 1 dc in each st.

Round 6 (dec): (Dc2tog, 4 dc) 5 times (25 sts).

Round 7 (dec): (Dc2tog, 3 dc) 5 times (20 sts).

Stuff the leg before continuing.

Round 8 (dec): (Dc2tog, 2 dc) 5 times (15 sts).

Round 9 (dec): (Dc2tog, 1 dc) 5 times (10 sts).

Round 10 (dec): (Dc2tog) 5 times (5 sts).

Fasten off and thread the tail of yarn through the last round of stitches. Pull tightly on the end of yarn to close and fasten off.

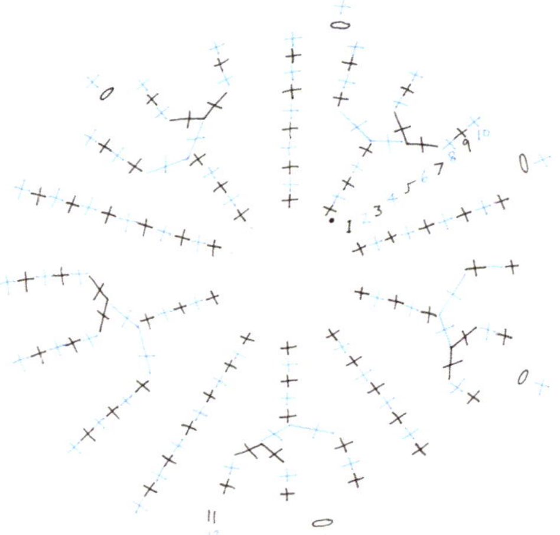

SHAPE LOWER LEG
ROUNDS 1–10

KNEE JOINT ROUNDS
ROUNDS 11–12

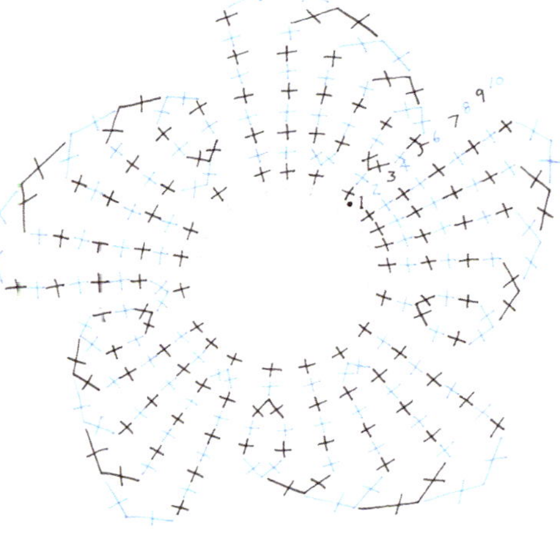

SHAPE THIGH
ROUNDS 1–10

ARMS
(make 2)

ELBOW JOINT

With 2.5mm hook and B, make a magic loop.

Round 1: 1 ch, 6 dc into loop (6 sts).

Round 2 (inc): (Dc2inc, 1 dc) 3 times (9 sts).

Pull tightly on short end of yarn to close loop.

Round 3 (inc): (Dc2inc, 2 dc) 3 times (12 sts).

Round 4 (inc): (Dc2inc, 1 dc) 6 times (18 sts).

FOREARM

Round 5: 1 dc in next 4 dc, skip next 10 dc, 1 dc in next 4 dc.

Continue on these 8 sts.

Rounds 6–7: 1 dc in each st.

Round 8 (dec): (Dc2tog, 2 dc) twice (6 sts).

ELBOW JOINT
ROUNDS 1–4

FOREARM
ROUNDS 5–8

HAND

Change to 2.25mm hook.
Round 9: 1 dc in each st.
Round 10 (inc): (Dc2inc, 2 dc) twice. Join D in last dc (8 sts).
Continue with D.
Round 11 (inc): (Dc2inc, 1 dc) 4 times (12 sts).

SHAPE FIRST FINGER

The following is worked in rows.
Row 1: 1 dc in next 2 dc, turn, leaving the remaining 10 sts unworked.
Row 2: 1 ch, 1 dc in next 4 sts, turn, leaving the remaining 8 sts unworked.
Continue on these 4 sts.
Rows 3–5: 1 ch, 1 dc in each st, turn.
Fasten off, leaving a long tail of yarn.

SHAPE MIDDLE FINGER

With RS facing and 2.25mm hook, join D with a sl st to the first of the 8 unworked sts.
Row 1: 1 dc in the same dc as the sl st, 1 dc in next dc, skip next 4 dc, 1 dc in next 2 dc, turn.
Continue on these 4 sts.
Rows 2–4: 1 ch, 1 dc in each st, turn.
Fasten off, leaving a long tail of yarn.

SHAPE THIRD FINGER

With RS facing and 2.25mm hook, join D with a sl st to the first of the 4 skipped sts.
Row 1: 1 dc in the same dc as the sl st, 1 dc in next 3 dc, turn (4 sts).
Rows 2–4: 1 ch, 1 dc in each st, turn.
Fasten off, leaving a long tail of yarn. Thread the tail of yarn through last round of stitches. Pull tightly on end of yarn to close and sew the side seam together. Repeat to finish the other two fingers.
Lightly stuff the hand. The fingers can be left unstuffed. Stuff the arm before continuing.

UPPER ARM

With RS facing and 2.5mm hook, join B with a sl st to the first of the 10 skipped sts of the elbow joint.
Round 1: 1 dc in same dc as sl st, 1 dc in next 9 dc (10 sts).
Rounds 2–3: 1 dc in each st.
Stuff the upper arm before continuing.
Round 4 (dec): (Dc2tog) 5 times (5 sts).
Fasten off and thread tail of yarn through last round of stitches. Pull tightly on end of yarn to close and fasten off.

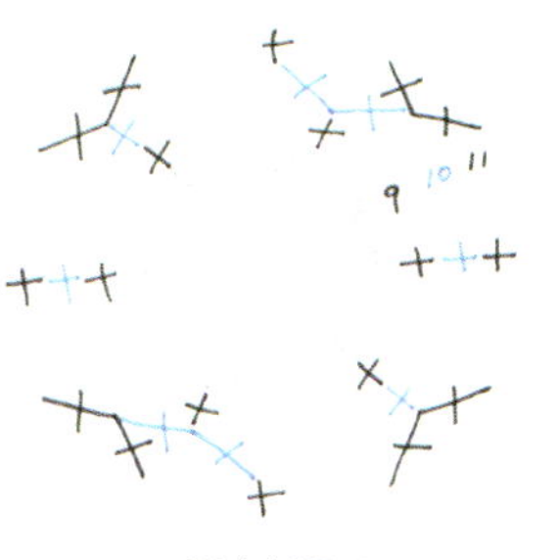

HAND
ROUNDS 9–11

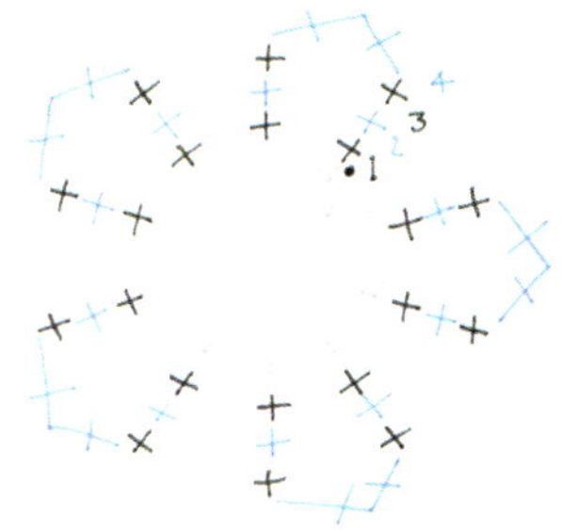

UPPER ARM
ROUNDS 1–4

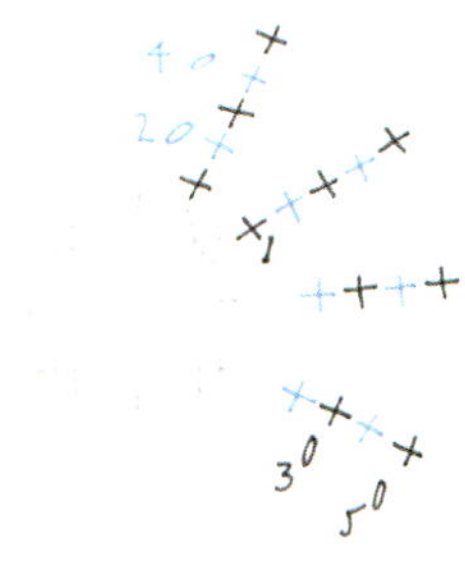

SHAPE FIRST FINGER
ROWS 1–5

SHAPE MIDDLE FINGER
ROWS 1–4

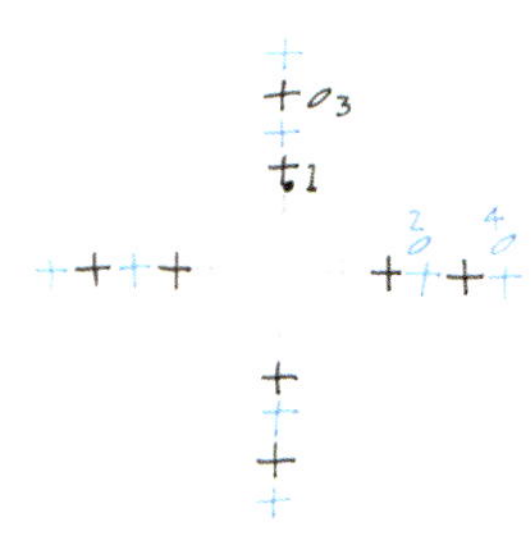

SHAPE THIRD FINGER
ROWS 1–4

RIGHT ARM FEATHERS

COVERT

With 2.5mm hook and B, make 12 ch.

Row 1 (RS): 1 tr in fourth ch from hook, 1 tr in next 2 ch, 2 tr in next ch, 1 tr in next ch, 2 htr in next ch, 1 htr in next ch, 1 dc in next ch, 3 dc in end ch. Join C in last dc and carry the unused yarn along the line of stitches (see page 161), turn (13 sts).

Row 2 (WS) (inc): With C, 1 ch, dc3inc, 1 dc in next 6 sts, dc2inc, 1 dc in next 5 sts, turn (16 sts).

Row 3 (inc): With B, 1 ch, 1 dc in next 15 sts, dc3inc, turn (18 sts).

Do not fasten off.

FEATHERS

Row 1 (WS): With C, 8 ch, 3 dc and 2 htr in second ch from hook, 1 htr in next 3 ch, 1 dc in next 3 ch, skip first dc of row 3 of covert and sl st in next dc with B, turn (11 sts).

On the following rows, carry the unused yarn along the line of stitches.

Row 2 (RS): With B, 1 dc in back loop only of next 8 sts, turn, leaving the last 3 sts unworked (8 sts).

Row 3: With C, 1 ch, 3 dc and 2 htr in next dc, 1 htr in next 3 dc, 1 dc in next 4 dc, skip next dc of covert and sl st in next dc with B, turn (12 sts).

Row 4: With B, 1 dc in back loop only of next 8 sts, turn, leaving the last 4 sts unworked, turn (8 sts).

Row 5: As row 3.

Row 6: With B, 1 dc in back loop only of next 7 sts, turn, leaving the last 5 sts unworked (7 sts).

Row 7: With C, 1 ch, 3 dc and 2 htr in next dc, 1 htr in next 3 dc, 1 dc in next 3 dc, skip next dc of covert and sl st in next dc with B, turn (11 sts).

Row 8: With B, 1 dc in back loop only of next 6 sts, turn, leaving the last 5 sts unworked (6 sts).

Row 9: With C, 1 ch, 3 dc and 2 htr in next dc, 1 htr in next 2 dc, 1 dc in next 3 dc, skip next dc of covert and sl st in next dc with B, turn (10 sts).

Row 10: With B, 1 dc in back loop only of next 4 sts, turn, leaving the last 6 sts unworked (4 sts).

Row 11: With C, 1 ch, 3 dc in next dc, 1 dc in next 3 dc, skip next dc of covert and sl st in next dc with B, turn (6 sts).

Row 12: With B, 1 dc in back loop only of next 4 sts, turn, leaving the last 2 sts unworked (4 sts).

Row 13: As row 11.

Row 14: With B, 1 dc in back loop only of next 3 sts, turn, leaving the last 3 sts unworked (3 sts).

Row 15: With C, 1 ch, 3 dc in next dc, 1 dc in next 2 dc, skip next dc of covert and sl st in next dc with B, turn (5 sts).

Row 16: With B, 1 dc in back loop only of next 2 sts, turn, leaving the last 3 sts unworked (2 sts).

Row 17: With C, 1 ch, 3 dc in next dc, 1 dc in next dc, skip next dc of covert and sl st in next dc with B, turn (4 sts).

Fasten off, leaving a long tail of B.

COVERT (RIGHT ARM)
ROWS 1–3

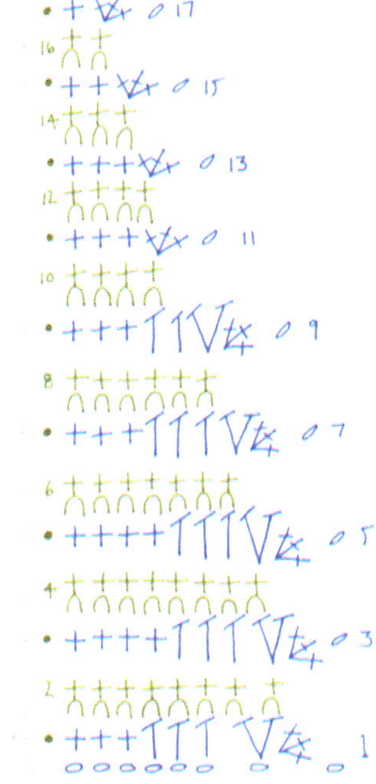

FEATHERS (RIGHT ARM)
ROWS 1–17

LEFT ARM FEATHERS

COVERT

With 2.5mm hook and B, make 10 ch.

Row 1 (RS): 3 dc in second ch from hook, 1 dc in next ch, 1 htr in next ch, 2 htr in next ch, 1 tr in next ch, 2 tr in next ch, 1 tr in next 3 ch. Join C in last dc and carry the unused yarn along the line of stitches, turn (13 sts).

Row 2 (WS) (inc): With C, 1 ch, 1 dc in next 5 sts, dc2inc, 1 dc in next 6 sts, dc3inc, turn (16 sts).

Row 3 (inc): With B, 1 ch, dc3inc, 1 dc in next 15 sts, turn (18 sts).

Do not fasten off.

FEATHERS

Row 1 (WS): With C, 3 ch, 3 dc in second ch from hook, 1 dc in next ch, skip first dc of row 3 of covert and sl st in next dc with B, turn (4 sts).

On the following rows, carry the unused yarn along the line of stitches.

Row 2 (RS): With B, 1 dc in back loop only of next 3 sts, turn, leaving the last st unworked (3 sts).

Row 3: With C, 1 ch, 3 dc in next dc, 1 dc in next 2 dc, skip next dc of covert and sl st in next dc with B, turn (5 sts).

Row 4: With B, 1 dc in back loop only of next 4 sts, turn, leaving the last st unworked (4 sts).

Row 5: With C, 1 ch, 3 dc in next dc, 1 dc in next 3 dc, skip next dc of covert and sl st in next dc with B, turn (6 sts).

Row 6: With B, 1 dc in back loop only of next 4 sts, turn, leaving the last 2 sts unworked (4 sts).

Row 7: As row 5.

Row 8: With B, 1 dc in back loop only of next 6 sts, turn (6 sts).

Row 9: With C, 1 ch, 3 dc and 2 htr in next dc, 1 htr in next 2 dc, 1 dc in next 3 dc, skip next dc of covert and sl st in next dc with B, turn (10 sts).

Row 10: With B, 1 dc in back loop only of next 7 sts, turn, leaving the last 3 sts unworked (7 sts).

Row 11: With C, 1 ch, 3 dc and 2 htr in next dc, 1 htr in next 3 dc, 1 dc in next 3 dc, skip next dc of covert and sl st in next dc with B, turn (11 sts).

Row 12: With B, 1 dc in back loop only of next 8 sts, turn, leaving the last 3 sts unworked (8 sts).

Row 13: With C, 1 ch, 3 dc and 2 htr in next dc, 1 htr in next 3 dc, 1 dc in next 4 dc, skip next dc of covert and sl st in next dc with B, turn (12 sts).

Row 14: With B, 1 dc in back loop only of next 8 sts, turn, leaving the last 4 sts unworked (8 sts).

Row 15: As row 13.

Row 16: With B, 1 dc in back loop only of next 7 sts, turn, leaving the last 5 sts unworked (7 sts).

Row 17: With C, 1 ch, 3 dc and 2 htr in next dc, 1 htr in next 3 dc, 1 dc in next 3 dc, skip next dc of covert and sl st in next dc with B, turn (11 sts).

Fasten off, leaving a long tail of B.

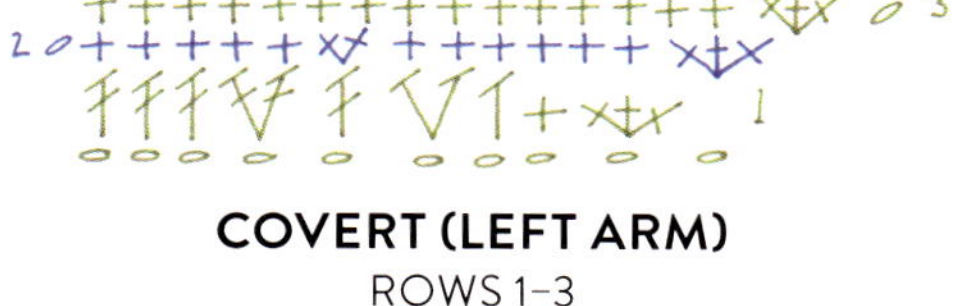

COVERT (LEFT ARM)
ROWS 1–3

FEATHERS (LEFT ARM)
ROWS 1–17

MAKING UP

HEAD

If using looped glass eyes, poke the loop of an eye through the centre of each eye socket before attaching each one to the head using 23⅝in (60cm) length of clear invisible or strong sewing thread (see page 163).

Use the tail of yarn left after fastening off the eyebrow to neatly sew the unworked loops of the socket to the head.

Embroider the nostrils in satin stitch (see page 164), using two strands of embroidery thread.

ARMS AND LEGS

Sew together the gaps between the toes and at the bend in the arms. Bend back the sickle-clawed toe and use yarn D to sew the toe to the foot so that it stands upright. Using yarn A, embroider a bullion stitch (see page 165) for each claw on the remaining toes.

Embroider a claw on each finger with a bullion stitch. Position the top edge of the covert so it runs down the centre of the arm, in line with the middle finger. Using the tail of yarn left after fastening off, sew along the edges of the covert to attach it to the top of the shoulder and down the arm, leaving the feathers unattached.

TAIL

Use the tail of yarn left after fastening off to sew the uppertail to the underside. Stitch the straight, lower edge in place, and then sew along the centre of the chain stitches to attach the uppertail to the underside of the tail.

Follow the instructions on page 164 to attach the limbs, using a 51in (130cm) length of yarn A or strong thread for the arms and 59in (150cm) length for the legs.

Weave in all the yarn ends.

TECHNIQUES

GETTING STARTED

BEFORE STARTING, GATHER ALL THE MATERIALS LISTED AT THE BEGINNING OF THE PATTERN TO MAKE YOUR CROCHETED DINOSAUR OR PREHISTORIC REPTILE. USE THE FOLLOWING INFORMATION TO HELP YOU GET STARTED.

HOOKS

Crochet hook sizes vary widely, from tiny hooks that produce a very fine stitch when used with threads, to oversized hooks for working with several strands of yarn at one time to create a bulky fabric. Using a larger or smaller hook will change the look of the fabric; it will also affect the tension and the amount of yarn required. The projects in this book use 1.25mm (UK3:US8), 2.25mm (UK13:USB/1) and 2.5mm (UK12:US-) crochet hooks.

NEEDLES

A blunt-ended yarn needle is used to sew the projects together. The large eye makes it easy to thread the needle and the rounded end will prevent any snagging.

SUBSTITUTING YARNS

When substituting yarns, it is important to calculate the number of balls required by the number of yards or metres per ball, rather than the weight of the yarn, because this varies according to the fibre. Tension is also important. Always work a tension swatch in the yarn you wish to use before starting a project.

READING CHARTS

Each symbol on a chart represents a stitch; each round or row represents one round or row of crochet.

For rounds of crochet, read the chart anti-clockwise, starting at the centre and working out to the last round on the chart.

For rows of crochet, the chart should be read back and forth, following the number at the beginning of each row.

The charts are shown in alternate rounds or rows of blue and black. The last round or row from a previous chart is shown in grey. Where multiple colour changes are used, the stitches on the charts are shown in different colours to represent each yarn.

TENSION

It is vital to check your tension before starting a project, as this will affect the size and look of the dinosaur or prehistoric reptile, as well as the amount of yarn you will use. The tension is the number of rows and stitches per square inch or centimetre of crocheted fabric. Using the same size hook and type of stitch as in the pattern, work a sample of around 5in (12.5cm) square and then smooth it out on a flat surface.

STITCHES

Place a ruler horizontally across the work and mark 4in (10cm) with pins. Count the number of stitches between the pins, including half stitches. This will give you the tension of stitches.

ROWS

Measure the tension of rows by placing a ruler vertically over the work and mark 4in (10cm) with pins. Count the number of rows between the pins.

If the number of stitches and rows is greater than those stated in the pattern, your tension is tighter and you should use a larger hook. If the number of stitches and rows is fewer than those stated in the pattern, your tension is looser, so you should use a smaller hook.

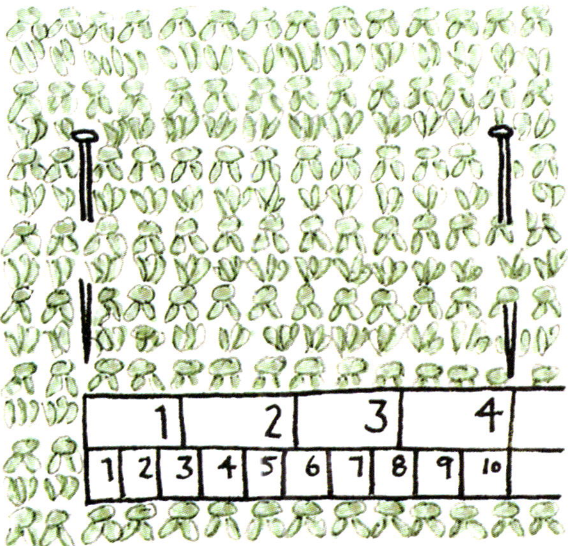

Stitches

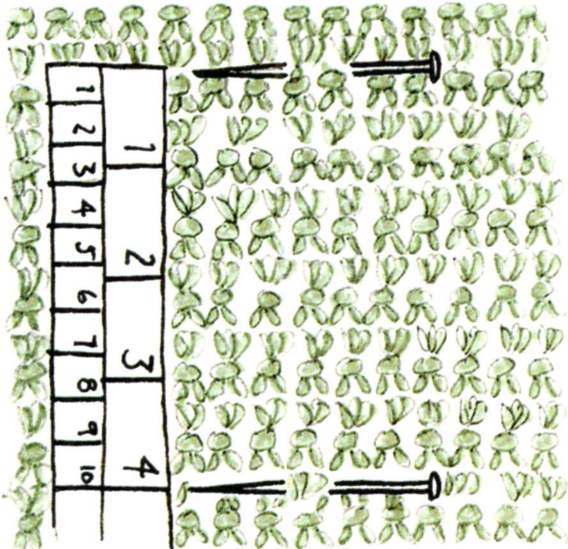

Rows

CROCHET STITCHES

HERE YOU WILL FIND MORE DETAILS ON THE TECHNIQUES USED TO CROCHET THE DINOSAURS AND PREHISTORIC REPTILES, INCLUDING HOW TO HOLD THE HOOK AND YARN, CROCHETING THE VARIOUS STITCHES AND WORKING IN MULTIPLE COLOURS.

SLIP KNOT

Take the end of the yarn and form it into a loop. Holding it in place between thumb and forefinger, insert the hook through the loop, catch the long end that is attached to the ball, and draw it back through. Keeping the yarn looped on the hook, pull through until the loop closes around the hook, ensuring it is not tight. Pulling on the short end of yarn will loosen the knot, while pulling on the long end will tighten it.

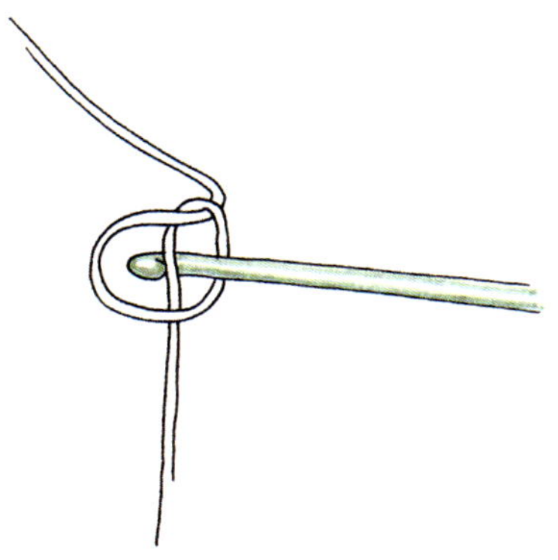

HOLDING THE HOOK

Hold the hook as you would a pencil, bringing your middle finger forward to rest near the tip of the hook. This will help control the movement of the hook, while the fingers of your other hand will regulate the tension of the yarn. The hook should face you, pointing slightly downwards. The motion of the hook and yarn should be free and even, not tight. This will come with practice.

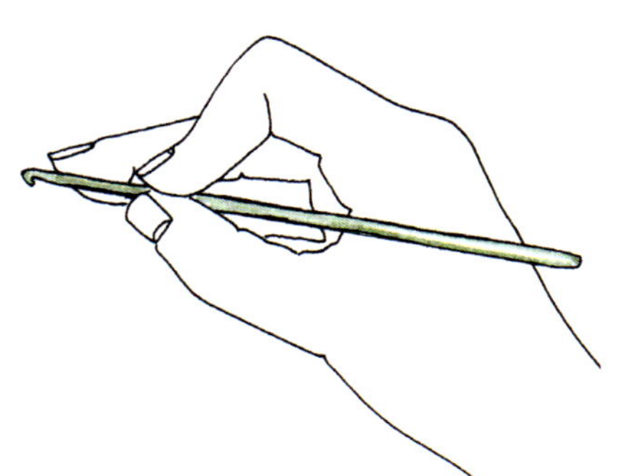

HOLDING THE YARN

To hold your work and control the tension, pass the yarn over the first two fingers of your left hand (right if you are left-handed), under the third finger and around the little finger, and let the yarn fall loosely to the ball. As you work, take the stitch you made between the thumb and forefinger of the same hand.

The hook is usually inserted through the top two loops of a stitch as you work, unless otherwise stated in a pattern. A different effect is produced when only the back or front loop of the stitch is picked up.

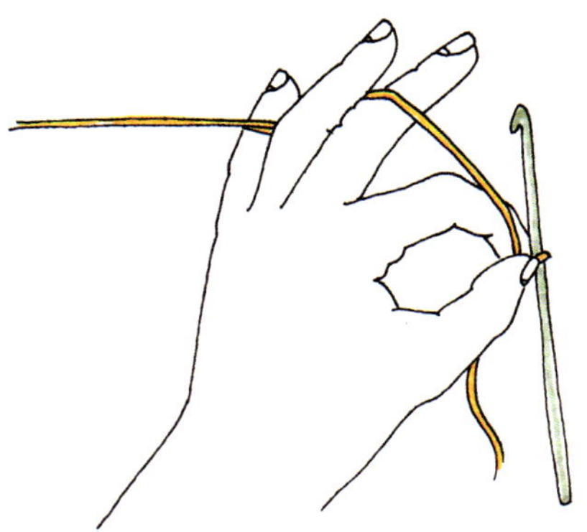

MAGIC LOOP

Many of the crocheted pieces start with an adjustable loop of yarn. To make the loop, wind the yarn around a finger, insert the hook, catch the yarn and draw back though the loop. After a couple of rounds have been crocheted, covering the loop of yarn, the short end of yarn is pulled tight to close the centre. An alternative method is to make four chain stitches and then slip stitch to the first chain to form a ring. However, this technique does leave a hole in the middle.

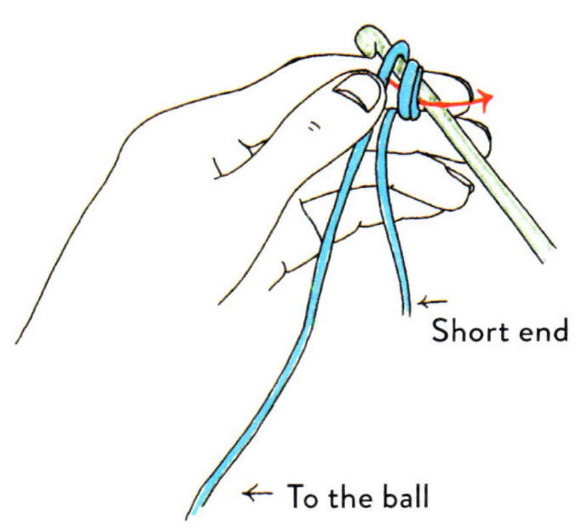

CHAIN (ch)

1 Pass the hook under and over the yarn that is held taut between the first and second fingers. This is called 'yarn round hook' (yrh). Draw the yarn through the loop on the hook. This makes one chain (ch).

2 Repeat step 1, keeping the thumb and forefinger of the left hand close to the hook, until you have as many chain stitches as required.

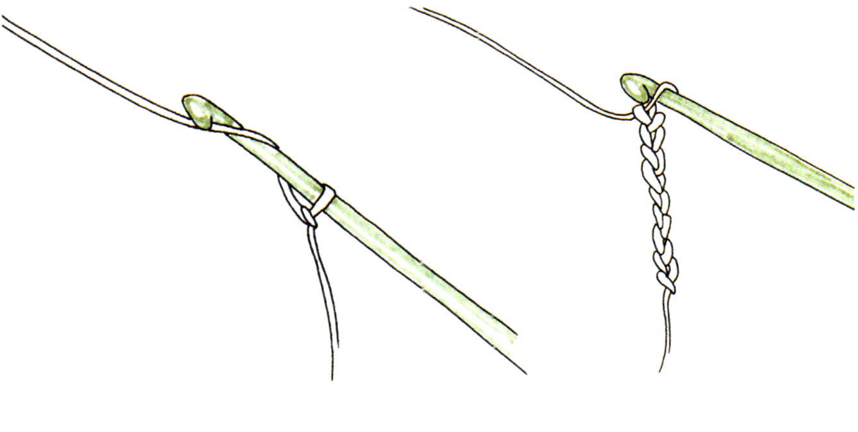

SLIP STITCH (sl st)

Make a practice chain of 10.

Insert hook into first stitch (st), yrh, draw through both loops on hook. This forms one slip stitch (sl st).

Continue to end. This will give you 10 slip stitches (10 sts).

DOUBLE CROCHET (dc)

Make a practice chain of 17. Skip the first ch.

1 Insert hook from front into the next stitch, yrh and draw back through the stitch (two loops on hook).

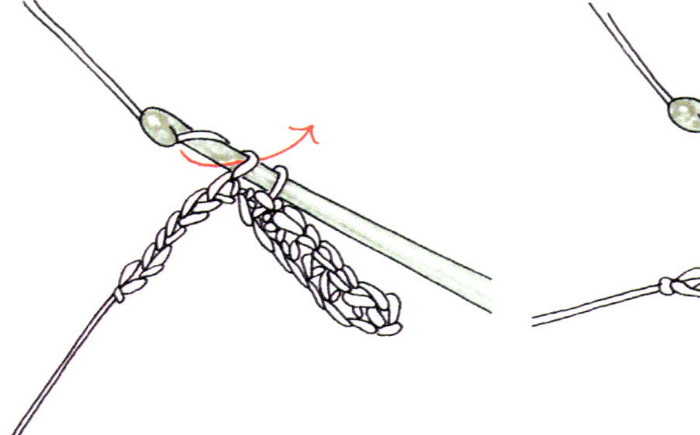

2 Yrh and draw through two loops (one loop on hook). This makes one double crochet (dc).

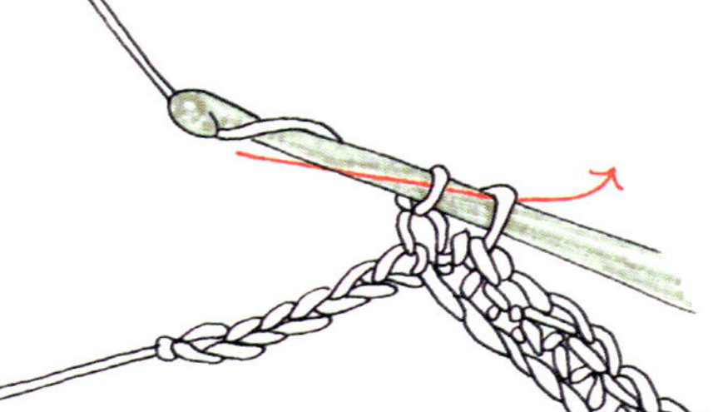

Repeat steps 1 and 2 to the end of the row. On the foundation chain of 17 sts, you should have 16 double crochet sts (16 sts).

NEXT ROW

Turn the work so the reverse side faces you. Make 1 ch. This is the turning chain; it helps keep a neat edge and does not count as a stitch. Repeat steps 1 and 2 to the end of the row. Continue until the desired number of rows is complete. Fasten off.

FASTENING OFF

When you have finished, fasten off by cutting the yarn around 4¾in (12cm) from the work. Draw the loose end through the remaining loop, pulling it tightly.

Plesiosaurus, page 52

Pterodactyl, page 42

HALF TREBLE (htr)

Make a practice chain of 17. Skip the first 2 ch (these count as the first half treble stitch).

1 Yrh, insert hook into the next stitch, yrh and draw back through stitch (three loops on hook).

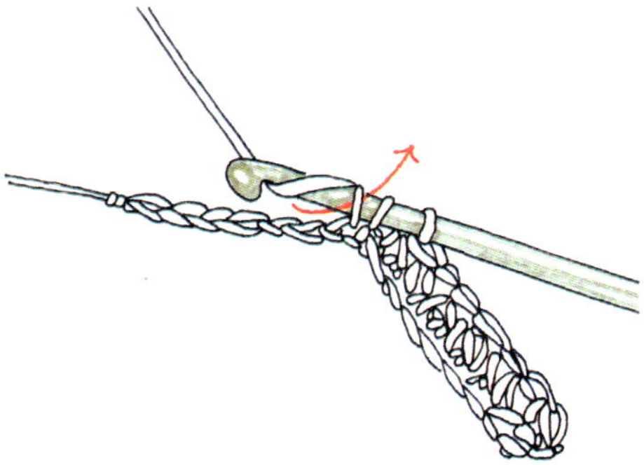

2 Yrh, draw through all three loops (one loop on hook).

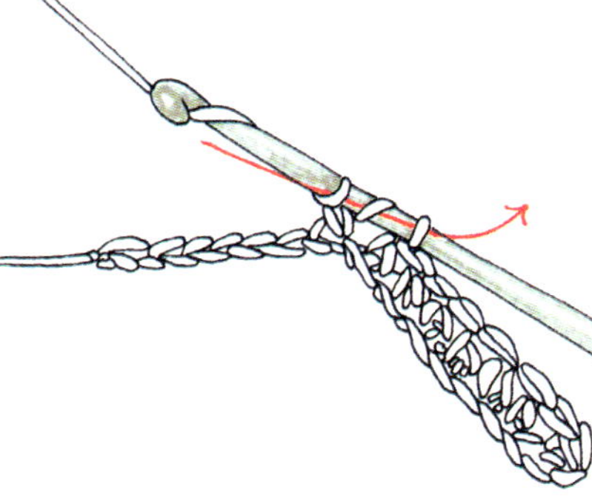

This forms 1 half treble (htr).

Repeat steps 1 and 2 to the end of the row.

On the foundation chain of 17 sts, you should have 16 half trebles (16 sts), including the 2 ch at the beginning of the row, which is counted as the first stitch.

NEXT ROW

Turn the work so the reverse side faces you. Make 2 ch to count as the first half treble. Skip the first stitch of the previous row. Repeat steps 1 and 2 for the next 14 htr of the last row, work 1 htr in the second of the 2 ch at the end of the row. Continue until the desired number of rows is complete. Fasten off.

TREBLE (tr)

Make a practice chain of 18. Skip the first 3 ch stitches (these count as the first tr).

1 Yrh, insert hook into the next stitch, yrh and draw back through the stitch (three loops on hook).

2 Yrh, draw through two loops (two loops on hook).

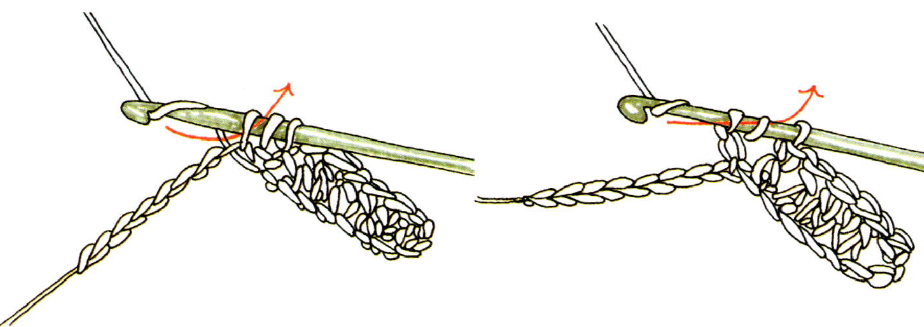

3 Yrh, draw through two loops (one loop on hook). This forms 1 treble (tr).

Repeat steps 1–3 to end of row.

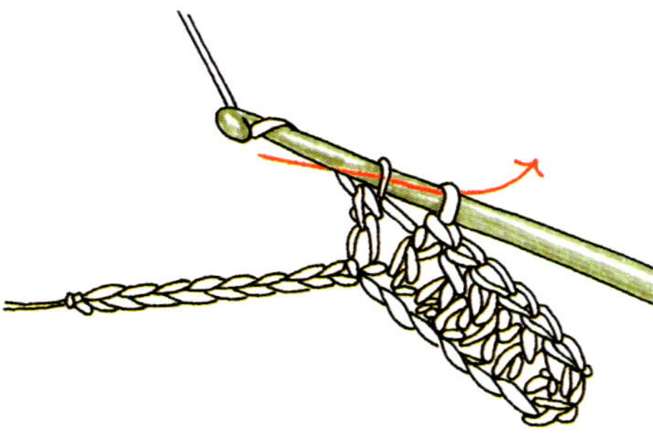

On the foundation chain of 18 sts you should have 16 trebles (16 sts), including the 3 ch at the beginning of the row, which is counted as the first stitch.

NEXT ROW

Turn the work so the reverse side faces you. Make 3 ch to count as the first treble. Skip the first stitch of the previous row. Repeat steps 1–3 to the end of the row, working 1 tr into the third of the 3 ch at the beginning of the last row. Continue until the desired number of rows is complete. Fasten off.

Tyrannosaurus Rex, page 24

BOBBLES

The bobbles appear on the reverse side of the work. This will be the right side.

MAKE BOBBLE (mb)

This stitch is used to create the ridges over the Tyrannosaurus's head and forms the toes of most of the dinosaurs. The bobble is formed by working three treble stitches together in one stitch.

1–2 Follow steps 1–2 of treble stitch.

3 *Yrh, insert hook into same st, yrh and draw back through stitch (four loops on hook), yrh and draw through two loops (three loops on hook)*; rep from * to * (four loops on hook) yrh, draw through all four loops (one loop on hook). This forms one bobble.

Ankylosaurus, page 122 Stegosaurus, page 10 Triceratops, page 78

6-TR BOBBLE

This stitch is used to create the large bony plates over the Ankylosaurus' back. The bobbles are made by working six treble stitches together in the same stitch.

1–2 Follow steps 1–2 of treble stitch.

3 Rep from * to * of step 3 of make bobble five times (seven loops on hook) yrh, draw through all seven loops (one loop on hook). This forms one 6-tr bobble.

2-HTR PUFF

This stitch is used for the markings over the Stegosaurus's body (page 10) and the spikes that run down the back of the Diplodocus (page 64). The puff stitch is formed by working two half treble stitches together in one stitch.

1 Follow step 1 of half treble stitch twice in the next stitch (five loops on hook).

2 Yrh, draw through all five loops (one loop on hook). This forms one 2-htr puff stitch.

3-HTR PUFF

This stitch is used for the markings over the Triceratops' body. The puff stitch is formed by working three half treble stitches together in one stitch.

1 Follow step 1 of half treble stitch three times in the next stitch (seven loops on hook).

2 Yrh, draw through all seven loops (one loop on hook). This forms one 3-htr puff stitch.

Diplodocus, page 64

INCREASING

To increase one double crochet (dc2inc), one half treble (htr2inc) or one treble stitch (tr2inc), work two stitches into one stitch of the previous row. To increase two double crochet (dc3inc), work three stitches into one stitch of the previous row.

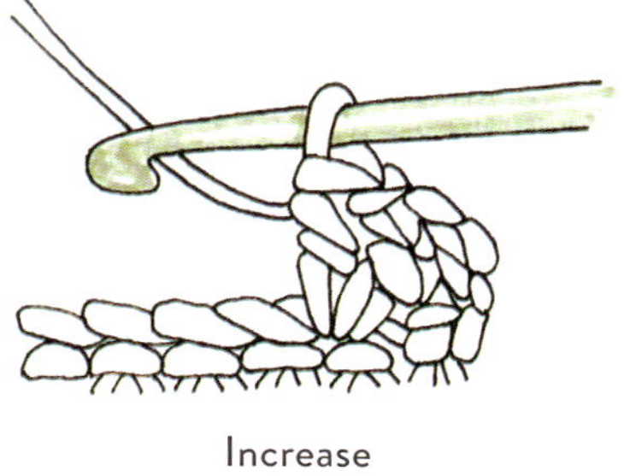

Increase

DECREASING

DECREASE ONE DOUBLE CROCHET (dc2tog)

1 Insert the hook into the next st, yrh and draw back through the stitch (two loops on hook).

2 Insert the hook into the following st, yrh and draw back through the st (three loops on hook).

3 Yrh and draw through all three loops.

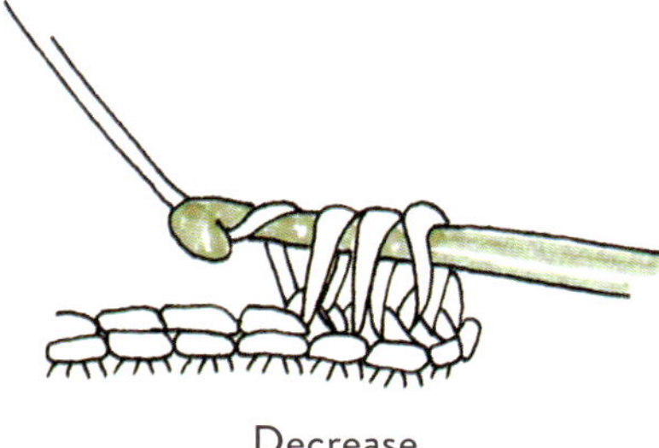

Decrease

DECREASE ONE HALF TREBLE (htr2tog)

Yrh, insert the hook into the next st, yrh and draw back through the stitch (three loops on hook); yrh and insert the hook into the following st, yrh and draw back through the stitch (five loops on hook), yrh and draw through all five loops on the hook.

DECREASE ONE TREBLE (tr2tog)

1 Follow steps 1–2 of treble stitch.

3 Yrh, insert hook into the following stitch, yrh and draw back through the stitch (four loops on hook).

4 Yrh, draw through two loops (three loops on hook).

5 Yrh, draw through all three loops.

Velociraptor, page 136

WORKING INTO THE BACK OR FRONT LOOP ONLY

The front loop of a stitch is the one closer to you; the back loop is the stitch further away. Generally, the hook is inserted into both loops of a stitch, but when only one loop is crocheted into, the horizontal bar of the remaining loop is left on the surface of the fabric.

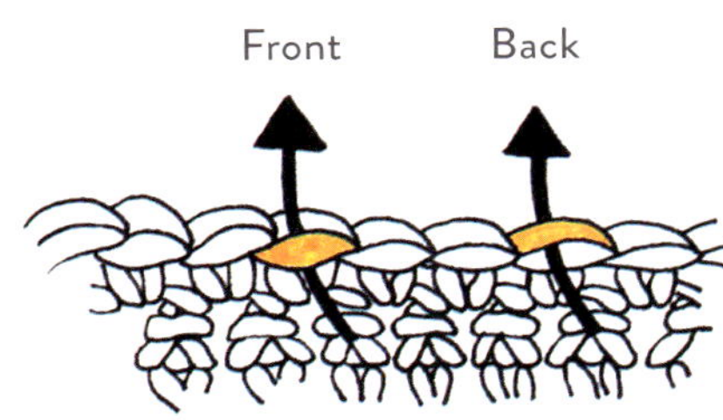

WORKING WITH MULTIPLE COLOURS

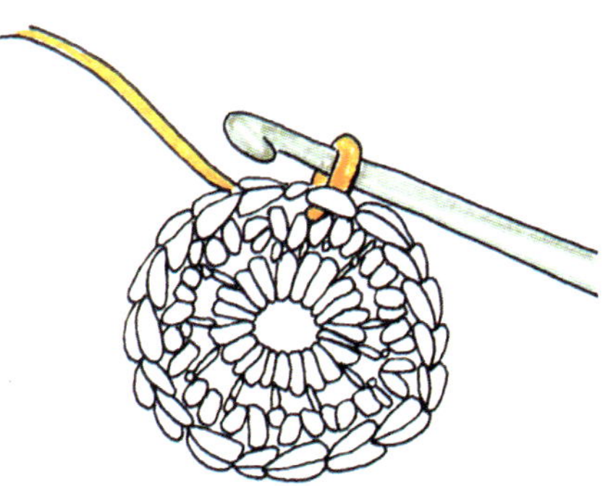

Joining a colour at the beginning of a round

Joining a colour in the middle of a row

JOINING A NEW COLOUR

When joining in a new colour at the beginning of a round or middle of a row, work the last step of the stitch in the new colour. Catch the yarn in the new colour and draw through the loops on the hook to complete the stitch.

CARRYING UNUSED YARN ACROSS THE WORK

When the colour that is not in use is to be carried across the wrong side of the work, it can be hidden along the line of stitches being made by working over the unused strand every few stitches with the new colour. When both sides of the work will be visible, the unused strand is worked over on every stitch, keeping the crocheted fabric neat on both sides. Lay the strand not being used on top of the previous row of stitches and crochet over it in the new colour, covering the unused colour.

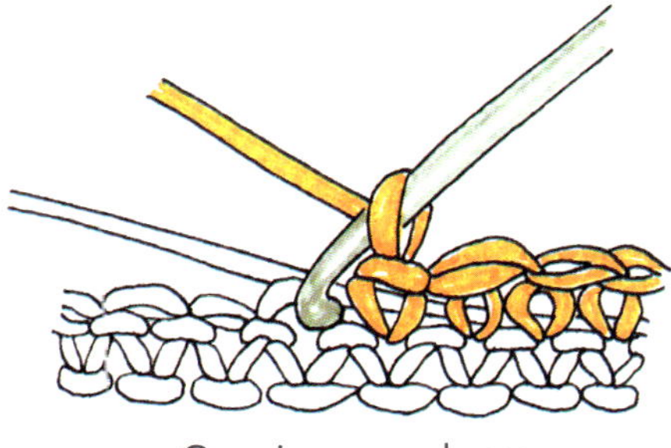

Carrying unused yarn across the work

FINISHING TOUCHES

THIS GUIDE PROVIDES DETAILED INSTRUCTIONS FOR COMPLETING YOUR PROJECT, INCLUDING STUFFING, SEWING THE CROCHETED PIECES TOGETHER AND ADDING EMBROIDERED DETAILS.

STUFFING

Polyester stuffing is a synthetic fibre that is lightweight and washable. It can also be found in black, which won't be so visible through the crocheted fabric in darker shades of yarn. Pure wool stuffing is a lovely, natural fibre. Durable and soft, it can be washed by hand but cannot be machine-washed as it will shrink and felt. Kapok is a natural fibre with a soft, silky texture. It comes from a seedpod that is harvested from the Ceiba tree.

Before stuffing your dinosaur or prehistoric reptile, tease the fibres by pulling them apart with your fingers to make them light and fluffy. Use small amounts at a time and line the inside of the crocheted fabric with a layer of stuffing before building up the filling in the centre. This will prevent the crocheted piece from looking lumpy.

SEWING THE PIECES TOGETHER

MATTRESS STITCH

This method produces a strong, flat and almost invisible seam. It can be used to sew together the open edges in the bodies. It is worked on the right side of the crocheted fabric, using matching yarn, or the tail of yarn left after fastening off.

Insert the needle from back to front through a stitch at the edge of the first piece, then insert the needle from back to front of the corresponding stitch on the second piece.

Insert the needle from back to front through the next stitch on the first piece, then from back to front of the corresponding stitch on the second piece. Continue to the end, pulling tightly on the yarn after every few stitches to close the seam.

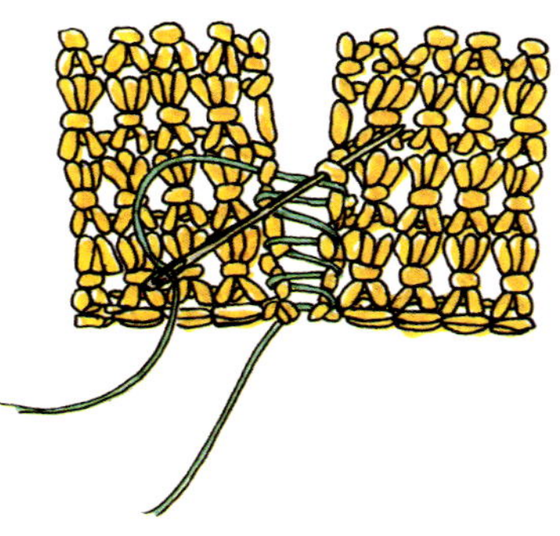

WHIP STITCH

Whip stitch can be used to sew together the edges of the Triceratops's horns, page 78, and the sickle claws of the Velociraptor, page 136.

Thread the tail of yarn, left after fastening off, onto a blunt-ended yarn needle. With wrong sides held together, insert the needle, from back to front, through a stitch on both sides at the same time and draw the yarn through the stitch. Insert the needle through the next stitch on both sides, from back to front, as before and continue to the end. The yarn will be wrapped around the edges, joining the two sides.

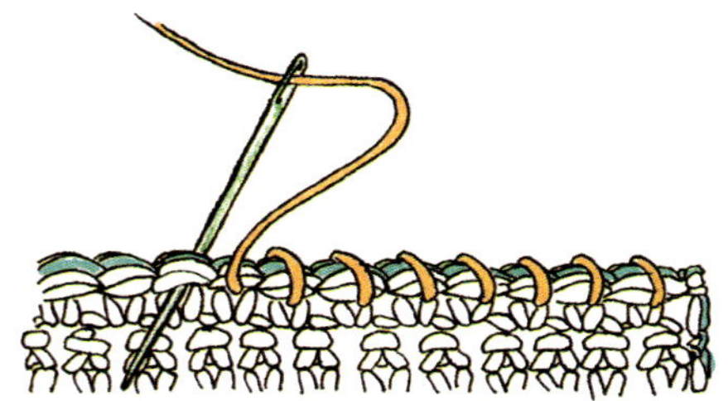

EYES

Looped glass teddy bear eyes or safety eyes are used on these projects. The loop or stem of the eye is poked through the centre of the crocheted eye socket before attaching to the head.

Alternatively, the eyes may be embroidered. Use satin stitch for the pupils and surround them with straight stitches to create the irises (see page 164).

ATTACHING SAFETY EYES

Stuff the head and mark the position of the eyes with a glass-headed dressmaker's pin. Remove the stuffing before attaching the eyes.

1 On the right side of the head, insert the stem of the eye at the desired position.

2 On the inside of the head, place the safety washer on the stem, with the flat side facing the crocheted fabric. Push the washer down the stem until it locks in place.

Repeat to attach the other eye.

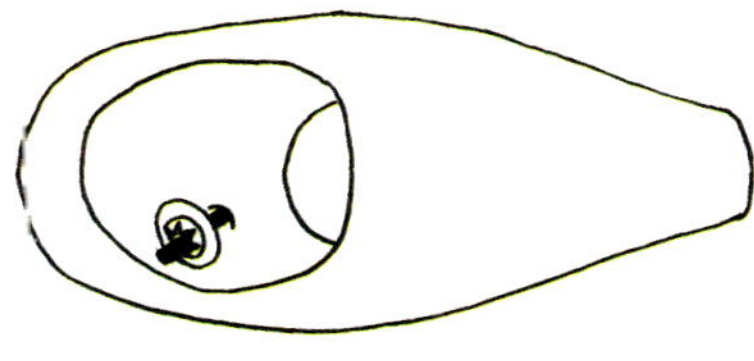

ATTACHING LOOPED GLASS EYES

1 Cut a 23⅝in (60cm) length of clear invisible or strong thread. Double the thread and pass both loose ends through the wire loop of the glass eye.

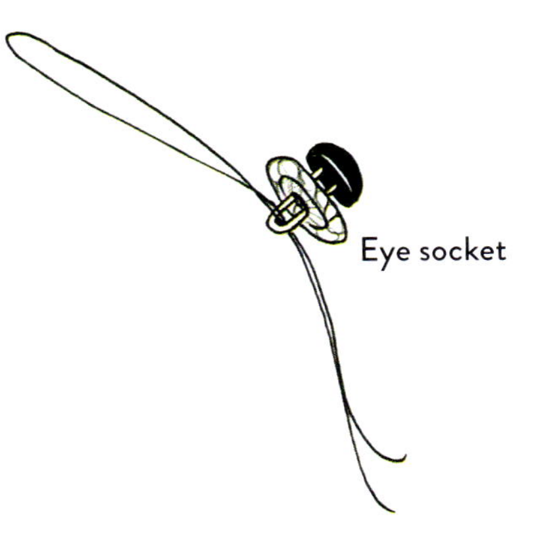

2 Thread both the ends of thread onto a needle and insert the needle into the head at the position of the eye, right through to the back of the head, so the needle emerges between the stitches. Leave the ends of the thread of the first eye hanging at the point where they emerged. Attach the second eye in the same way, pulling the threads through, close to the threads of the first eye.

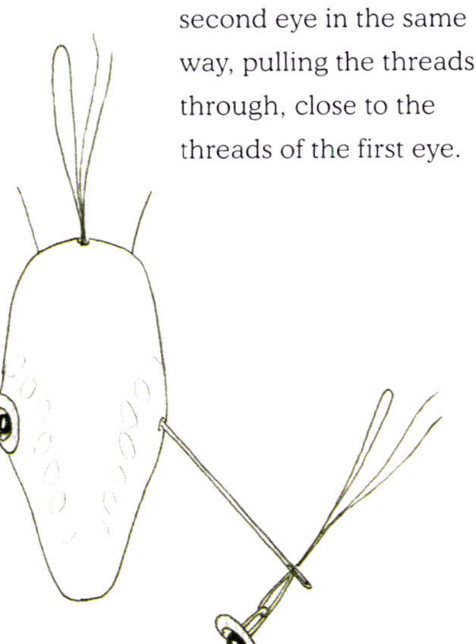

3 Remove the needle and check the position of the eyes. Tie the threads together, knotting them securely. Thread all the strands onto the needle and pull them through to the inside of the head to hide the ends. Trim the excess ends that poke out of the head.

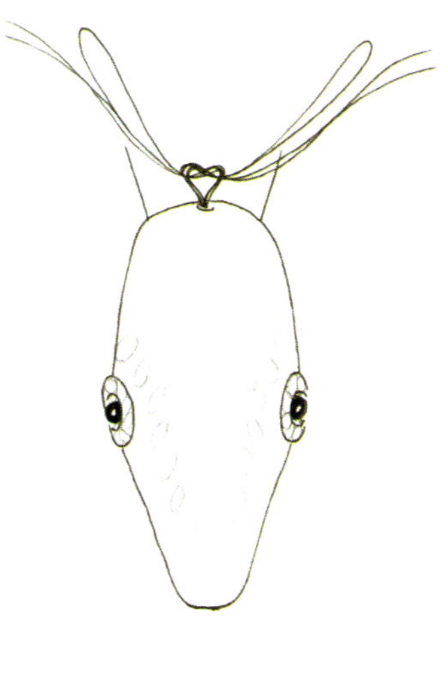

ATTACHING LIMBS

Use matching yarn or strong thread, such as crochet thread, to attach the arms and legs. Refer to the pattern for the required length of yarn or thread.

1 To attach the limbs, cut the specified length of yarn or strong thread. Double the yarn or thread and thread both loose ends onto a needle, so there are four strands of equal length. Insert the needle through the inner side of one limb, where the stitch will be hidden against the body. Insert the needle into the body, where the limb is to be attached, and pull all four strands through to the other side of the body, at the position of the second limb.

2 Thread the needle through the inner side of the second limb and back into the body, where the needle emerged. Pull the yarn right through to the first side.

3 Remove the needle and pull tightly on the strands. Tie the ends of the yarn or thread together, knotting them securely. Thread all the strands back onto the needle and pull them into the body to hide the knot and the ends. Trim any excess ends.

EMBROIDERY STITCHES

Embroidered stitches are used to add the details to the dinosaurs, such as satin stitch for the nostrils.

SATIN STITCH

Work straight stitches side by side and close together across a shape. Take care to keep the stitches even and the edge neat. The finished result will look like satin.

Velociraptor, page 136 uses satin stitch and bullion stitch

BULLION STITCH

This embroidered stitch is used to create the claws on the Velociraptor's hands and feet, page 149.

1 Bring the needle through to the right side of the work at the position of one end of the finished stitch (a). Insert the needle into the work, a little way back, at the desired length of the stitch (b) and then bring the tip of the needle back through to where it first emerged (a).

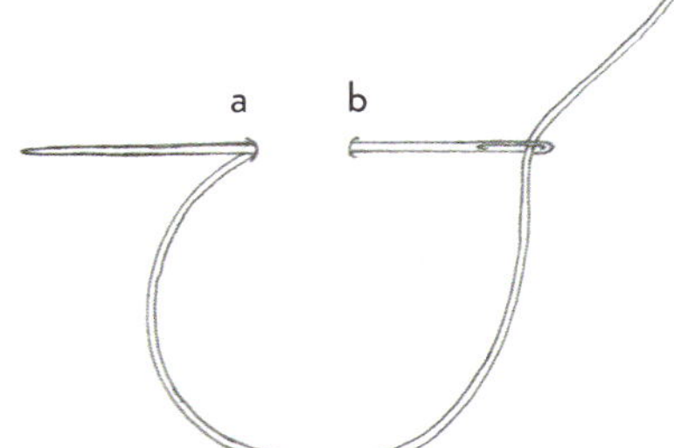

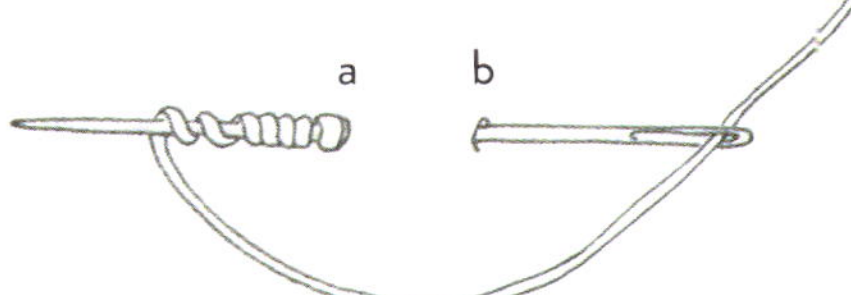

2 Wind the yarn around the needle, so the wraps cover the distance between where the needle is inserted and emerges.

3 Holding the wound yarn in place, gently pull the needle through until the wraps lay flat against the work. Insert the needle back through the work at the end of the stitch (b).

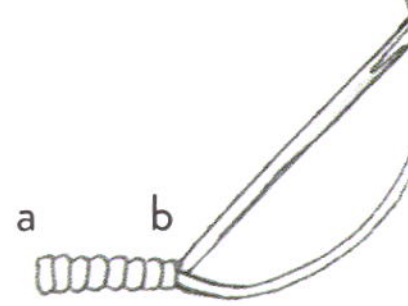

FRENCH KNOT

The bumps over the snout of the Pachycephalosaurus, page 92, are worked in French knots.

1 Bring the yarn through to the right side of the work at the desired position where the French knot is to be made and hold it down with your thumb. Wind the yarn twice around the needle, still holding it firmly in place.

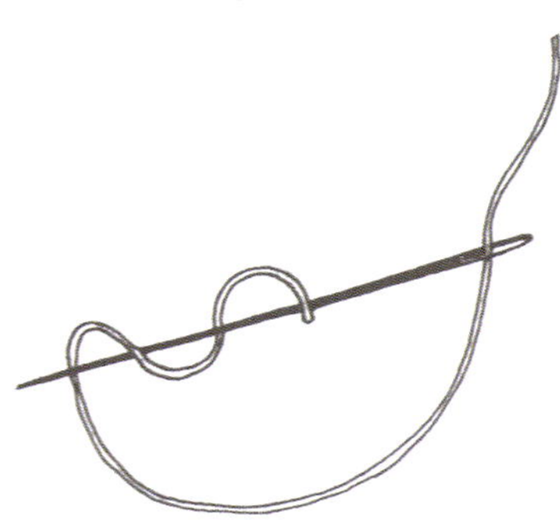

2 Insert the needle back into the work, close to the point where the yarn first appeared. Pull the yarn through to tighten the knot and bring the needle back through to the front of the work to start another French knot.

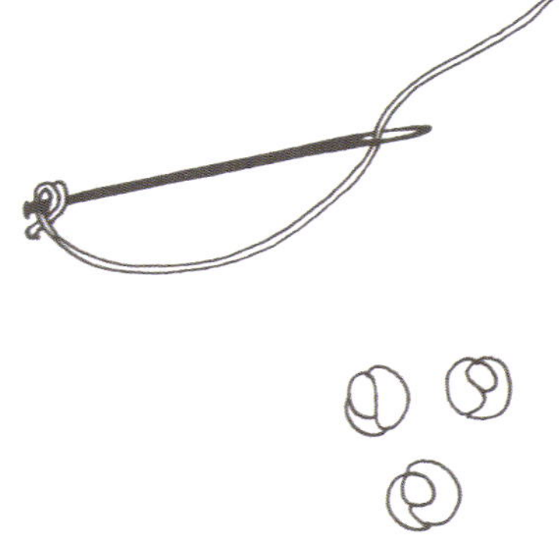

LAZY DAISY STITCH

Lazy Daisy stitch is used on the plates of the Stegosaurus, page 10.

Bring the yarn through to the front of the work at the position where the stitch is to be made; insert the needle back through at the same point to form a loop. Hold the loop down with your thumb. Bring the needle back through to the front of the work, a little way down according to the length of the stitch you wish to make, keeping the yarn under the needle. Reinsert the needle over the yarn and into the same point it emerged to form a small stitch to anchor the loop.

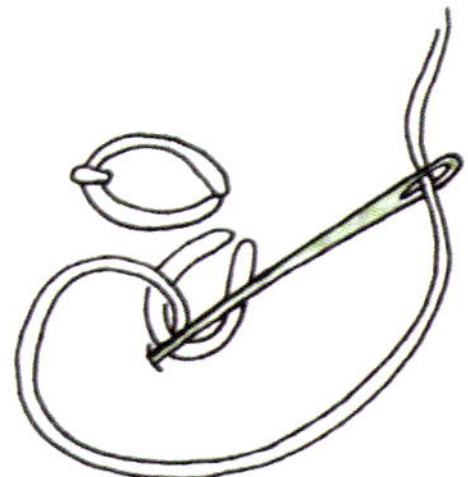

FASTENING OFF

To fasten off embroidery, make a small knot in an area of the same colour where it won't show, or hide it where two pieces are joined. Weave in the ends.

ABBREVIATIONS

ch chain
cm centimetre(s)
dc double crochet
dc2inc work 2 double crochet stitches into the next stitch to increase
dc2tog work 2 double crochet stitches together to decrease
dc3inc work 3 double crochet stitches into the next stitch to increase
dec decrease
htr half treble
htr2inc work 2 half treble stitches into the next stitch to increase
htr2tog work 2 half treble stitches together to decrease
2-htr puff yrh, insert hook into next st, yrh, draw back through st; yrh, insert hook into same st, yrh, draw back through st, yrh, draw through all 5 loops
3-htr puff yrh, insert hook into next st, yrh, draw back through st; (yrh, insert hook into same st, yrh, draw back through st) twice, yrh, draw through all 7 loops
in inch(es)
inc increase
m metre(s)
mb make bobble
mm millimetre(s)
rep repeat
RS right side
sl st slip stitch
sp space
st(s) stitch(es)
tog together
tr treble
tr2inc work 2 treble stitches into the next stitch to increase
tr2tog work 2 treble stitches together to decrease
6-tr bobble yrh, insert hook into the next stitch, yrh and draw back through the stitch, yrh, draw through two loops; (yrh, insert hook into same st, yrh and draw back through stitch, yrh and draw through two loops) 5 times, yrh, draw through all 7 loops
WS wrong side
yd yard(s)
yrh yarn round hook
* work instructions following the asterisks, repeating them as many times as directed
() repeat instructions inside brackets as many times as directed

UK/US CROCHET TERMS

UK	US
Double crochet	Single crochet
Half treble	Half double crochet
Treble	Double crochet

Note: This book uses UK crochet terms

CONVERSIONS

STEEL CROCHET HOOKS

UK	Metric	US
6	0.60mm	14
5½	–	13
5	0.75mm	12
4½	–	11
4	1.00mm	10
3½	–	9
3	1.25mm	8
2½	1.50mm	7
2	1.75mm	6
1½	–	5

STANDARD CROCHET HOOKS

UK	Metric	US
14	2mm	–
13	2.25mm	B/1
12	2.5mm	–
–	2.75mm	C/2
11	3mm	–
10	3.25mm	D/3
9	3.5mm	E/4
–	3.75mm	F/5
8	4mm	G/6
7	4.5mm	7
6	5mm	H/8
5	5.5mm	I/9
4	6mm	J/10
3	6.5mm	K/10.5
2	7mm	–
0	8mm	L/11
00	9mm	M–N/13
000	10mm	N–P/15

ACKNOWLEDGEMENTS

Thank you Jonathan Bailey, Sara Harper and all at GMC. Thank you to Andrew Perris for the fabulous photography. Thank you to my wonderful husband and family for their continuous support and encouragement. I dedicate this book to my beautiful grandchildren who are an inspiration to me. My grandson, Leo, is an aspiring palaeontologist who happily helped me envision how dinosaurs and prehistoric reptiles might have appeared.

First published 2025 by
Guild of Master Craftsman Publications Ltd,
Castle Place, 166 High Street, Lewes,
East Sussex, BN7 1XU, UK
www.gmcbooks.com

ISBN 978 1 78494 700 2

Reprinted 2026

The EEA authorised representative is
Authorised Rep Compliance Ltd.
Ground Floor, 71 Baggot Street Lower,
Dublin, DO2 P593, Ireland
www.arccompliance.com

A catalogue record for this book is available from the British Library.

PUBLISHER Jonathan Bailey
PRODUCTION Jim Bulley
SENIOR PROJECT EDITOR Sara Harper
PATTERN CHECKER Jude Roust
DESIGN MANAGER Robin Shields
DESIGNER JC Lanaway
PHOTOGRAPHY Andrew Perris
ILLUSTRATIONS & CHARTS Vanessa Mooncie

Colour origination by GMC Reprographics
Printed and bound in China

FSC
www.fsc.org
MIX
Paper | Supporting responsible forestry
FSC® C193369

To order a book, contact:
GMC Publications Ltd
Castle Place, 166 High Street
Lewes, East Sussex
BN7 1XU
United Kingdom
Tel: +44 (0)1273 488005
www.gmcbooks.com
THE GUILD OF MASTER CRAFTSMAN
PUBLICATIONS